Contemporary Latin American Cinema

Contemporary Latin American Cinema

Breaking into the Global Market

Edited by Deborah Shaw

ROWMAN & LITTLEFIELD PUBLISHERS, INC.
Lanham • Boulder • New York • Toronto • Plymouth, UK

ROWMAN & LITTLEFIELD PUBLISHERS, INC.

Published in the United States of America
by Rowman & Littlefield Publishers, Inc.
A wholly owned subsidiary of The Rowman & Littlefield Publishing Group, Inc.
4501 Forbes Boulevard, Suite 200, Lanham, Maryland 20706
www.rowmanlittlefield.com

Estover Road, Plymouth PL6 7PY, United Kingdom

British Library Cataloguing in Publication Information Available

Library of Congress Cataloging-in-Publication Data
Contemporary Latin American cinema : breaking into the global market / edited by
Deborah Shaw.
    p. cm.
  Includes bibliographical references and index.
  ISBN-13: 978-0-7425-3914-3 (cloth : alk. paper)
  ISBN-10: 0-7425-3914-8 (cloth : alk. paper)
  ISBN-13: 978-0-7425-3915-0 (pbk. : alk. paper)
  ISBN-10: 0-7425-3915-6 (pbk. : alk. paper)
  1. Motion pictures—Latin America. I. Shaw, Deborah.
  PN1993.5.L3C66 2007
  791.43'098—dc22

                                                                        2006027739

Printed in the United States of America

∞™ The paper used in this publication meets the minimum requirements of
American National Standard for Information Sciences—Permanence of Paper
for Printed Library Materials, ANSI/NISO Z39.48-1992.

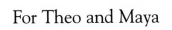

For Theo and Maya

Contents

             Piñeyro's *Kamchatka*   105
             David William Foster

Chapter 7   Soapsuds and Histrionics: Media, History, and
             Nation in *Bolívar soy yo*   117
             Geoffrey Kantaris

Chapter 8   Killing Time in Cuba: Juan Carlos Tabío's
             Lista de espera   135
             Rob Stone

Chapter 9   The Power of Looking: Politics and the Gaze in
             Salvador Carrasco's *La otra conquista*   153
             Miriam Haddu

Chapter 10   Peruvian Cinema and the Struggle for
             International Recognition: Case Study on *El
             destino no tiene favoritos*   173
             Sarah Barrow

             Selected Bibliography   191

             Index   193

             About the Contributors   199

Acknowledgments

Thanks to Sue Harper for her wise advice with the planning of this project and to colleagues at Portsmouth University for their support and friendship. I would also like to thank Susan McEachern at Rowman and Littlefield for her help throughout the project, and another big thank you to all the wonderful staff at Portsmouth nursery who allowed me to work with a peaceful heart. Thanks also to my mother, Lesley, for her love and support, and to Verena Wright for her help with the index.

Images from *Los diarios de motocicleta* appear courtesy of Pathe Pictures International © FilmFour Limited 2004, all rights reserved; images from *Nueve reinas* appear courtesy of Optimum Releasing; images from *Y tu mamá también* appear courtesy of Icon Films; images from *Lista de espera* appear courtesy of Tornasol films; images from *La otra conquista* appear courtesy of Carrasco & Domingo Films; images from *Cidade de Deus* are reproduced with the permission of Fernando Meirelles; and images from *El Destino no tiene favoritos* are reproduced with the permission of Alvaro Velarde.

Latin American Cinema Today
A Qualified Success Story
Deborah Shaw

In little more than a decade, Latin American cinema has been transformed in terms of international visibility and recognition. As recently as 1988, the well-known Chilean author Antonio Skármeta, lamenting the absence of films from Latin American in Europe, wrote, "Latin American cinema is not seen in Europe, except in cinema clubs and on cultural television channels in absolutely minimal and insufficient proportions."[1]

Today, there are more Latin American films than ever before on screens in big cities in Europe, the United States, Australia, Russia, Israel, and Latin American countries such as Mexico, Argentina, Brazil, Colombia, and Chile. There has never been such visibility for films from the region: New box-office records are being broken regularly; there are more DVDs available than ever before through large retail outlets, such as Blockbuster, and online companies, such as Amazon.com. Important Latin American directors, in particular Mexican directors, are being feted by Hollywood with Alejandro González Iñárritu, Alfonso Cuarón, and Guillermo del Toro all making films in the United States.[2]

A combination of factors is behind this change in fortunes for films from Latin America, but in broad terms, directors and producers are more aware of the international market and have learned how to raise funds, create more audience-friendly films, and market their finished products. As a result, more production companies are investing in Latin America, and coproductions are a central factor in this internationalization process. This looks set to continue with companies encouraged by the profits generated by films such as

Walter Salles's *Central do Brasil* (*Central Station*, 1998), Iñárritu's *Amores perros* (*Love's a Bitch*, 2000), and Cuarón's *Y tu mamá también* (*And Your Mother, Too*, 2001).

This is a dynamic time for filmmakers, with more international funding opportunities for new directors and screenwriters. There are a number of programs to help to foster filmmaking cultures that can benefit Latin American cineastes. These include funds from the Sundance Institute, the Hubert Bals project of the Rotterdam Film Festival, which supports proposals from non-Western countries, and the Cannes screenwriting residency awards, which focus on writers from countries with less access to financial support. In addition, the Ibermedia program, actively seeks to encourage filmmaking from Latin America, and the fact that it funded thirty-two projects in 2004 and thirty-six in 2005 demonstrates that it is succeeding.[3] Its stated aims are to "promote the development of projects directed [toward] the Ibero-American market [and to] create a favorable environment for the development and integration of Ibero-American productions companies."[4]

In addition to grants or loans available from the aforementioned bodies, there are more independent production companies, which have also been instrumental in furthering this boom in Latin American films. These include companies such as Patagonik, which coproduced both Fabián Bielinski's, *Nueve reinas* (*Nine Queens*, 2000) and Marcelo Piñeyro's *Kamchatka* (2002), which are featured in this volume; Videofilmes, which coproduced Fernando Meirelles's and Kátia Lund's *Cidade de Deus* (*City of God*, 2002) and Karim Ainouz's *Madame Satã* (2002), which are also featured in this volume; and Altavista Films, which produced *Amores perros* as well as a number of other Mexican hits. International distribution companies are also developing an interest in films with companies, such as Buenavista International, Sony Pictures, Miramax Films, and 20th Century Fox, distributing some of the most commercially successful films of recent years. In this way, filmmaking from Latin American countries is not forced to depend on state subsidies, which while potentially a positive source of income, can vanish suddenly with changes in administrations and have traditionally been inadequate to support a vibrant film culture.[5] There has also been an increase in scholarship on Latin American cinema. Academic publishers are responding to the developing market in Latin American film and are contracting more authors to produce monographs and edited works, such as this one, on the subject of Latin American film.[6] In conjunction with this, there are now more and more academic units at universities that incorporate films from Latin American into their program of study.

Nevertheless, the preceding scenario can present an over-celebratory picture of the current state of Latin American cinema. There are indeed films that are having unprecedented international success from a range of countries, including *Central do Brasil* and *Cidade de Deus* from Brazil, *Nueve reinas* and Lucrecia Martel's *La niña santa* (*The Holy Girl*, 2004) from Argentina, *Amores perros* and *Y tu mamá también* from Mexico, Andrés Wood's *Machuca* (2004) from Chile, and Juan Pablo Rebella and Pablo Stoll's *Whisky* (2004) from Uruguay. Yet, there are films from other Latin American countries that are rarely seen beyond their country of origin or have a limited release. There are many Latin American films whose potential to do well at the international box offices is never tested. Other films are simply not made; there may be more money available, yet projects deemed to be less commercially successful, more experimental, and with less obvious international appeal are unlikely to be taken on by large companies or able to raise sufficient funds to bring films to fruition; this point lends support to the argument for sustained state funding for such projects.

Latin American cinema is a generalized term, which while useful in creating a space in the market for films from the region, as will be seen, does not manage to include all of Latin America, as revealed by a scan through major film retail outfits and the tables of contents of books, such as this and others on the subject. Such venues and books rarely, if ever, include films from many Latin American republics, including Bolivia, Paraguay, Venezuela, Guatemala, Costa Rica, Nicaragua, El Salvador, or Honduras, because films from these countries are either not being made or not being distributed across national borders. It is, then, as important to ask why international audiences are not seeing films from these countries as it is to celebrate the films that audiences in industrialized countries are able to see. Other unseen works are documentaries produced on digital cameras, a common form of contemporary filmmaking in Latin America. These films are almost never released outside their national borders, despite the fact that there have been great advances in documentary filmmaking in recent years.[7] Likewise, films made on video by indigenous communities have limited audiences; although they are outside the remit of a book of this nature, it is important to recognize that such films are being made outside the confines of globalized film markets.[8]

It is also worth keeping a sense of perspective when celebrating advances made at the box office. Even films that do well are often only exhibited in small art house cinemas, and many mainstream cinemagoers would not have heard of even the most successful Latin Americans films previously mentioned. A comparison of two successful Latin American– and U.S.-financed films of 2001, *Y tu mamá también* and *Lord of the Rings: The Fellowship of the Ring*, reveals the enormous difference in budgets, distribution arrangements, and audience figures. The Mexican film was made with an estimated $5,000,000; it grossed $408,091 in its opening weekend in the United States and was shown on 40 screens.[9] The first of the *Lord of the Rings* films was made with a budget of approximately $93,000,000; it grossed $66,114,741 at the box office in its first weekend in the United States and was seen on 3,359 screens.[10]

I have questioned the term Latin American cinema in that it renders certain countries invisible, yet the term is clearly used and useful to discuss films from Latin America, not least as a marketing label. As Andrew Higson has noted in his discussion of British cinema, notions of national cinema in terms of the international and domestic marketplace are used to sell films by using national identity as a distinctive brand name.[11] In the international film market, Latin American continental identity has become such a brand, with popular film critics talking enthusiastically about Latin American cinema and drawing (rather forced) comparisons between films as diverse as *Cidade de Deus* and *Amores perros*.[12] Indeed, individual films may have little in common with each other and be made in countries that are geographically and culturally at some distance; it is, in fact, important to acknowledge that there are many forms of filmmaking coming from Latin America, with each director employing a unique visual style and addressing specific themes. Nevertheless, the notion of Latin American film has been useful as each success creates an opening in the market for other films, with production and distribution companies more likely to keep investing in films from the region.

Despite the wide range of approaches that lie behind such generalizing terms as Latin American cinema, there are some common points in a number of the films that have proven most successful in commercial terms. Many films released from the end of the 1990s to the present have managed to retain a social conscience, so characteristic of New Latin American cinema of the 1960s and 1970s. The most profitable films of recent times—*Cidade de Deus, Central do Brasil, Y tu mamá también,* and Walter Salles's *Los diarios de motocicleta* (*The Motorcycle Diaries,* 2004)—have a clear sociopolitical agenda. And unlike more explicitly political filmmaking of the earlier era, this agenda is filtered through a personal, intimate, character-driven focus and shares high production values and an emphasis on an entertaining plot. Party political agendas are avoided with politicians and political institutions unnamed, yet these films tackle such issues as social injustice, police corruption, political corruption, and poverty. It is also no coincidence that even though these films engage with social issues, many borrow conventions from

genre formats. *Los diarios de motocicleta* and *Y tu mamá también* share many ingredients with more traditional road movies; *Nueve reinas* is rooted within
the tradition of the scam movie; and even *Cidade de Deus*, a film so rooted in
the realities of the Brazilian *favelas*, owes some of its success, in part, to the
fact that it could be read, erroneously in Elsa Vieira's view, from within the
conventions of the gangster film. The strength of some of the most successful films from Latin America, in contrast to many (but not all) of its Hollywood counterparts, is that high-quality entertainment is produced without
the loss of a socially committed agenda.

Latin American Cinema and the International Market

This collection of essays by major scholars in the field of Latin American
cinema highlights the diverse strengths of some of the most important films
to emerge in the first years of the new millennium and draws attention to
an extraordinary period in the history of Latin American film in terms of its
presence in the international market. The chapters provide readings that
explore film text, social context, and production conditions to gain a fuller
picture of the state of contemporary filmmaking in a range of Latin American countries. The readings in this book provide invaluable material for students and scholars of Latin American film and contribute to the growing
field of research on Latin American cinema with a focus on some of the
most recent films to emerge. Films such as *Nueve reinas*, *Y tu mamá también*,
Cidade de Deus, and *Los diarios de motocicleta* are already finding their way
into film-studies and Hispanic-studies programs, and this book includes
readings of other films that would be fruitful texts for study both at under-
graduate and postgraduate levels. The chapters are organized into three sec-
tions. Chapters 1 to 4 examine films that have had an unprecedented impact on a global level; chapters 5 to 8 consider films that have been
exhibited principally at film festivals, in limited runs, and few theaters in
other national contexts but have failed to secure widespread international
distributions deals; and chapters 9 and 10 take as their subject films that
have failed to attract international support, despite local interest, and look
at the reasons for this. All of the essays provide in-depth analysis and are
grounded in an understanding and explanation of the films' geo-historical
context and show that, despite the emphasis on transnational practices of
production and distribution, it is still possible to talk in terms of national
cinemas in a Latin American context.

Thus the readings of the films demonstrate that, despite their relationships with the international market, they are deeply rooted in national

preoccupations. In chapter 6, David Foster examines *Kamchatka* (2002) and demonstrates the way in which the family unit acts as a metaphor for Argentine society during the time of the military dictatorship. Foster argues that despite an approach influenced by Hollywood in terms of style and narrative conventions, the film is an example of a cultural exploration of national trauma. In chapter 8, in his analysis of Juan Carlos Tabío's *Lista de espera* (*The Waiting List*, 2000), Rob Stone argues that the coach station, in which the action takes place and which is geographically situated between Havana and Santiago, comes to represent an imagined Cuba that can fulfill its Revolutionary ideals. For Stone, a critique of Castro's Cuba is combined with a faith in the founding Socialist ideals of the Revolution. In chapter 9, in her analysis of Salvador Carrasco's *La otra conquista* (*The Other Conquest*, 1999), Miriam Haddu analyzes the ongoing concern to represent Mexican history from the point of view of the indigenous population; while in chapter 1, in her analysis of *Los diarios de motocicleta*, Claire Williams explores the way in which the notion of a Pan-Latin American identity is combined with the realities of social inequality uniting diverse republics.

National contexts are important even with the films in this collection of essays that are not explicitly about a specific national issue. Jorge Alí Triana's *Bolívar soy yo* (*Bolívar is Me*, 2002) examines the role of the mass media in contemporary Colombia through the dramatization via *telenovela* of the exploits of Simon Bolívar; Peru's obsession with telenovelas is sent up in Alvaro Velarde's *El destino no tiene favoritos* (*Destiny Has No Favorites*, 2003), *Madame Satã* indirectly explores the heterogeneous body of Brazil through its focus on an Afro-Brazilian homosexual transvestite, who is both masculine and feminine; the diverse faces of Mexico are a constant background to the two teenage boys' adventures in *Y tu mamá también*; even *Nueve reinas*, a film that appears to be rooted in a generic tradition, has at its heart the national preoccupations of crime and corruption.[13]

These national contexts have, in many cases, proven no obstacle to spectators' enjoyment of the films in other countries, and many of the essays in this collection examine the relationship between films and the international market and analyze the forces behind international hits. In chapter 5, Lisa Shaw considers *Madame Satã* and, among other aspects, reflects on how a film that focuses on a fascinating marginalized character from the Brazilian underworld struck a chord with both national and foreign audiences. In chapter 2, Nuala Finnegan's study of *Y tu mamá también* examines the relationships between the local and the global in the film, and she reveals the ways in which the two concepts coexist. The chapter highlights the way in which the film speaks to national concerns and simultaneously presents and undermines a tourist vision of Mexico. In a related approach, in chapter 4 in my study of *Nueve reinas*, I argue that different readings of the film are encouraged through the marketing processes depending on the national context in which it is seen. *Nueve reinas* can be read as a generic scam movie, or it can be viewed as an Argentine film rooted in a national tradition and concerned with contemporary sociopolitical issues. In this way, I explain how both national and international markets have embraced this film. In chapter 1, Williams demonstrates how romantic representations of the iconic figure of Che Guevara as a young idealistic student, coupled with spectacular scenery of Latin American landscapes, provide an example of an approach to filmmaking that is bound to secure commercial success and critical acclaim. Likewise, in chapter 3, Else Vieira hails the extraordinary success of *Cidade de Deus*; she argues that it has been enormously influential in terms of innovations in style and demonstrates how it has both contributed to the internationalization of Brazilian film and helped to provide a new language for the social film while renovating generic traditions associated with Hollywood.

A darker, often untold side to Latin American cinema is that of the commercial failures and films that never make it to our screens. Several of the chapters in this volume provide fascinating explanations for this and consider the difficulties faced by filmmakers, particularly in terms of distribution. In chapter 10, on *El destino no tiene favoritos*, Sarah Barrow looks at the importance of mechanisms of support for filmmakers in the Peruvian context and presents a detailed analysis of the failings in terms of financial and marketing support for national filmmakers. The chapter demonstrates that *El destino no tiene favoritos* is a film with great commercial potential; but the aforementioned failings mean that this potential cannot be exploited. In a similar vein, Haddu's study of *La otra conquista* and its failure to secure an international distribution deal, despite its success in national terms, points to a worrying side effect of the reliance on international finance: the failure of filmmakers to take risks on less glossy, less Europeanized, viewpoints on national identity. Stone's chapter on *Lista de espera*, rather than lamenting the lack of international recognition awarded to the movie, demonstrates the value of a more local approach to filmmaking. This is a film that is specifically Cuban in its focus and aims to appeal to national audiences or to those with a particular interest in Cuban culture. It is, in Stone's words: "an insular work in subject and theme that offers a self-diagnosis of Cuban cinema as a self-reflexive national cinema that is neither intended nor intelligible for international audiences" (p. 135–36). It is important to argue for a space for this kind of cinema in these profit-driven times of globalized film markets.

Another linking theme seen in a number of chapters is the exploration of new forms of representation that run counter to more traditional forms seen in previous films. The chapters by Shaw and Haddu highlight such new departures. In her analysis of *Madame Satã*, Shaw provides an insightful reading of the film's central figure, Joao Francisco de Santos (Madame Satã), a black homosexual transvestite who defies easy categorization and transcends traditional understandings of racial identity, masculinity, and femininity. Haddu focuses on the way in which *La otra conquista* departs from the dominant filmic representations of Europeanized, middle-class Mexicans, and foregrounds the experiences of the indigenous *mexica* during the period of the conquest of Mexico.[14]

Vieira also explores marginalized groups and demonstrates how they are placed center stage in her reading of *Cidade de Deus*. She highlights the ways in which professional actors are largely bypassed in the attempt to represent life in the favelas from the point of view of the favela population. In chapter 7, Geoffrey Kantaris is also concerned with other issues relating to representation; in his reading of the Colombian film *Bolívar soy yo*, he focuses on postmodern questioning of notions of reality in favor of representation. The chapter highlights the way in which the great champion of independence, Bolívar, is seen through a comic filter and used as a vehicle to parody mass media entertainment, principally the telenovela.

Taken together, the chapters in this collection demonstrate the vitality of much contemporary Latin American film culture, both in terms of film production and scholarship. While there are common threads, there are a range of styles, approaches, and themes that speak of a rich and varied culture of filmmaking. This book aims to contribute to this culture by both helping to disseminate knowledge of these important films to a wider audience and offering interpretations that will help fans and researchers gain a deeper understanding of the films.

Notes

1. Antonio Skármeta, "Europe: An Indispensable Link in the Production and Circulation of Latin American Cinema," in *New Latin American Cinema*, vol. 1, *Theory, Practices and Transcontinental Practices*, ed. Michael T. Martin (Detroit: Wayne State University Press, 1997), 263–269, 267. I would like to thank Sue Harper for her helpful comments on the draft of this introduction.

2. Cuáron directed *A Little Princess* (1995), *Great Expectations* (1998), and *Harry Potter and the Prisoner of Azkaban* (2004), shot in the United Kingdom, and starring mainly British actors but produced by Warner Bros. Del Toro directed the Hollywood films *Mimic* (1997) and *Blade II* (2002), and Iñárritu directed *21 Grams* (2003).

3. A number of films funded by this program have been successful; these include: Carlos Carrera's *El crime del padra Amaro* (*The Crime of Father Amaro*, 2002) from Mexico, Lucrecia Martel's *La ciénaga* (*The Swamp*, 2001) from Argentina, and Beatriz Flores Silva's *En la puta vida* (*In This Tricky Life*, 2001) from Uruguay. For more information, see www.programaibermedia.com/esp/htm/home.htm.

4. Information taken from Tamara Falicov, "Ibermedia: The Strengths and Pitfalls of the Ibero-American film Co-Production Fund," paper presented at the New Latin American Cinemas: Contemporary Cinema and Filmmaking Conference, University of Leeds, June 2005.

5. For further discussion on the changing relationship between filmmaking that is supported by the state and privately financed in Latin American contexts, see my conclusion in *Contemporary Latin American Cinema: Ten Key Films* (London: Continuum, 2003), 183–185.

6. Recent monographs and edited volumes on Latin American cinema include: Marina Díaz López and Alberto Elena, eds. *The Cinema of Latin America* (London: Wallflower Press, 2003); Stephen Hart, *A Companion to Latin American Film* (Ipswich, England: Boydell and Brewer, 2004); Lúcia Nagib, *The New Brazilian Film* (London: Tauris, 2003); David William Foster, *Queer Issues in Contemporary Latin American Cinema* (Austin: University of Texas Press, 2003); Deborah Shaw, *Contemporary Cinema of Latin America: 10 Key Films* (London: Continuum, 2003); Lisa Shaw and Stephanie Dennison, eds. *Latin American Cinema Modernity, Gender and National Identity* (Jefferson, N.C.: McFarland, 2005).

7. Michael Chanan, "Contemporary Documentary Currents in Latin America," paper presented at the New Latin American Cinemas: Contemporary Cinema and Filmmaking Conference, University of Leeds, June 2005. Chanan focuses on the work of the Brazilian filmmaker Eduardo Coutinho and *cine piquetero*, which are the works of Argentine filmmakers that documented the financial and political crisis of 2001.

8. Michael Chanan writes of the indigenous groups in Brazil who are making videos to document their traditions and struggles, "Contemporary Documentary Currents."

9. Internet Movie Database (IMDB), Business data for *Y tu mama también*, www.imdb.com/title/tt0245574/business (accessed October 10, 2005).

10. IMDB, Business data for *Lord of the Rings: The Fellowship of the Ring*, www.imdb.com/title/tt0120737/business (accessed October 10, 2005).

11. Andrew A. Higson, "The Limiting Imagination of National Cinema," in *Cinema and Nation*, eds. Mette Hjort and Scott Mackenzie (London: Routledge, 2000), 69.

12. For example, Peter Bradshaw, the respected film reviewer for the *Guardian*, draws a comparison between the two films that is, at best, tenuous. He writes, "*Amores Perros*—increasingly the touchstone of the Latin new wave—began with a car chase and a dead animal. Director Fernando Meirelles's *City of God* [. . .] has something similar, but invests his images with more overtly mythic qualities, irresistibly potent from the very beginning." Peter Bradshaw, "*Cidade de Deus* and *Amores*

Perros," film.guardian.co.uk/News_Story/Critic_Review/Guardian_Film_of_the_week/ 0,4267,867669,00.html (accessed October 15, 2005).

13. There may appear to be some omissions in this book relating to other recent landmark films; there is for example no chapter on either of the two highly influential films by Lucrecia Martel (*La ciénaga* and *La niña santa*), and there is no chapter on *Amores perros*. The reason for these omissions in both cases is that there are other excellent studies either existing or about to be published. The study on Martel's films is included in Joanna Page's *The Aesthetics of Survival: Cinema and the Argentine Crisis* (forthcoming); for an excellent study of *Amores perros*, see Paul Julian Smith's volume in the BFI Modern Classics Series, *Amores perros* (London: BFI, 2003).

14. *La otra conquista* is the only film to be released before 2000; it was first shown in Mexico in 1999, just one year before this period and is included as it offers a counterpoint to the more commercial forms of filmmaking associated with films such as *Amores perros* and *Y tu mamá también*.

CHAPTER ONE

Los diarios de motocicleta
as Pan-American Travelogue

Claire Williams

Walter Salles's film *Los diaros de motocicleta* (*The Motorcycle Diaries*, 2004) is a truly pan-American film. It was put together with funding from Argentina, Chile, Peru, France, the United Kingdom, and the United States; the screenplay was written by a Puerto Rican, José Rivera; it was directed by a Brazilian; and it starred the Mexican actor Gael García Bernal and Argentine actor Rodrigo de la Serna. Furthermore, the project involved local crews and production companies and used actors from across the continent to work in the eleven main locations.[1] And the biggest stamp of approval came from Hollywood royalty in the shape of the executive producer Robert Redford. When Redford invited Salles to direct the story of the young Ernesto "Che" Guevara's travels round Latin America in 1952, the Brazilian reputedly jumped at the chance, even though this would be his first experience of filming in Spanish rather than Portuguese. Guevara's revised version of diaries and letters chronicling the trip, together with the volume published by his co-adventurer (and owner of the motorbike), Alberto Granado, would be the basis of Rivera's script.[2]

The film can be read on many levels: as a road movie, a voyage of self-discovery, a historical travel documentary, a travelogue and guide to sites of symbolic or tourist significance (the lakes of Bariloche, the largest open-pit copper mine in the world at Chuquicamata, the Inca fortress of Machu Picchu, the Amazon jungle), and a representation of two young men's rites of passage as they mature emotionally and politically, learning from the people they meet along the way. This chapter will analyze these various dimensions of the film and consider the construction of a Latin American identity that recognizes differences but celebrates similarities and common struggles. Furthermore, the effects of the journey on the characters, particularly on Ernesto, will be examined in considering the construction of a hero in the making. The last words of the film are Ernesto's, and they emphasize the transformation. In voice-over he recognizes that "I'm not the person I once was" after wandering around "Our America with a capital A."[3]

Salles, originally known in Brazil for his documentaries, is seen by many as the man responsible for the recent popularity of Brazilian cinema on an international scale. The impact of *Central do Brasil* (*Central Station*, 1998), which was nominated for several categories in the 1999 Oscars, encouraged critics to take a closer look at the challenging new films coming out of Latin America. It also became much easier for filmmakers to secure contracts with distributors and thus ensure a worldwide audience. In fact, *Los diarios de motocicleta* was sold for the record sum of $4 million the day after it was launched.[4] Together with his brother, the documentary filmmaker João Moreira Salles, Walter runs a production company, Videofilmes, which has been involved in some of the more recent Brazilian box-office hits at home and abroad, notably Fernando Meirelles's *Cidade de Deus* (*City of God*, 2003).[5] He is known for his commitment to realism, his interest in social themes, and his willingness to improvise scenes and work with untrained actors, like Vinícius de Oliveira, the shoeshine boy who was chosen to star in *Central do Brasil*.

In 1999 Salles said, "it is true that somehow all of my films are about wandering, and this involves two evident consequences: firstly, the idea of loss, for all running forward necessarily involves some loss; and secondly, the possibility of finding people, the possibility of change."[6] This quote captures the essence of his filmmaking: the touch of melancholy and loss, the restless search, and the unexpected encounter that transforms subsequent events. It also resonates with the nomadic spirit of Ernesto, who never really settled after his first transcontinental trip, which left him always trying to reconcile "the two I's struggling inside me: the socialist and the trave[ler]."[7] The road movie provides the perfect structure for stories of self-discovery, and this one, filmed chronologically in eighty-four days, following the route taken fifty years earlier, turned out to be a voyage of discovery for cast and crew, too. Salles declared that he felt that as well as being a Brazilian filmmaker, he now knew that he was a Latin American filmmaker. García Bernal felt like a "*biógrafo*" (biographer) in the way he was recreating the journey and seeing things through his character's eyes.[8]

Thus, the spectator accompanies Ernesto, Alberto, Gael, Rodrigo, and Walter through arid desert, snowy mountains, lush pastures, humid jungle, and along endless highways as they observe the changes in landscape, customs, food, accent and dialect, music, and clothes. The last section of the real journey, through Colombia and Venezuela, does not appear in the film maybe because of difficulties with filming permission but probably because of time restrictions: It shows a wide enough selection of adventures and cultural differences in 126 minutes to make its point. The evocative soundtrack features regional music, from panpipes to a *charango* guitar, from mambo to tango, as the travelers journey from one country and culture to another.

Salles capitalized on the actors' reactions to the scenery, architecture, and natural wonders and made the most of serendipitous encounters, or what he calls "miracles of improvisation" along the way, as he had done in previous films.[9] In *Central do Brasil* he included footage of a religious festival and filmed real people dictating their letters, unrehearsed, to Dora, the protagonist. In *Los diarios de motocicleta*, unscripted, improvised meetings with curious passersby add to the sense of authentic interaction between Ernesto and Alberto and the "real" Latin America. The scenes in the market in Chile and the conversations with "Don" Nestor and the Quechua women were totally spontaneous and filmed with the minimum of equipment. The use of local

Ernesto (Gael García Bernal) and Alberto (Rodrigo de la Serna) in the desert. Los diarios de motocicleta/The motorcycle diaries *(Walter Salles, 2004). Photo: British Film Institute.* Images from The Motorcycle Diaries *appear courtesy of Pathé Pictures International,* © *FilmFour Limited 2004, all rights reserved.*

Ernesto and Alberto on la Poderosa. Los diarios de motocicleta/The Motorcycle Diaries *(Walter Salles, 2004). Photo: British Film Institute. Images from* The Motorcycle Diaries *appear courtesy of Pathé Pictures International, © FilmFour Limited 2004, all rights reserved.*

people in bit parts and as crew members created jobs, albeit temporary ones, and some of the installations that were built for the film at the leper colony were left in place for the inhabitants.[10]

A certain amount of poetic license also fleshed out the plot, in two instances in particular. In the film, Ernesto's girlfriend Chichina gives him fifteen dollars to buy her a bikini when he reaches the United States. This helps to categorize Chichina as a material girl who is ideologically incompatible with her boyfriend. The frivolousness of the errand becomes a way of making it easier for him to cope with her rejection of him, as well as tempering his romanticism. The episode is not mentioned in either diary, but in the film it is an excuse for Alberto to tease Ernesto about his submission to Chichina, calling her "*La patrona*" (the boss) and joking that she has got him "by the balls."[11] Fifteen dollars could buy them comfort and good food or the medical treatment Ernesto requires at one point. Yet he stays true to his beloved until she betrays him, at which point he is finally prepared to give the money to someone who truly needs it. Secondly, the swim across the Amazon becomes symbolic of Ernesto's refusal to recognize borders and inspired the song that plays through the closing credits. In his *Sight and Sound* review of the film, Geoffrey Macnab comments sarcastically that "not since Byron crossed the Dardanelles has a swim been invested with such meaning."[12] Ernesto did swim the Amazon, but according to the diaries, it took him two hours and did not take place either on his birthday or at night.[13] Both of these fictionalized episodes are believable in the context of the film, however, and they contribute toward the representation of the maturing of Ernesto's conscience and personality and to the idealized Che he will become.

Several of Salles's previous films are typical of the road movie, in that they chart a journey from A to B in which the most important factors are the journey, rather than the destination, and the encounters that take place along the way.[14] The open road offers liberation, escape, and discovery of new experiences and environments in comparison to home and the past. *Terra Estrangeira* (*Foreign Land*, 1996) showed the tribulations of a young couple who ran away from the economic crisis in Brazil in 1990 to try to make their fortunes in Portugal—a reversal of the voyages of the Portuguese navigators in the 1500s and also of Portuguese economic emigration to Brazil from the nineteenth century onward. In *Central do Brasil* a middle-aged woman hardened by a lifetime of disappointments rediscovers faith in humanity during her journey from Rio de Janeiro to a village in the rural Northeast, taking a young boy on a kind of pilgrimage to find his father. It is a film that shows the influence on Salles of the *Cinema Novo* films of the 1960s, suffused with social realism and bleak black-and-white images of human suffering in both urban and rural settings. He was to rework these images in *O Primeiro Dia* (*Midnight*, 1999), *Abril Despedaçado* (*Behind the Sun*, 2002) and *Los diarios de motocicleta*. The journey to the center of Brazil suggested by the title *Central do Brasil* mirrors the protagonists' discovery of a country they did not know existed. Not surprisingly, Salles has been lined up by Francis Ford Coppola to direct a film version of Jack Kerouac's seminal road novel *On the Road*, published five years after Guevara's journey. The antiestablishment themes are particularly appealing to the director, who sees them as just as relevant now in the face of a new kind of fundamentalism affecting the world.[15]

On the Road with Ernesto and Alberto

Salles develops the theme of the eventful journey in *Los diarios de motocicleta*. Alberto Granado, a twenty-nine-year-old biochemist, and his friend Ernesto Guevara de la Serna, a twenty-three-year-old medical student, set off to discover their continent and do some good and have some fun at the same time.

The odd couple thrown together on a journey (like Dora and Josué in *Central do Brasil* or Paco and Alex in *Terra Estrangeira*) and the fluctuations in their relationship are, of course, a typical feature of the road movie. These two are not averse to a bit of romance or joining in with any party or football (American soccer) game they may come across. Their limited resources mean they often have to rely on the kindness of strangers, and they are frequently touched by the generosity of their humble hosts. By traveling the cheapest way, they come into contact with the poorest members of society and are able to observe how they live and how they survive against the threats of progress. Ernesto is honest, loyal, and principled and becomes outraged at the injustices he sees committed against his fellow man. The film becomes a kind of hagiography, relating the trials and revelations of the idealistic young man of the people, as will be discussed later in the chapter.

Salles researched *Los diarios de motocicleta* for three years, meeting the families of Ernesto and Alberto in Cuba, retracing the journey to find suitable locations in the spots the pair visited, consulting experts in asthma and leprosy, listening to music from the 1950s, and studying Aymara and Inca history and culture. Despite the attention to period detail, the film has a timelessness to it, because it focuses on sites of natural beauty or historical importance and also because in many of the locations little has changed over the last fifty years. The underlying messages of the film (and the published diaries) are timeless, too: the value of friendship and the need for charity, hospitality, and dignity, lacking in an unjust society. "This is not a story of heroic feats" warns the voice-over and subtitle (it is a direct quote from Guevara's diary) that begin the film "but the story of two lives that ran parallel for a time." It was undoubtedly the combination of spectacular scenery, humor, and humanism that confirmed success for *Los diarios de motocicleta* on the international circuit. It is not a documentary or biopic but a text that was open (or, in Salles's words "porous"[16]) to a certain amount of improvisation as filming progressed and situations arose along the way—improvisation also being the method Ernesto claims, during the first minutes of the film, that the pair will use to complete their trip. The interpolated testimonies of people encountered during the trip (rather like the flashbacks in *Y tu mamá también*) increase the sense of authenticity of the film and emphasize that the same problems affect the area as they did fifty years before.

The protagonist of this film is not "El Comandante," the revolutionary who fought alongside Fidel Castro in Cuba in the late 1950s, addressed the United Nations General Assembly in 1964, traveled to China, the Soviet Union, and around Africa, was assassinated in 1967, and became the face that launched a thousand T-shirts. This is Che before the beard, the cigar, and the beret. He is not yet the self-proclaimed Latin American who traveled from Chile to Mexico, became a revolutionary in Guatemala, fought in Cuba, and was killed in Bolivia. This is the story of twenty-three-year-old Argentine Ernesto Guevara de la Serna, known to his friends as "Fuser" (a contraction of *furibundo*, which means frenzied and Serna, his surname), the nickname he earned playing violent games of rugby that tested his asthmatic lungs to full capacity.[17] This is an idealistic, adventurous young man prepared to suspend his degree in medicine to study people firsthand. However, the figure of who he was to become informs the focus on his reactions to episodes of exploitation of the poor by the powerful. He is still at the stage of being a dreamer (often seen gazing, half-frowning, into the distance or writing thoughtfully in his diary) and although he has a pistol his father gave him, the extent of his anger is to throw a stone at the truck of the foreman of the Anaconda Mining Company. The journey helps him to realize that as a doctor he can only treat the consequences and not the causes of the continent's problems, that "a revolution cannot take place without guns." The film does not concentrate exclusively on Ernesto but also chronicles the ways in which the journey shapes his fellow traveler: Alberto Granado (Mial to his rugby pals), whose younger brother was Ernesto's best friend.[18] Their already firm relationship develops as they tease and argue with each other but look after each other's welfare. They work as a double act when chatting up girls or trying to get a square meal or a bed for the night by using the exaggerated article they managed to get published in the *diário austral*, or the "anniversary" routine Guevara describes in his diaries.[19] Initially, Alberto's barefaced cheek and "*la infalible lábia de Alberto*" (bullshitting) contrast with Ernesto's inability to tell a lie, but this honesty wears off at moments when their financial situation becomes more precarious.

Although in the late twentieth and early twenty-first centuries it seems like there is a constant flow of backpackers and students on gap years traveling around South America, the habits, means of transport, and border restrictions were extremely different in the 1950s. Then, as now, a trip round South America that includes a return ticket to university or a job is only accessible to the more privileged traveler. Alberto and Ernesto had the background and education to make their journey possible, but their experiences of hardship and danger (as for many travelers) were temporary and bearable because of that. When they were unable to obtain money from their families, they used their skills, their titles, their luck, and their audacity. In the 1950s, television had not yet arrived in European-influenced Argentina, and people knew and cared little about their neighboring countries. Alberto and Ernesto knew more about distant and ancient civilizations, like the Greeks and

Phoenicians, than they did (beyond broadly stereotyped ideas) about the great founding civilizations of their own continent or about their contemporaries in Brazil, Peru, or Mexico.[20] The eight-month, 8,000-mile journey they undertook crossed almost the length of the continent of South America, from Córdoba in the south to Caracas on the north coast, passing through Argentina, Chile, Peru, Colombia, and Venezuela. Brazil, the largest country in South America, was not on the route, presumably because of the language barrier as well as for logistical or bureaucratic reasons.

In the first scenes of the film the two young men declare their intention to explore a continent they had only known in books, and Alberto confidently draws their route on a map, unaware that it will not be as easy getting from A to B as he thinks. At the end of the film, the map serves as a physical reminder of the life-changing journey, and Alberto presents it to Ernesto as a keepsake. Symbolically Ernesto takes the map and all he has learned with him into the future. He is the one who flies away to great things, while Alberto watches the plane disappear and chooses to stay behind in Venezuela. A final shot of the real, octogenarian Alberto Granado gazing into the distance and remembering his friend shows what he has become all these years later. Guevara's fate is described in a subtitle (as are Granado's achievements), but no images of him post-1952 are shown, avoiding explicitly politicizing the film and capturing instead the idea of Ernesto as he was before he was "El Che."

The continuous line drawn by Alberto on the map is also the narrative thread of the film, framed by the departure and an arrival that is simultaneously a departure toward new horizons. The objective of the trip, to explore the continent, propels the pair forward along with the deadlines they have to respect: Alberto's thirtieth birthday and the start of the new academic year. They choose movement and the unknown over stagnation and the familiar. Alberto teases Ernesto by pointing at an overweight, balding, older man, nodding off over his drink and saying: "You don't want to end up like that guy over there, do you?"[21] Like Don Quixote and Sancho Panza (or General San Martín), they set off for adventure.[22]

A road movie offers the director multiple opportunities for lingering panoramic shots of the backdrop. This film is shot with loving attention to the spectacular mountains, plains, desert, and jungle, the geographical variety of the continent. The straight, parallel lines of the highways across the plains and desert provide opportunities to focus on the vanishing point of the horizon, simultaneously representing the journey and its destination. As the motorcycle adventure proper begins, the camera follows the road from the viewpoint of a biker, creating a symmetrical picture in which the lines of perspective lead into the distance and the future. After a few seconds of this hypnotic symmetrical view, Ernesto and Alberto overtake on *La poderosa* (mighty lady) and splutter ahead. The motorbike, which in road movies like Dennis Hopper's *Easy Rider* (1969)[23] represents modernity and speed, is soon overtaken by a pair of *gauchos* on horseback; just as the exhausted protagonists are overtaken by a Peruvian peasant while ascending a mountain road on foot later in the film. Modernity and youth are ironically shown wanting in comparison with the traditional skills of the horsemen and the stoic stamina of a native Andean. The hairpin bends that encircle more undulating countryside allow a fixed camera to observe the bike in motion from various angles, against stunning backdrops.

A variety of means of transport must be used once Alberto's beloved machine can no longer be "operated on" and repaired.[24] An optimistic Ernesto concludes that a journey on foot and by hitching rides will bring them more opportunities to meet people. When the pair is entering the Atacama desert, the camera shoots them from the dusty booted feet upward to emphasize the change in transport and environment. The camera is always handheld when they are on foot, the jolts of the low-angle shots matching their steps and ensuring that the spectator always shares their viewpoint. From the diaries, we know that through Chile, Peru, Colombia, and Venezuela they stowed away on cargo ships and cadged lifts on long-distance trucks carrying a variety of produce; but few truck scenes appear in the film, perhaps because they are unnecessary to the plot or aesthetically uninteresting.[25] When Ernesto and Alberto travel through the Peruvian Andes, there are shots of indigenous people on mountain paths contrasted with reverse shots of Ernesto's frowning face looking down on them, framed in a truck window that fills the screen. He travels in relative comfort, at a greater speed than them and from choice, whereas they are forced to emigrate: "homeless in their own land." The scenes in the jungle, both on the boat and on the raft, show Ernesto and Alberto observing the mighty river as well as the humble dwellings that appear on the banks from time to time. The camera circles the boat and the raft, showing the humans immobile on their crafts, at the mercy of the forces of nature.

The film alternates between scenes of the travelers in motion and pauses for the stops along their way or for conversations with passersby. In this way the road symbolically opens up into a land. Two vital breaks in the action are the campfire conversation with the mining couple in the Atacama desert and the visit to Machu Picchu. The encounter with the economic migrants shocks Ernesto into a reevaluation of his journey; they were evicted from their land, persecuted for being Communists, and forced to migrate to find work, whereas he had the luxury of traveling "just to travel." The gaunt faces of the Chilean and his wife in the flickering light from the campfire remind us of the "faces dark with hunger" Ernesto expected to encounter when he set out and prefigure the black-and-white portraits that provide an emphatic end to the film. The excursion to Machu Picchu, still one of South America's most visited sites, is another example of how the cast's experience replicates the characters' and most likely affects the spectator. There are several minutes of silence as with shared amazement the viewer watches their awestruck faces taking in the monumental remains. Both men are unkempt, and Ernesto has the beginnings of the beard that will become part of his revolutionary image. It cannot be by chance that a glimpse of the future icon is engineered in the place where he observes "the pure expression of the most powerful indigenous race in the Americas."[26] The imposing ruins remind Ernesto and Alberto of the glory of the South American people (prior to the arrival of the *conquistadores*) and lead them to wonder about alternative pasts that would have changed their present. Despite the aesthetic and historical importance of the landscape, the last scenes of the film dwell on the faces of the people encountered along the journey rather than on the views. Salles has carefully made it clear, through his choice of the episodes and faces depicted, that it is the people and their suffering that inspire Ernesto to fight.

As he travels onward, the transformation in Ernesto takes place visibly, through his gradual observations and realizations and by implication as he learns from people and from books. The asthma attacks that debilitate him enable him to empathize with the sick and mean that his bedside manner is extremely effective. He tends to the dying Doña Rosa and the young leper Silvia respectfully, calmly, and in semidarkness, which creates intimacy and trust between doctor and patients. He becomes more and more assertive, whereas Alberto, formerly the bold leader of the expedition, starts to ask Ernesto's advice and take it. Ernesto is no longer content to stand passively by while he witnesses inequality. Finally, in the leper colony of San Pablo, he is prepared to do something about it; he swims the Amazon that separates sick from well so that he can celebrate his birthday with the patients as well as with the doctors, excluding nobody. This idealization of Ernesto runs parallel with the simplified politics of the film. Ernesto is the obvious hero, but who are the villains? They are the invisible landlords, land speculators, and managing directors of foreign companies who employ foremen to do their dirty work. They are professionals who abuse their status, the "snobs" who exploit their workers, and they are even the nuns at the leper colony who blackmail people into attending Mass. The film avoids direct accusations but shows the strengthening of Ernesto's resolve and his indefatigable humanism that cannot help but inspire optimism: he will do something about it. Of course, there is no explanation of exactly what he did next or any suggestion that it might have been wrong.

Ernesto is seen writing in his diary after moments that have particularly affected him: in the tent at Miramar after observing class prejudice in action during dinner, after treating Doña Rosa, on an Inca wall at Machu Picchu, on the riverboat after observing the differences between first- and second-class travel, and in the colony at San Pablo. We also hear his words in voice-over to explain his observations and realizations. He and Alberto compare the countries they have visited and contrast the great civilizations of the past with the injustices of the present wrought by greed, exploitation, and capitalism. Alberto captured his friend's words in his diary: "This is how it is. Heads and tails, always the two sides of the coin. The beauty of the landscape and the natural wealth of the land set against the poverty of those who work it."[27] Ernesto and Alberto hear stories of eviction, slave labor, abuse, the slide into passivity, and self-loathing of the indigenous people of the continent. They begin to think about their common heritage and habitat, beyond political and national frontiers. In Machu Picchu, Alberto (whom Ernesto teased about wanting to "get laid in every country in Latin America") jokes that he should marry a girl descended from the Incas and found an Indo-American dynasty, but Ernesto, in his birthday speech, is less flippant. He declares that "the division of [Latin] America into unstable and illusory nations is completely fictional" and that "we constitute a single mestizo race, which from Mexico to the Magellan Straits bears notable ethnographic similarities," ending with a toast to a "United Latin America."[28] The film itself, as a transnational cooperative project, represents just such a dream come true.

Even before they have left Argentina, Alberto and Ernesto are conspicuous outsiders "outlaws," "commanding attention" wherever they go. They stand out because of their accent and shabby appearance (part of their playing the role of *vagabundos* [tramps]), which make them objects of curiosity and sometimes suspicion. Alberto wears baggy *gaucho* trousers. They drink *hierba mate* from a *cimarrón* gourd, the sure sign of a Southerner. And they use the interjection *che*, so distinctively Argentine that it became Ernesto's nickname, given to him by Cuban and Mexican friends, which he eventually adopted. During their farewell at the airport in Caracas, Alberto deliberately and prophetically addresses Ernesto as *Che*, reminding the audience of who he will become. They play at being ambassadors for their country, trying to persuade the mechanic in Temuco that by mending the bike he will be "doing incalculable service to the bilateral relations between our countries," or joking about Argentine customs and Chilean traits.

On the road, they learn that there are cultural manifestations that transcend borders, nationalities, race, and class: sport and music. Wherever they go, people have heard of Argentine footballers and know the words to popular tangos (this is made clear in Alberto's diary). In the leper colony, they play football with the sick and join in with them making music. They progress from simply sharing their *mate* or blankets with fellow travelers to sharing a more human warmth, represented by their refusal to use the gloves and coats that mark the difference between doctor and patient.

The idealistic young travelers become more and more aware of the borders that construct, categorize, and stratify society according to nation, race, language, creed, class, and state of health. Ernesto makes a conscious decision to reject all these borders and to treat all men and women as equals. The first stop on their journey is the holiday resort of Miramar, where the privileged relax in their reproduction Swiss chalets. The travelers feel out of place among the snobbishness and prejudice of the upper classes. Further along the way, they try to impress people by introducing themselves as doctors. Yet when they are not in need of a favor, they introduce themselves plainly as Ernesto and Alberto—open, friendly, and interested in everyone they meet. The portrayal of different classes in the film tends to suggest that the poor are inherently generous, and the rich are naturally ignorant and prejudiced. However, the upper classes are only portrayed in the scenes at Miramar. The published diaries are more balanced and provide accounts of encounters with soldiers, firemen, policemen, prisoners, sailors, truck drivers, students, diplomats, and doctors who vary in their attitudes toward the indigent Argentines.

It is important that this rediscovery of Latin America is made by Latin Americans rather than by the foreigners who have traditionally represented it, from Columbus to Darwin and modern travel guides (never mind Hollywood films). Alberto Granado described his motivation behind his journey thus: "I needed to see the world, but first I wanted to see Latin America, my own long-suffering continent—not through the eyes of a tourist, interested only in landscapes, comforts, and fleeting pleasures but with the eyes and spirit of one of the people, someone wanting to know about the continent's beauty, its riches, the men and women who live there."[29] He and Ernesto stayed true to this proposal, although they were never able to provide more than companionship, food, and maybe medical help. They could not help but be tourists to a great extent: interested in seeing the famous sights, describing them to their families in letters, and taking photos for posterity. Many of those photos still exist in archives and collections and served as templates for the film, such as Ernesto framed by an Inca doorway in Machu Picchu or the launch of the Mambo Tango raft.[30]

Twenty-first century spectators cannot fail to be impressed by the beauty and variety in the landscape of South America as portrayed in the film. Each setting is identified by a white subtitle giving the location, the name of the country, the date, and the distance traveled by Ernesto and Alberto on reaching it. The views, labeled thus, could be taken for postcards, were it not for the information about kilometers traveled. Because it displays important sites in the continent that viewers from around the world will have heard of for their geographical, ecological, aesthetic, or historical significance, the film provides an almost comprehensive introductory travel guide to Latin America; this helps to explain the film's transnational appeal. In fact, in the same week that the film went on general release in the United Kingdom, a special *Los diarios de motocicleta* tour offered by Journey Latin America was advertised in the *Observer* magazine. The twenty-three-day tour, "aiming to be as faithful as possible" to the original trip, includes visits to "the places that had the most impact on Che" as well as "some of the region's highlights," and promises reassuringly "the travel infrastructure of 2004 not the 1950s."[31] The film has undoubtedly inspired tourism to South America and even motorcycle journeys, although whether the increased flow of visitors benefits the inhabitants economically remains to be seen.[32] Almost a year after the film went on general release in the United Kingdom, British travel journalist Stanley Stewart admitted that "I hadn't realized I even had an inner biker until I saw *The Motorcycle Diaries*. . . . As cultural icons, motorcycles and Che are made for one another—rebellious, romantic, dangerous."[33]

The final sequence of the film is a series of black-and-white shots of the people encountered along the journey through Argentina, Chile, and Peru. A few shots interrupted the action earlier on in the film: on the river boat, where the third-class passengers travel in a communal boat with the livestock, and in Lima, after Ernesto started to read César Vallejo and José Carlos Mariátegui on the recommendation of leprosy specialist Dr. Pesce.[34] These texts, it is implied, help Ernesto to clarify his thoughts about the inequalities he has witnessed on his travels and to start deciding what he will do about them. Mariátegui's theories about the "revolutionary potential" of the indigenous people and the claim that "we are too few to be divided, everything unites us," both quoted in the film, prove to Ernesto that not only Europeans think along Marxist lines. The twelve living photos that linger on the screen for several seconds are carefully composed to present human beings against landscapes associated with their lives or in their workplaces with their colleagues and the tools of their professions. They are reminiscent of the striking and emotive studies of workers and the dispossessed by Brazilian photographer Sebastião Salgado, the eyes of the people not accusing, begging, or smiling but simply stating their existence.[35] Salles explains that he was in-fluenced by the work of Martin Chambi, a Peruvian photographer of the 1920s, "who was the first to take the camera out of the studio and photograph people in the streets. He treated people you would never have seen before as citizens, anticipating what the Italian neorealists did in the 1940s and '50s."[36] These are not stills, however, because there are movements to indi-cate that these people are alive and that their problems exist. It is the faces rather than the views that remain in Ernesto's mind (especially the last one: the Chilean emigrant worker they met in the desert) and are the last images of the journey presented to the audience. The faces display the range of eth-nicities native to South America, but because they are shown sequentially there is no need for a comment on their nationality. Their identity is clear. They, like Ernesto and Alberto, are Latin American.[37]

Notes

1. The filming of the journey was a logistical nightmare that required detailed planning, according to producer Michael Nozick, interviewed on the DVD version of the film. As a transnational cooperative production, *Los diarios de motocicleta* has much in common with Fernando Solanas's *El Viaje* (*The Voyage*, 1991), although Salles's political message is far subtler and less didactic. For a reading of Solanas's search for Latin American identity through this film, see Deborah Shaw, "Heroes, Villains and Women: Representations of Latin America in *The Voyage*," in *Contemporary Latin American Cinema: Ten Key Films* (London: Continuum, 2003), 159–87.

2. Ernesto "Che" Guevara, *The Motorcycle Diaries: Notes on a Latin American Journey* (London: Fourth Estate, 2004). In the wake of the film's success, the cover of the book was changed to feature Bernal and Serna in action on the bike. Alberto Granado's complementary account, *Traveling with Che Guevara: The Making of a Revolutionary* (London: Pimlico, 2003), was first published in 1978. Italian journalist Gianni Minà obtained the rights to Guevara's diaries and intended to make a film of Granado making the journey fifty years later, but he was unable to finance it until Redford and FilmFour stepped in (Geoffrey Macnab review in *Sight and Sound* 14, no. 9 [September 2004], 70, 72). Granado, an energetic octogenarian, did accompany the crew during the filming of some scenes, as he relates in the preface to the revised edi-tion of his memoir.

3. Unless attributed to the original diaries, quotes are taken from the subtitles of the DVD version of the film. *Los diarios de motocicleta*, DVD, directed by Walter Salles (Universal Studios, 2005).

4. Neca de Araújo Ribeiro and Juliano Zappia, "Making Up for Lost Time," *Jungle Drums* 10 (March 2004), 20–27.

5. In the wake of *Los diarios de motocicleta*, much in the spirit of pan-Latin American cooperation, Videofilmes is collaborating in projects with documen-

taries by some of the non-Brazilian crew who worked on the film (the composer, Gustavo Santaolalla, the Chilean assistant director Samuel León, and the Argentine assistant director Julia Solomonoff), according to an interview with Salles by Jaime Biaggio ("*Caminhos tortuosos*," *O Globo* 11 [August 2005], 1 [Segundo Caderno]).

6. Walter Salles, quoted by Alberto Elena in "*Terra Estrangeira*," in *The Cinema of Latin America*, ed. Alberto Elena and Marina Díaz López (London: Wallflower, 2003), 211–19, 215.

7. This quotation is taken from a letter Guevara wrote to his mother on May 10, 1954, which is reprinted in *Back on the Road: A Journey to Central America*, trans. Patrick Camiller (London: Vintage, 2002), 61.

8. Interview with Gael García Bernal for the "Cast and Crew Interviews" section of the DVD version of the film.

9. Anthony Kaufman, "On the Road with Walter Salles, Director of *Central Station*" (an interview with Salles), *Indiewire*, www.indiewire.com/people/int_Salles_Walter_981118.htm (accessed August 13, 2004).

10. In the preface to the English translation of his diaries, Granado explains proudly that "in each of the countries where the film was shot, it was done using local bit players, workers, and advisers for each category, thus creating jobs at a time when there is massive unemployment as a result of the neo-liberal policies of those countries' governments. And a further cause for satisfaction is the fact that installations built at Santa María—the electricity supply, the meeting rooms, the pathways made of timber, the distribution of running water, all the grid that provides lighting to the village, and all that was built for the film—remain in place for the enjoyment of the local inhabitants and as a result will enhance the living conditions of each and every one of them," Granado, *Traveling with Che Guevara*, xv–xvi.

11. In the film Chichina tries to use Ernesto's desire for her as a way of making him stay longer, despite her parents' disapproval of him. As they embrace, she tells him "I'd like you to stay like this—silent," and the audience realizes that because he cannot stay silent, the romance will not last.

12. Macnab, "The Motorcycle Diaries," 72.

13. Guevara, *Notes on a Latin American Journey*, 150, 155.

14. There are many definitions of the genre, but Timothy Corrigan's, the one used as a template for the postwar U.S. road movie in *The Road Movie Book*, relies on four related features: the "destabilization of male subjectivity and masculine empowerment" resulting from the breakdown of the family unit; "events act upon the characters during the journey"; the protagonist "readily identifies with the means of mechanized transportation"; it promotes "a male escapist fantasy . . . defining the road as a space that is at once resistant to while ultimately contained by the responsibilities of domesticity: home life, marriage, employment." Steven Cohan and Ina Rae Hark, "Introduction" in *The Road Movie Book* (London: Routledge, 1997), 1–14. Corrigan's definition appears in his study *A Cinema Without Walls: Movies and Culture after Vietnam* (New Brunswick, N.J.: Rutgers University Press, 1991).

15. Biaggio, "*Caminhos tortuosos,*" 1. In the same interview, Jaime Biaggio asks Salles about the making of *Dark Water* (2005) (a Hollywood remake of a successful Japanese horror film) the first English-language film he was invited to direct. Ever the diplomat, Salles is careful not to confirm or deny rumors that he was not pleased about the studio's interference with his work and pressure to please the market, but he does admit that the final cut was not his. He wanted to try a genre film, and he accepted that at some point he would work in Hollywood. However, the experience confirmed for him that he is not a Hollywood director: "*Filmar fora me deu ainda mais certeza de ser um cineasta brasileiro. É aqui que quero trabalhar.* . . . On the Road *é um pouco a exeção que confirma a regra*" (Filming abroad made me even more certain that I am a Brazilian director. I want to work here. *On the Road* is a bit like the exception that proves the rule.)

16. Geoff Andrew, "Guardian/NFT interview: Walter Salles," *Guardian Unlimited*, August 26, 2004, film.guardian.co.uk/interview/interviewpages/0,6737,1291387,00 .html (accessed August 19, 2005).

17. Che had various nicknames including *pelao* (baldy), because he used to wear his hair short and *chancho* (pig), his pen name in the school rugby magazine. This name came from his claim not to wash for weeks on end. See Ruben Ayala, "Rugby en Argentina," www.geocities.com/cherugby/historia01.html (accessed August 13, 2004).

18. Lúcia Álvarez de Toledo writes this footnote to the "Preface to the English Language Edition" of Granado's diaries: "Mial: a nickname given to [Granado] by Guevara. It is a contraction of Mi Alberto, which is what his grandmother used to call him," *Traveling with Che Guevara*, xvi.

19. Guevara, *The Motorcycle Diaries*, 130–31.

20. Granado affirms this in the interview included on the DVD version of the film. See also the film's official Web site at www.motorcyclediaries.movie.com/ home.html (accessed August 28, 2005).

21. During their goodbyes, Señor Guevara gives his son a revolver that he never uses. The only other reference to firearms is in Machu Picchu when Ernesto solemnly informs Alberto that in his opinion a revolution without guns can never succeed—a foreshadowing of his explosive political actions in the future.

22. José de San Martín (1778–1850) is the Argentine hero who successfully led the fight against the Spaniards and helped secure the independence of Argentina, Peru, and Chile.

23. The ad campaign for *Easy Rider* proclaimed "A man went looking for America and couldn't find it anywhere." Ernesto and Alberto went looking for Latin America and found a continent they did not expect.

24. *La poderosa* turns out to be as reliable as Chichina, who coincidentally breaks up with Ernesto by letter shortly after they abandon the bike. It is described in human terms: it "pees oil," needs operations, and eventually is laid to rest as *La defunta* (the deceased woman).

25. Writer Matthew Parris describes the discomforts of traveling on Peruvian trucks in *Inca-Kola: A Traveler's Tale of Peru* (London: Phoenix, 1993).

26. Guevara, *The Motorcycle Diaries*, 111.

27. Granado, *Traveling with Che Guevara*, 15.

28. Guevara, *The Motorcycle Diaries*, 149.

29. Granado, *Traveling with Che Guevara*, xvii.

30. Some of the photos appear as the final credits roll. Others are reproduced in the Fourth Estate paperback copy of *The Motorcycle Diaries: A Journey Around South America* (London: Fourth Estate, 1996).

31. Advertisement: "Your Chance to Follow Che," *Observer*, August 29, 2004, 4. The London-based company is still running the tours. See www.journeylatinamerica .com/motorcycle/tour.shtml (accessed August 29, 2005).

32. As admissions tutor for Hispanic studies courses running at the University of Liverpool, I have noticed that a considerable number of applicants cite *Los diarios de motocicleta* as a film that inspired them either to travel through Latin America or to study Spanish at the university level.

33. Stanley Stewart, "CC the World: Top Trips on Two Wheels" *Times*, June 12, 2005, 8–9. The microsite developed by Channel 4 and FilmFour includes a section about intrepid graduates Ben Lawrie and Karl Rees, who made their own motorcycle journey "In Che's Tyre Tracks" and "like Che, wanted to do something that would change [them] fundamentally," using the trip to raise money for the British Leprosy Relief Association. See www.channel4/film/cinemadvd/microsites/M/motorcycle_ diaries/index.html (accessed August 28, 2005).

34. Ernesto is seen reading Jose Carlos Mariátegui's, trans. by Marjori Urquidi, *Seven Interpretative Essays on Peruvian Reality* (*Siete ensayos de interpretación de la realidad peruana* [1928]) (Austin: University of Texas Press, 1971), which is, according to James Higgins "a Marxist analysis of Peruvian society and history. The thrust of Mariátegui's argument was that as a result of the colonial experience Peru had failed to produce either a capitalist bourgeoisie or an industrial working class. He . . . proposed that national progress could only be achieved through a [program] of agrarian reform, which would restore land to the indigenous communities, whose collective traditions would be built on to construct a new society." See José Carlos Mariátegui, *Lima* (Oxford: Signal, 2005), 177–78.

35. I am thinking particularly of Sebastião Salgado's *Other Americas* (New York: Pantheon, 1986) and *Workers: An Anthology of the Industrial Age* (London: Phaidon, 1993).

36. Nick James, "Against the Current," *Sight and Sound* 14, no. 9 (September 2004): 8–9.

37. I am grateful to Claire Taylor for assistance with technical terms and to Núria Triana Toríbio, with whom I first saw the film and discussed many of the ideas explored in this essay.

CHAPTER TWO

"So What's Mexico Really Like?"
Framing the Local, Negotiating the Global in Alfonso Cuarón's Y *tu mamá también*

Nuala Finnegan

The question posed here—so what's Mexico really like?[1]—captures the predicament often experienced by filmmakers making films about the national. Examples abound in which directors are accused of betrayal, fabrication, cynicism, or naiveté when it comes to the vexed question of the representation of the national in a cinematic context.[2] What is of interest in this chapter is this virtual intervention into the debate about Alfonso Cuarón's successful feature, Y *tu mamá también,* and the assumption made by the anonymous reviewer that the film, while clearly on one level about the nature of teenage friendship and sexuality in what is often a prototypical coming-of-age road movie, is also certainly about Mexico.[3] Here, thus, is a film that fuses its obvious international focus with a story about modernity and more specifically, Mexico's tumultuous path toward first-world integration. How then to analyze this focus on the national within what is clearly a global framework with regard to plot, genre, and distribution?[4] Indeed the juxtaposition of the global and the local constitutes one of the primary sources of fascination in a film that while "apparently artless"[5] on one level still attempts, in a self-referential way, to comment on the way Mexico's youth negotiate and interact with certain aspects of modern Mexico.

It is, of course, widely acknowledged that the effects of globalization are far-reaching and that moreover, as Nestor García Canclini attests, it is in the terrain of the visual that its effects are most striking.[6] It is also the case that when analyzing the juxtaposition of local and global, caution must be exercised in any uncritical acceptance of the pairing as binary opposites.[7] As Inderpal Grewal and Caren Kaplan assert:

> What is lost in an uncritical acceptance of this binary division is precisely the fact that the parameters of the local and global are often indefinable or distinct—they are permeable constructs. How one separates the local from the global is difficult to decide when each thoroughly infiltrates the other.[8]

Thus in analyzing Y tu mamá también, it is the infiltration of both categories by the other that is of interest. García Canclini maintains that the general process of deterritorialization marked by globalization is accompanied by strong movements of "reterritorialization."[9] This trend has also been noted with regard to recent Mexican cinema when Paul Julian Smith observes that Y tu mamá también is an example of an "emergent promotion-innovation paradigm (in which art and commerce are no longer held to be antagonistic in the elaboration of a new national style)."[10] He goes on to note that this model, from which Y tu mamá también is so clearly derived, leads not to "homogeni[zation] but to a reinforcement of territorial markers such as land and language."[11] What is so interesting about this observation is how clearly it seems to match Cuarón's vision in the film. What we might term the quintessential presence of the global appears in a kind of dual focus with an often overdetermined national presence that begs as many questions as it poses. In a discussion of a postmodern capitalist era, in which transnational practices overcome the pretenses of national sovereignty, mixed with the widely acknowledged dislocation between filmmaker and nation occurring in Latin America, just what is at stake in Cuarón's overdetermined envisioning of Mexico?[12]

This chapter argues that the film is an archetypal product of a globalized culture industry following Smith's contention that this, in fact, leads to an increased local stamp on the product itself.[13] How this plays itself out will be documented through detailed examination of the envisioning of Mexico in the film. What is perhaps most interesting about the continuous bombardment of images and references (both visual and aural) to contemporary Mexico is that all too often, the images destabilize themselves, shifting continually between what might be called a "globalized" local and a more "localized" local, with its more critical and often sensitive depiction of a local life that quite literally tells another story. The first version constitutes a "visión de turista" ("tourist vision")[14] or a veritable "guided tour"[15] of Mexico's hot spots and high moments, encapsulated by the characters' jubilant toast at the end of the film, "¡Por México lindo! ¡Por México mágico!" ("To beautiful Mexico!

To magical Mexico!"). However, as shall be seen, the film constantly undermines its own positions, shifting focus quite literally from shot to shot and from voice-over back to plot. In this way *Y tu mamá también* actually exemplifies the permeability of the global and local constructs through the seemingly effortless fusion of both. Ultimately, this chapter contends that this undermining of global/local oppositions is where the film's political charge lies, an undermining that leads to a profound ambivalence evident at every level: character, camera work, plot, and genre. Thus the Mexico that emerges is unstable and unable to be represented, joyful and pitiful, anchored in an ambivalence constructed by a filmmaker who himself embodies the contradictions and tensions inherent in the local/global paradigm.[16]

Global Traces

The obvious presence of the global is shown at various levels in the film. The film first uses the road movie genre, derived historically from the Hollywood film tradition[17] in combination with some of the essential elements of the genre: the use of the road as an open space free from the hegemonic norms prevalent in the town or city; escapism; the clash between modernity and tradition; the quest for identity; and, indeed, the homoerotic subtext.[18] The second genre that clearly infuses the text is the teenage sex movie, popular in Hollywood since the 1980s. Early examples of this kind of film include the *Porky's* series, released in the early 1980s, that set the tone for many other teen films of that era. The film (and its sequels) takes a humorous look at the sex lives of a group of teenage boys in 1950s Florida in all their obsessive, unfulfilled glory. More recent successes include *American Pie* (1999) and *American Pie 2* (2001) and perhaps in a closer parallel to *Y tu mamá también*, *Road Trip* (2000), which also combines the road movie plot with the sexual adventures of its protagonists. Key to the success of *Y tu mamá también* was its juvenile humor, which proved immensely appealing to its audience, and like Hollywood films pitched at teenage audiences, ensured that viewers returned again and again. Interestingly, the film was ironically placed in Categoría C (sólo para mayores de 18 años) (Category C [only for those over 18]) "*para tratar de que los adolescentes no la vean*" ("to ensure that teenagers couldn't see it").[19] This was, however, largely ignored by many Mexican cinemas, ensuring its extraordinary commercial success.[20] The ruling also brought widespread publicity to the film through the insatiable marketing campaign waged by the film's producer Jorge Vergara Madrigal, who designated it "*el primer acto de censura del gobierno del presidente Vicente Fox*" ("the first act of censorship of the Vicente Fox government").[21] This alleged "censorship" of the film further cemented its popularity in capturing a kind of Mexican zeit-geist. However, the film's colorful language, replete with sexual jokes and ju-venile humor, attracted opprobrium from other quarters, and Mexican critic, Vicente García Tsao labeled it *"una versión chilanga de Beavis y Butthead"* ("a Mexico City version of 'Beavis and Butthead'"), which is another interesting reference to its clear indebtedness to North American genres and conven-tions.[22]

Other evidence of globalized style and production can be found in the film's hybrid soundtrack, incorporating artists as diverse as Frank Zappa, Brian Eno, Natalie Imbruglia, La Revolución de Emiliano Zapata, Flaco Jiménez, and Café Tacuba.[23] Furthermore, the film includes a major Spanish character (Luisa) who at times, literally, translates the local *chilango* dialect for Spanish-speaking viewers outside of Mexico City. The high-speed use of Mexican city slang, the in-jokes, and private vocabulary prompt Luisa on many occasions to ask them to explain what they mean. Other questions fol-low later in her dialogue with the boys about their lovemaking. Her insistent questioning and probing of the boys' Mexican cowboy (*charolastra*) code un-ravels the dense dialogue and explains some of its more arcane arrangements. The slang, it may be argued, functions both as defensive mechanism and a verbal vehicle for the boys' *machismo*, which is constantly exposed by Luisa in the same way that their impenetrable language is teased out and ex-plained. Thus the use of intensely local language is juxtaposed against the more widely recognizable Spanish of the mediator, Luisa. In this way not only is the global seamlessly fused again with the local, but it is the sense of the local that emerges triumphant. The local is demystified by the global but is in no way effaced by it, thereby ensuring its prominence and, in fact, helping to illuminate it on a global stage.

Alongside the evident presence of the global in terms of plot, soundtrack, language, and genre, therefore, the film is already framing the local while ne-gotiating global frameworks and contexts. Even from within the countless images of Mexico that saturate the film, we detect a globalized local, a film that enacts the kind of guided tour discussed by French critic Serge Daney in some of his comments on postmodern cinema. Taking his cue from Daney, Smith maintains that in this kind of cinema, "the director displays his cine-matic props for the consumerist delight of the spectator."[24] In some ways, *Y tu mamá también* is an almost clichéd example of this trend, as, time and again, the film indulges in scenes of folkloric picturesqueness. There are nu-merous examples of these scenes that span both the rural and urban facets of modern Mexico. They include the lavish wedding ceremony, complete with a *mariachi* band, featuring an appearance by the national president flanked by bodyguards. The trend is further emphasized by the search for paradise embodied in the name of the beach, *Boca del cielo* (Heaven's mouth) and the glorious cinematography of the beach scenes that stress the glittering waters, the bright blue skies, and the idyllic nature of the surroundings. Many other elements contribute to this vision: the attractive authentic music often accompanying similarly authentic local events or images, such as when the car is forced to a halt because the road has been taken over by cows. Again, these kinds of scenes bring into sharp relief the contrasts of urban and rural Mexico and quite literally slow the car down to immerse it in local rural color. Furthermore, the inclusion of certain scenes of native innocence and optimism, such as the collection by the villagers for the *Reina del pueblo* (Village Queen) contribute to this sense of Mexico as colorful, exotic, and beautiful. This vision is perhaps best exemplified through the exuberant excesses of the characters' final drunken night together, during which Luisa calls a toast: *"Tenéis una suerte de vivir en un país así. Sabes . . . es que México . . . mira . . . se respira vida por todos lados. ¡Por México lindo! ¡Por México mágico!"* ("You're so lucky to live in Mexico! Look, it breathes with life. To beautiful Mexico! To magical Mexico!"), a sentiment that is enthusiastically echoed by her companions. This tourist vision thus echoes Daney's argument about a postmodern cinema in which there is a parodic overdetermination—not just a showing but a demonstrating, "heavily gesticulating with its directorial hand."[25]

Destabilizing the Global Frame

It becomes clear, therefore, as the film progresses, that alongside the clear global framing there is an intensely overdetermined local presence. What is more, this local is incorporated neatly within the global frame in a way that contests and destabilizes the binary pairing. The next section of this chapter documents the more interesting ways in which this occurs, paying particular attention to the points at which seeming tensions between the two are resolved. This fusing of the global and the local is evident from the beginning of the film, illustrated during the wedding of Tenoch's cousin, at which the president of Mexico is present, evidence of the high social standing of Tenoch's family. The voice-over explains the president's early exit from the wedding:

> The President left an hour later. He had an urgent meeting with the leaders of his ruling party to appoint the candidates for the upcoming national elections. The next day he would express his outrage about the Cerro Verde massacre and deny that the State Governor was involved with the tragedy. After offering

condolences to the victims' relatives he would fly to Seattle for a conference on globalization.[26]

Here, the politics of the local and the global are sutured together from the start in the plot in a clear and explicit way. Furthermore, what frequently occurs in scenes like this is that the tourist vision explored in the previous section is actually undercut by other motifs and details. In the case of the wedding, there is a sense of the ridiculous attached to this formal situation in a way that humorously undermines the participants' authority. There is a similar irony in the explanation of the presidential agenda, as Cuarón points out, "When he relates the schedule of the Mexican president out of context, it's actually funny. There's a lot of irony to it: In one day the president goes from grieving about a massacre, of course created by the government—the narrator only mentions there was a massacre, he doesn't blame anyone—to a conference on globalization in Seattle. I think that schedule was real, too."[27] The follow-up shot of the presidential bodyguards receiving their lunch also merits further examination. Indeed the mise-en-scène makes curious use of the bodyguard figures. Their dominant presence, the rapid cutting from close-ups to medium close-ups, and the variety of angles used indicate not only their numbers but also their hugeness. The juxtaposition of the mariachi saturates this moment with irony, as though the bodyguard is protecting this archetype of national identity.[28] Thus, here we are confronted with a seemingly playful merging of local and global concerns, but one that skillfully manages to puncture the narrative with a political charge that becomes more forceful as the film progresses. Thus, while the heavy gesticulation of Cuarón's hand is evident in this aspect of his envisioning of Mexico, its parodic overdetermination ensures that the tourist vision so artfully displayed is interrogated and ultimately undermined.

Death—Mexican Style

A sense of death permeates the entire narrative of Y tu mama también, and it is through the compelling exploration of death that the film most effectively merges its global and local concerns. The most obvious example—the death of Luisa at the end of the film—constitutes a classic plot twist and one that poignantly plays with spectator expectations.[29] Luisa's death, however, and death in general, is clearly a thematic concern of the film overall and warrants further exploration. On the one hand, there is the universal tale of Luisa's death by cancer. Cancer figures here in its universal manifestation: a disease that attacks at random, one that is cross-cultural and cross-classed, though largely a Western phenomenon. It also contains interesting gender inflections; notwithstanding the obvious threat to men by cancer, it is on women that most media and indeed much medical research have focused. In particular, breast, ovarian, and uterine cancer, which attack the obvious sexual and reproductive areas of the female body, renders it a particularly sensitive and sexualized subject of discussion.[30] It is a narrative immediately understood by a global audience and plays on Western fears of the seemingly uncontrollable disease. In this way Luisa, as the European female protagonist, is embedded within the film's global structure as we retrospectively understand her journey (the main stumbling block in the plot's plausibility thus far) as her "final fling." This fling incorporates the return to the ocean with its myriad psychoanalytical interpretative possibilities, including the severing of ties with her past glimpsed through the breakdown of her marriage to Jano and her yearning for family, fulfilled at the end when we are told that she passes away in the company of the humble fisherman Chuy, his wife Mabel, and their daughter Lucero, to whom she becomes attached. Other details contribute to this "universal" reading of Luisa's tragic tale: the clinic where she goes to receive her test results has sterile blue seats and blinds, the walls are covered in anatomical posters, and there is a computer on the doctor's desk. His silent rise to close the door signifies, in classic filmic terms, the ensuing bad news that is to come. This depiction points to the clinic as a stereotypical example of the impersonal highly technological nature of Western medicine. Furthermore, much of Luisa's discourse during the film is shot through with personal reflections on life and death as the spectator comes to understand that Luisa, too, is on a final journey of discovery:

> Luisa thought that even after people die, they are still present. She wondered how long she would continue to live in the memory of others. But she preferred not to think about death.[31]

She later asks the boys, "¿Quisieraís a veces vivir para siempre?" ("Do you ever wish you could live forever?"), and her final words to them are, "La vida es como la espuma. Por eso hay que darse como el mar" ("Life is like the surf, so give yourself away like the sea"). However, this archetypal global tale of a life tragically snuffed out in its prime is undercut in the film by the emphasis on the Mexicanness of death. The particularities of Mexican attitudes to death are well-documented, of course, particularly in relation to the Mexican celebration, el día de los muertos (Day of the Dead) celebrated on All Souls Day, November 2nd.[32] The colorful and exotic presence of skulls in multiple forms (as candy, brooches, costumes, and such) ensures that this festival has a unique appeal to an international audience. The fact that this authenticity is, in itself, under threat is also extremely interesting in the context of the film's representation of death, which eschews any obvious references to the famous festival.[33] The death emphasis thus is more subtle and happens in various ways, visually through the numerous shots of crosses, and in a more comprehensive way through the film's multiple microstories about tragic deaths, often in road accidents. The first voice-over intrusion in the narrative tells the story of migrant worker Marcelino Escutia. Escutia, late for work and unwilling to walk the extra two kilometers to the pedestrian flyover, tries to cross one of Mexico City's perilous multilane highways and is killed by a speeding bus. It takes four days for Marcelino's body to be identified, presumably because of his anonymity in the big city and the lack of contact with any relatives. This story highlights a major preoccupation in Mexico in the 1990s, namely the dangers faced on a daily basis by Mexico City's pedestrians. As Rubén Gallo points out, "Pedestrians can no longer walk more than a few blocks without running into formidable obstacles like retaining walls for elevated highways and concrete ramps. Poor planning makes getting across ubiquitous expressways a life-threatening experience: Pedestrians either dart across these roads, running for the[ir] lives and dodging cars racing at 80 mph (not an uncommon sight on the *Periférico*), or they climb several stories to reach poorly planned bridges."[34] The story of Marcelino thus alerts the spectator to the dangerous excesses of urban Mexico, itself a recurrent motif of the film. This concept of excess is articulated at various times during the film: the exaggerated hedonism of the adolescent parties in the early scenes; their frequent drug-taking; and Tenoch's mother's esoteric leanings toward spiritual excesses. Even Julio's sister's involvement in the student demonstrations points to the notion that the urban connotes all that is dangerous, exciting, and excessive.

The death narrative continues as the spectator learns that Luisa's life encompasses a number of deaths, including that of her aunt, whom she nurses to the end, and also that of her first boyfriend—again in a road accident. The telling of the loss of her first love coincides with a shot of a cross and the recounting of a horrific car crash at the scene ten years earlier:

> If they had passed this spot ten years earlier they would have encountered a pair of cages lying on the road and then driven through a cloud of white feathers. Five yards later, they would come across a pile of broken cages filled with bleeding chickens flapping their wings. And after that, a truck on its side, still smoldering. Beyond, they would see two bodies on the road, one smaller than

the other, barely covered by a jacket. And next to them, a woman crying inconsolably.[35]

The camera pans a number of painted crosses at the scene, the first one a vivid blue, reminiscent once more of the clinic, and also interestingly, Luisa and Jano's apartment with its blue seating and floors. Perhaps the overwhelming emphasis on road accidents may be read as a playful irony in a film that is, in so many ways, a conventional road movie. The focus on the car as a vehicle of destruction is itself interesting as the viewer witnesses the destructive bent of the boys' relationship, which is narrated almost entirely from within the confines of the car. The viewer is perhaps privy here to yet another political comment as the car, an obvious marker of modernity, literally encases the destruction of Luisa's young life, followed shortly by the total disintegration of the boys' relationship. Other references to death abound: After the car coughs and splutters to a halt and the passengers are forced to make a stop in a rather disheveled, if pleasant, village, Luisa strikes up a conversation with Doña Martina, and her eye is drawn to a tiny soft mouse, also called Luisa, on the woman's table. We are informed by a later voice-over that the great-grandchild of this woman dies in Arizona from heatstroke, a stark reference to the conditions in which she undertakes her perilous journey from Mexico.[36] The death of the little girl is mirrored directly in the later scene in which Luisa teaches Mabel's daughter how to swim, holding her like a corpse, "A ver cómo haces la muerta—a ver. ¡Whuy! ¡Qué muerta está!" ("Let's see you float like a corpse, whoa, she's really dead"). This prompts a further meditation on the nature of life and death in a way that, again, the spectator understands only retrospectively, when learning of Luisa's fate in the final scene. It also directly connects with the earlier tale of the woman's great-grandchild as though in homage to that particular tragic death. This connection is further compounded by Luisa's presenting of the mouse called Luisa to the little girl, again signaling an imminent death (her own). In this way, the little mouse functions metonymically to signify the multiple deaths of the Luisas in the film. Aside from the more obvious political critique attempted here (and of those throughout the film), through the insistence on death as a particularly Mexican experience, Cuarón merges both global and local spheres in a striking way.

Other Mexicos

Death thus functions as a kind of unifying force between the multiple narratives unfolding throughout the film, narratives that hint at other Mexicos hidden behind the filmic image. These stories merit further examination not least because of what they say about Cuarón's vision of Mexico and also how they fit into the film's constant negotiation between its local and global contexts. We saw earlier how some of the visual references to the nation may be analyzed as a kind of clichéd guided tour during which Mexico is configured as a series of luscious, exotic images in which the beaches are gleaming, the weather perfect, and where everyone "breathes life." It is clear, however, that there is more to see and that the spectator is bombarded with a multitude of heterogeneous and fragmented signs that make up the confused portrait of the nation that emerges by the end of the film. This portrait is communicated cinematically in two principal ways: through the oddly distant voice-over (with its informative, bizarre, and strangely irrelevant pieces of information) and through the use of the "straying camera" (or "wandering eye") that emphasizes and draws attention to the inane ordinariness of Mexican life.[37] Some of these references may be construed as overtly critical of a modern Mexico portrayed as the brutal perpetrator of ongoing social and economic injustices. A primary example in this category is the story of Chuy and Mabel Carranza, which chronicles a familiar story: aggressive development of tourist infrastructure in the form of luxury hotels that, in turn, lead to the disappearance of Chuy's living as fisherman. Shortly after being introduced to Chuy and his family, the voice-over announces, in prophetic style, that in a year from then, Chuy's living will have disappeared forever:

> At the end of the year, Chuy and his family will have to leave their home to make way for the construction of an exclusive hotel to be built on the nature preserve of San Bernabé. They will relocate to the outskirts of Santa María Colotepec. Chuy will attempt to give boat tours but a collective of Acapulco boatmen supported by the local Tourism Board will block him. Two years later, he'll end up as a janitor at the hotel. He will never fish again.[38]

This explicit reference to the rapid modernizing of Mexico's tourist industry and the predatory impulses of the various local vested interests bears eloquent testimony to the perilous nature of life on the margins of modern Mexico. A few minutes later, when the boys and Luisa's camp is trampled by local pigs, the voice-over again intrudes:

> The twenty-three pigs had escaped from a nearby ranch. Over the next two months, fourteen would be slaughtered. Three of them would provoke an outbreak of trichinosis among those who attended a festival at Chavarín ranch.[39]

This rather odd addition to the narrative might be said to detract from the solemn misfortunes of Chuy and Mabel, but the connection with slaughter and death clearly locates it as one of the many other Mexican death stories bearing testimony to the difficulties of everyday life. The reference to disease is also interesting in that it links the narrative to a wider context of animal welfare and market pressures, thus again ensuring the global stamp on local events.

Other examples of the hazardous conditions of the life of Mexico's poor described to the spectator by the all-knowing voice-over, include the sad story of the great-grandchild killed en route to life in the United States and the story of Leodegaria Victoria, or Leo, the indigenous nanny still resident in Tenoch's household. As the boys make their way to the sea, they pass the village of Tepelmeme where Leo was raised, prompting the following voice-over insertion:

> Tenoch realized he had never visited Tepelmeme, the birthplace of Leodegaria Victoria, his nanny who immigrated to Mexico City when she was thirteen. She found work at Tenoch's family and had cared for him since he was born. He called her 'mommy' until he was four years old. Tenoch did not share this with the others.[40]

This often forgotten narrative of the indigenous maid/wet nurse/nanny sent at a young age to the city is inserted into the narrative in a self-conscious fashion. The early shots of Leo in the film show her waiting on Tenoch, serving him his favorite sandwich, *"Hiciste tu sandwich favorito. Puse el queso que te gusta"* ("I made your sandwich. It has your favorite cheese"); answering the phone for him *"Es para ti, amor"* ("it's for you, darling"); and patting him affectionately on the head. His reaction is to dismiss her in an offhand manner, *"Gracias nana"* ("Thanks, Leo") and clearly portrays how she is now relegated merely to the role of servant. Tenoch's betrayal of his mama, thus, connotes, by metonymic association, the betrayal of the indigenous (and by extension the motherland—*madre patria*) by the Mexican upper classes and constitutes a clear political critique despite Cuarón's distancing himself from any "cinema of denunciation."[41] This episode comprises one of a few incursions into the film of indigenous characters, a telling reminder of the insistent presence of the indigenous in both urban and rural Mexico. Their destabilizing ability to pierce the national conscience, thus, is signaled in *Y tu mamá también* by Tenoch's uneasy recollection of his early emotional attachments.[42] These stories, obviously and directly communicated through the voice-over, clearly constitute political critique, however lukewarm in nature, and document the eruption of the marginalized into the ostensibly central narrative of the relationship between the boys and Luisa.

"Straying Camera"

The other major storytelling form employed in Y tu mamá también involves the use of a straying camera to hint at the many stories beyond the reach of the film. This technique succeeds in painting a complex portrait of modern Mexican life. These narratives are purely visual and crucially involve only the viewer, excluding the boys completely. Thus the banality of the scene in which the bodyguards receive their lunch at the wedding or the indigenous cooks followed by the camera away from the restaurant and into the kitchen of their home testify to the defiant presence of people other than the principal characters of the main story. What, then, is the viewer to make of these mini-narratives? The fact that they are silent, serving in many cases, as picturesque backdrop to the main story of the middle-class protagonists, could in itself be interpreted as a profound political statement. Thus the story of Tenoch and Julio's friendship and their obsession with loyalty, betrayal, and sexual adventure is privileged at all times, as in national terms, over the microstories of Mexico's poor. On the other hand, this straying camera comprises a large part of the film and thus cannot be easily dismissed from any interpretation of the text. If we return to the notion that globalization actually leads to a more intense local presence, then that is clearly one explanation for what is happening here. The more the central story advances, the more the local intrudes. On another level, however, by allowing the camera away from the main story so early on in the film, the viewer is forced into the often uncomfortable situation of seeing and yet not knowing or understanding what he or she is seeing. This undermining of the viewer's position provokes a strange longing for another mediator or translator figure like Luisa or indeed more voice-overs that will somehow explain what is going on. The thwarted desire for knowledge is thus set up by the camera from the beginning of the film and is compounded by the use of doors and windows as blocking devices for this desire.

Serge Daney provides yet another interesting focus for analysis in this regard. He emphasizes the importance of doors and windows as pivots that repeatedly raise and frustrate the desire to "see more" beyond or behind the filmic image.[43] Clearly, parallels may be drawn between Daney's observations and the evolution of Y tu mamá también in which the windows of the car and doors play an integral part. Indeed Daney draws attention to what he calls the "restricted and pseudo-theatrical space of classical mise-en-scène to which the action constantly returns."[44] There are many scenes shot from either thresholds between rooms or outside doors and windows looking in. Examples include the boys watching Luisa through the window of the hotel and her first phone conversation with Jano on the trip, which is shot from outside. Julio's observation of Luisa and Tenoch having sex takes place at the doorway to the room. The explosive argument between Julio and Tenoch is shot from inside the car as Julio shouts and screams through the window at Tenoch, and the phone call in which Luisa bids a final good-bye to Jano is again in the phone booth and shot from the outside (as the boys play table soccer through a parallel window). Finally, the farewell between Julio and Tenoch is shot from inside the café in Mexico City but against a window. Daney interprets these pivots as desires to see beyond the filmic image; they work in a similar way here, too. The film relies on its privileging of the viewer as knowing more than the boys, particularly in relation to Luisa and the painful breakdown of her marriage to Jano. And yet by the end of the film, as already noted, the viewer has been betrayed to the extent that the death of Luisa is a shocking conclusion to her story, and one that has not been anticipated. In this way, the doors and windows function perfectly as barriers, which seem to open, but are ultimately impermeable. In many ways the prevalence of doors and windows and their function as barriers stand as testimony to the viewer's powerlessness—if seeing is knowing and knowledge is power, then the film playfully unmasks the viewer's comfortable sense of superiority and underlines the power of the camera to control and determine.

The longest example of this straying camera technique occurs early on in Luisa and the boys' journey and is perhaps worthy of exploration within the context outlined previously. This lengthy take features the anonymous tale of the road accident outlined previously shot against the background of Luisa's tale of her first boyfriend's death. This leads into a mumbled conversation over the batteries of the car radio cassette when, outside the car, the army is stopping vehicles to search for drugs. In the context of late-1990s Mexico, this is a telling political comment on the prevalence of these roadblocks, stepped up considerably by the Mexican army owing to pressure from the U.S. Drug Enforcement Agency.[45] The boys' insistent cry *"no mires, no mires"* ("don't look, don't look") is, of course, an ironic comment on their inability and unwillingness to look at any Mexican realities other than their own. The car passes by a building on which a picture of liberal president Benito Juárez (1806–1872) appears against a lush rural background, alongside the large letters, *el respeto al derecho ajeno es la paz* (respect for the rights of others is peace), probably Juárez's most famous pronouncement. This may again be read ironically as we listen to the boys' inane discussion over sexual positions and are yet again drawn away from the outside story back into the car and the drama unfolding there. This constant frustration of the viewer's desire to see, and therefore know more points, as outlined previously, to the national as ultimately unknowable. As the viewer skims by the slogan on the wall, back to the boys, back outside to the slow passage of cows, the viewer is reminded of how fragmented this national picture really is and once again, how it is only ever partially filtered through the glass of the car. As the cows disperse and the car goes on its way, it is overtaken by a police van or another military vehicle, and in a flash the camera focuses through the window on the lining up of peasant workers and their interrogation by armed police. The camera lingers for a brief moment on this and then, as the conversation about sexual technique builds to a "climax," the boys crash as Luisa humorously exposes their macho posturing, unmasking their claims of using "*todo el Kama Sutra entero*" ("the entire Kama Sutra") with a reference to "*culo*" ("ass"). The shock of the protagonists then forces the car to an abrupt halt. This take begs many questions; it is, on one level, about the eruption of the national into the personal story unfolding in the car. It is, also, an ironic comment on the disengagement of Mexico's urban youth from wider national debates and issues. The only outside happening registered by them is not surprisingly, given the relevance to their own lives, the drug search. The local is here but must be decoded and deciphered in ways that are often beyond the audience's reach. The withholding of information may also be read, therefore, as a directorial game designed to keep the viewer at bay and ultimately excluded from the national story, a strategy that works in both domestic and international arenas. The viewer is given tantalizing glimpses of a national way of life that is not explained and that he or she must, like the boys, ultimately bypass. This deliberate alienation of the viewer from participation in the national spectacle can thus be read as a self-referential gesture to the artifice of cinema itself and the triumph of the space within the car over the outside. If, as Daney maintains, cinema is haunted by the studio space in which it originated, then surely the film's constant return to the confined space of the car may be read as a negation or rejection of the national story that is quite literally beyond the camera's scope.[46]

Ambivalence

It hardly requires stating that the "national" story of Y *tu mamá también* does not constitute trenchant political critique. Ultimately what emerges from

Tenoch (Diego Luna) and Julio (Gael García Bernal) embrace Luisa (Maribel Verdú). Y tu mamá también/And your mother, too *(Alfonso Cuarón, 2001). Photo: British Film Institute.*

Julio and Luisa in the car. Y tu mamá también/And your mother, too *(Alfonso Cuarón, 2001). Photo: British Film Institute.*

the totality of its national references (through both the voice-over and the straying camera) is a confused political commentary. It testifies to corruption, the negative consequences of modernity, and the betrayal of rural Mexico; it also, however, constantly undermines its own positions. Much of the narrative is delivered either through a deadpan voice-over that attributes the same tone to the death of children as it does to the death of pigs or through a straying camera that deliberately frustrates the viewers' desires to see, and therefore know, more of what is going on. Thus the critique is couched in ambivalence, brought into vivid focus in the final scene in which news of Luisa's death is finally revealed, along with the news that the boys will never meet again.

In this scene with it shot-reverse-shot editing, Tenoch, despite previously vehemently rejecting economics, "*me cago en los putos economistas*" ("Fuck economists man, those pricks can suck my dick") and consequently his father's will and legacy, has now chosen economics. Julio has also entered college and thus the scene indicates a return to the patriarchal order that had been temporarily suspended during their journey to the beach. In this way the ending conforms to early U.S. road movies, which, according to Steven Cohan, concluded with "an imagined and ultimate reintegration of the road character into the dominant culture."[47] In this apparently resolved ending, the protagonists, now matured, are presented as following the route laid down for them by their class positions and social environments. And yet, once again, the film rejects any clear attempt at resolution. As the voiceover intervenes for one last time, it informs us that the ruling party, the *Partido Revolucionario Institucional* (PRI) has been defeated for the first time in seventy years in the national elections, and the viewer infers that Mexico stands on the brink of a new era. The end of the political era coincides with the end of Julio and Tenoch's friendship; proof, if proof were needed, that the threads of the personal and the political are now irrevocably intertwined. It is uncertain whether this new era is being heralded as positive, but because the information is given against the backdrop of the retreat into the entrenched class positions of Julio and Tenoch and the demise of their friendship, it surely suggests that while perhaps inevitable, it is certainly not "happy." The ambivalence that permeates this final scene is also perhaps the inevitable consequence of the complicit positions of filmmakers immersed in the cultural politics of filmmaking as they stake out their positions in a global market. This is an ambivalence that implies complicity from a filmmaker as versed in film sets outside Mexico as he is well-known in the domestic arena. While Smith contends that his "apparent lack of ideology becomes ideological,"[48] it is difficult to fix Cuarón's stance as anything more stable than the basis of his protagonists' friendship or Luisa's hold on life. Cuarón himself tellingly comments on the predicaments of artists working within the global environment when he says, "Saying 'I am against modernity' is like saying 'I am against the law of gravity.' You can be against them but there is no way around them."[49] In this way, Cuarón expresses his complicity in the project of *modernización*; a project that has succeeded in interpolating filmmakers into the nation-building project as it has, at the same time, copper-fastened the class divisions portrayed with such nuance in the film and which continues to ignore the indigenous question (in the same way as the film does) even after it has burst onto the national stage. The global/local divide so effectively destabilized throughout the narrative is thus perhaps the inevitable response from a filmmaker unable to step outside the constraints of the cultural and political project of modernization. In this way, the viewer is no closer to knowing what Mexico is really like and is instead forced to contemplate a Mexico that is fragmented, unstable, and ultimately unknowable from within the frustrating confines of the movie theater.

Notes

1. This quotation is taken from a virtual discussion board from www.imdb.com and was posed by Willowbrooksys on Friday May 23, 2003. The full text of the message is as follows: "I've never been to Mexico—after seeing the film, I'd like to go. But of course, the more that outsiders come, the more the hosts will try to make it more like where we came from, rather than preserving the authentic (I think) sense of modern Mexico that comes across. Like "Heaven's Mouth,'" www.imdb.com/title/tt0245574/board/nest/1638237 (accessed June 19, 2003).

2. Examples include Mel Gibson's *Braveheart* (1995) and *The Patriot* (2000), which sparked lively debates on this topic, and also Neil Jordan's *Michael Collins* (1996), which provoked similar reactions in Ireland with regard to the interpretation and portrayal of British and Irish histories.

3. This observation is reinforced by critics, Andrea Noble among them, who draw attention to the fact the film "insists that we read it in national cultural terms." Andrea Noble, "Seeing the Other Through Film: From *Y tu mamá también* to *¡Qué viva México!* And Back Again," in *Mexican National Cinema* (London: Routledge, 2005), 123–146, 141. By permission of the author. Also, Ernesto Acevedo Muñoz. "Sex, Class, and Mexico in Alfonso Cuarón's *Y tu mamá también*," *Film and History* 34, no. 1 (2004): 39–48.

4. *Y tu mamá también* was entirely financed with private money from various Mexican sources. For more information, see Paul Julian Smith, "Transatlantic Traffic in Recent Mexican Films," *Journal of Latin American Cultural Studies* 12, no. 3 (2003): 389–400. Ernesto Acevedo Muñoz also makes reference to this global framework. Referring to *Amores perros* (Love's a Bitch) and *Y tu mamá también* he says that, "In these

two films the language of violence and sexuality, and a postmodern generic malleability overtake the details and nuances of national topics as treated regularly in Mexican films, so they become 'universal,' while being allowed to keep their original Spanish titles," "Sex, Class, and Mexico," 39.

5. Paul Julian Smith, review of *Y tu mamá también*, "Heaven's Mouth," *Sight and Sound* (April 2002), from www.bfi.org.uk/sightandsound/2002_04/heaven.html (accessed February 23, 2004): 2.

6. *"Donde se ve más efectiva la globalización es en el mundo audiovisual: música, cine televisión e informática"* ("Globalization is at its most effective in the audiovisual world: music, cinema, television and information technology"), Néstor García Canclini, *La globalización imaginada* (Mexico: Paídos, 1999), 15.

7. The debate on globalization is wide-ranging and extensive. The terminology of global/local has emerged in popular and professionalized discourses of world-scale social relations. Many critics accept the formation global/local as a qualitative step forward in the search for an adequate vocabulary of power relations. However, when used metaphorically the binarism can be more problematic. See Mike Featherstone, ed., *Global Culture: Nationalism, Globalization and Modernity* (London: Sage, 1990) and *Global Formation: Structure of the World-Economy* (Oxford: Basil and Blackwell, 1989). See also Kathleen Newman, "National Cinema after Globalization: Fernando Solas's *Sur* and the Exiled Nation," in *Mediating Two Worlds: Cinematic Encounters in the Americas*, eds. John King and Ana M. Lopez Manuel Alvarado (London: BFI, 1993).

8. Inderpal Grewal and Caren Kaplan, eds., *Scattered Hegemonies: Postmodernity and Transnational Feminist Practices* (Minneapolis: University of Minnesota Press, 1994), 11. She further adds, "Global-local as a monolithic formation may also erase the existence of multiple expression of 'local' identities and concern and multiple globalities," 11.

9. "Will There Be Latin American Cinema in the Year 2000? Visual Culture in a Postnational Era," in *Framing Latin American Cinema: Contemporary Critical Perspectives*, ed. Ann Marie Stock (Minneapolis: University of Minnesota Press, 1997), 256.

10. "Transatlantic Traffic," 398.

11. "Transatlantic Traffic," 398–99.

12. For discussion on the dislocation between cinema and state in Latin America, see Chon Noriega, ed., *Visible Nations: Latin American Cinema and Video* (London: University of Minnesota Press, 2000).

13. Smith in his work on recent Mexican cinema is testing Manuel Castells's theory of "the interaction between technology-induced globalization, the power of identity . . . and the institutions of the state," "Transatlantic Traffic," 389. See Manuel Castells, *The Power of Identity* (Oxford: Blackwell, 1997).

14. The phrase, "tourist vision" is Leonardo García Tsao's and appears in his blistering critique of the film, *"Sólo con tu pajero"*: *"Quizá Cuarón (Alfonso) ha pasado demasiado tiempo en Hollywood, pues solo así se explica su visión de turista alivianado sobre*

una provincial pintoresca, poblada por acomedidos paisanos dispuestos a tratar como bwanas al par de gueritos" ("Perhaps Cuarón [Alfonso] has spent too much time in Hollywood. That's the only possible explanation for his tourist vision, set against a background of provincial picturesqueness, populated by aggressive peasants ready to treat the blonde city kids like a pair of bwanas"), www.jornada.unam.mx/2001/jun01/010622/15an1esp.html (accessed June 11, 2003).

15. The term "guided tour" is used by Paul Julian Smith citing French critic Serge Daney, in his fascinating discussion of Tomás Gutiérrez Alea's film, *Fresa y chocolate.* See *"Fresa y chocolate* (Strawberry and Chocolate): Cinema as Guided Tour" in *Vision Machines: Cinema, Literature and Sexuality in Spain and Cuba, 1983–1993* (New York: Verso, 1996), 81–98. I will return to Daney's theories at a later point in the chapter.

16. As is often noted in discussions on Mexico's so-called Renaissance of cinema, many of the most acclaimed directors—Guillermo del Toro, Alejandro Gonzalez Iñárritu, and Cuarón himself—are products of a new system of cinema direction and production that places them in many different national contexts at many different times. Cuarón's filmography bears testimony to this trend: *Sólo con tu parejo* (1991); *The Little Princess* (1995); *Great Expectations* (1998); *Y tu mamá también* (2001); and *Harry Potter and the Prisoner of Azkaban* (2004). He is currently working on several projects, including another road movie, *Memory of Running*; a film about the Tlatelolco student massacre provisionally entitled *Mexico '68,* and *Life of Pi,* based on Yann Martel's best-selling novel.

17. See Steven Cohan and Ina Rae Hark, eds., *The Road Movie Book* (London: Routledge, 1997) and, in the European context, Laura Rascaroli and Eva Mazierska, *From Moscow to Madrid: Postmodern Cities, European Cinema* (London: I. B. Tauris, 2003) and *Crossing New Europe: Postmodern Travel, European Cinema* (London: Wallflower Press, 2006).

18. The debt to the road-movie tradition is acknowledged by several critics, including Acevedo Muñoz, Noble, and Smith. Noble, in particular, maintains that the film is "in all but one dimension, generically exemplary," "Seeing the Other Through Film," 123.

19. David Sosa Flores, *"Para Y tu mamá también, el primer acto de censura del gobierno foxista,"* www.jornada.unam.mx/2001/jun01/010610/21an1esp.html (June 11, 2003).

20. *Y tu mama también* grossed $1.3 million from 250 theaters in its first three days of release, shattering Mexican opening weekend records. It was also a hit worldwide and took £1.3 million sterling in the United Kingdom, a record for a Spanish-language film. It remains behind both *Sexo, pudor y lágrimas* (1999), and *El crimen del padre Amaro* (2002) in terms of box-office success in its own country.

21. Sosa Flores, "Para *Y tu mamá también,"* www.jornada.unam.mx/2001/jun01/010610/21an1esp.html (accessed June 11, 2003).

22. *"Sólo con tu pajero,"* www.jornada.unam.mx/2001/jun01/010622/15an1esp.html (accessed June 11, 2003).

23. Tracks include "Here Comes the Mayo"—Molotov vs. Dub Pistols; "La Sirenita"—Plastilina Mosh and Tonino Carotone with Chalo from Volovan; "Insomnio"—Café Tacuba; "Cold Air"—Natalie Imbruglia; "Go Shopping"—Bran Van 3000; "La Tumba Será el Final"—Flaco Jimenez; "Afila el Colmillo"—Titan & La Mala Rodriguez; "Nasty Sex"—La Revolución de Emiliano Zapata; "By This River"—Brian Eno; "Si No Te Hubieras Ido"—Marco Antonio Solis; and "Watermelon in Eastern Hay"—Frank Zappa. For these and other tracks, see *Y tu mamá también* Soundtrack (2002, Volcano Label).

24. Smith, "*Fresa y chocolate*," 83.

25. Daney outlines in detail the difference between *montre* and *démontre* in this context in his review of *Ludwig*, in *Ciné Journal* (Paris: Cahiers du Cinéma, 1986), 167–168. Smith makes the same point in his discussion of the Cuban film "*Fresa y chocolate*," 87.

26. "*El presidente se fue una hora más tarde. Tenía una reunión urgente con el comité ejecutivo nacional de su partido para decidir los candidatos en las próximas elecciones. A las 10 de la mañana del día siguiente manifestaría su indignación por la masacre en Cerro Verde negando la participación del gobernador del estado en lo sucedido. Después de darles las condolencias a los familiares de las víctimas viajaría a Seattle a un encuentro mundial sobre globalización.*"

27. A. G. Basoli, "Sexual Awakenings and Stark Social Realities: An Interview with Alfonso Cuarón," *Cineaste* (Summer 2002), 26–29, 26.

28. I am indebted to Karen Downes for this insight and indeed am grateful to all the postgraduate students in SP523 Cultural Politics in Modern Mexico for their perceptive analysis of certain aspects of the film.

29. Noble draws attention to this betrayal of the spectator by the film's end as part of her wider argument that the film is all about betrayal (the boys' betrayal of each other, urban Mexico's betrayal of its rural counterpart, etc.), "Seeing the Other through Film," 141–142.

30. Recent examples of media concern include the furor over global icon, Kylie Minogue, and her revelation that she is suffering from breast cancer. For an excellent discussion on the sexualized nature of cancer discourse, see Jackie Stacey, *Teratologies: A Cultural Study of Cancer* (London: Routledge, 1997).

31. "*Luisa pensó que aun en la ausencia las personas siguen estando presentes. Se preguntó por cuanto tiempo ella seguiría en el recuerdo de los demás cuando dejara de existir. Pero Luisa no quería ocupar su mente con pensamientos de muerte.*"

32. For a comprehensive and fascinating discussion of this festival, see Elizabeth Carmichael and Chloe Sayer, *Skeleton at the Feast: The Day of the Dead in Mexico* (Austin: University of Texas Press, 1992).

33. Many studies attest to the creeping influence of Halloween in Day of the Dead celebrations in Mexico. Carlos Monsiváis writes, "Mexico has sold its cult of death and the tourists smile anthropologically satiated," Carmichael and Sayer, *Skeleton at the Feast*, 9. The excellent Web resource by The Consortium in Latin American & Caribbean Studies at the University of North Carolina at Chapel Hill and Duke also points to the new trend: "When children in the [U.S.] are shouting 'trick or treat'

and trying to terrify each other, Mexican children are home helping with the many preparations for the day. It is also possible that today, especially in urban areas, they are running through the streets with their plastic or squash carved like a skull asking "*no me da mi holloween?*" ("won't you give me my halloween?") www.duke.edu/web/carolinadukeconsortium/K-16_community/dayofdead.htm (accessed August 4, 2005).

34. Gallo adds, "Since the 1950s, the city's exponential growth has required the construction of multilane highways, inner expressway, *viaductos* and *periféricos*—public works that have had the unintended consequence of making life nearly impossible for anyone without a car." He draws attention to Santiago Sierra's artistic intervention on the subject, *Pedestrian Bridge Obstructed with Wrapping Tape* (1996) as a way of highlighting the problem. *New Tendencies in Mexican Art: The 1990s* (New York: Palgrave Macmillan, 2004), 107.

35. "*Si hubieran pasado por este mismo lugar diez años antes se habrían topado con un par de jaulas tiradas sobre el pavimento. Luego habrían cruzado por una nube de plumas blancas. Cinco metros después una pila de jaulas destrozadas con gallinas sangrantes aleteando arbónicas. Y más adelante un camión volteado echando humo. Al rebasarlo habrían visto dos cuerpos tirados, inertes, uno más pequeño mal cubiertos por una chamarra. Y una mujer desconsolada llorando a su lado.*"

36. *Doña Martina le regaló a Luisa la figura de la ratona que llevaba su nombre. Le explicó que había pertenecido a su biznieta, Luisa Obregón, quien había muerto de insolación al cruzar el desierto de Arizona junto con sus padres cuando iban en búsqueda de un mejor futuro* ("Doña Martina gave Luisa the figure of the mouse with her name on it. It had belonged to her great-grandchild, Luisa Obregón, who had died of a heatstroke fifteen years ago, while crossing the border in Arizona with her parents, seeking a better life").

37. Noble employs the term "straying camera" to describe this device in "Seeing the Other Through Film," 123–146, while Acevedo Muñoz prefers the term, "wandering eye," "Sex, Class and Mexico," 39–48.

38. "*Para fines de año, Chuy y su familia tendrán que abandonar su hogar cuando comienza la construcción de un hotel exclusivo sobre terrenos ejidales de San Bernabé. Se mudarán a la afueras de Santa María Colotepec. Chuy intentará dar servicio de lancha para turistas pero será bloqueado por el grupo de lancheros agremiados recien llegados de Acapulco favorecidos por el consejo local de turismo. Dos años después terminará como empleado de limpieza del hotel. Jamás volverá a pescar.*"

39. "*Los veintetrés puercos habían salido del corral de un rancho vecino. En los próximos dos meses, catorce serán sacrificados, tres de los cuales provocarían una infección de sisticercosis al ser consumidos durante una fiesta popular en la ranchería El Chavarín.*"

40. "*Tenoch pensó que nunca había visitado Tepelmeme, el pueblo natal de Leodegaria Victoria—Leo—su nana que a los trece años emigró a la ciudad de México. Leo encontró trabajo en la casa de los Iturbide y estuvo al ciudado de Tenoch desde recién nacido. Hasta los 4 años le decía mamá. Tenoch no hizo comentario alguno.*"

41. As Smith attests, "Cuarón himself is eager to disassociate himself from what he calls a 'cinema of denunciation'—the explicitly political output of an earlier

generation of engaged auteurs, such as Felipe Cazals' *Los motivos de Luz* (1985), which explores poverty and exploitation among the underclass, or Paul Leduc's *Dollar Mambo* (1993) which attacks U.S. imperialism." "Heaven's Mouth," www/bf .org.uk/sightandsound/2002_04/heaven.html, (accessed February 23, 2004): 2.

42. It should be remembered here that the turbulent political events of 1990s Mexico (the years preceding the making of this film) include the entry of the Zapatistas (FZLN) onto the national stage in the form of a grassroots struggle for indigenous civil rights. See Alma Guillermo Prieto, *Looking for History: Dispatches from Latin America* (New York: Vintage, 2002) for an excellent overview of this period. The story of Marcelino Escutia from Michoacán also figures in this set of references to either indigenous or *campesino* characters, plunged into an alien urban environment in which all contact with the local community is severed.

43. "*La Rampe* (bis)" in *La Rampe: cahier critique 1970–82* (Paris: Cahiers du Cinéma/Gallimard, 1983), 171.

44. "*La Rampe* (bis)," 173.

45. It is widely acknowledged that the coordination of United States and Mexican efforts to combat drug trafficking increased greatly during the terms of presidents Salinas (1988–1994) and Zedillo (1994–2000). According to various sources, Mexico widened the scope and intensity of its counter-narcotics effort, increasing personnel and budgets threefold between 1989 and 1993. For more information, see The Library of Congress Country Studies, www.photius.com/countries/mexico/national_security/mexico_national_security_concerns_fo~9999.html (accessed June 25, 2005). See also Alma Guillermoprieto, *Looking for History*.

46. "*La Rampe* (bis)," 173.

47. Cohan and Hark, eds., *The Road Movie Book*, 5.

48. Smith, "Heaven's Mouth," 4, www.bfi.org.uk/sightandsound/2002_04/heaven .html (accessed February 23, 2004).

49. Basoli, "Sexual Awakenings," 26.

CHAPTER THREE

Cidade de Deus
Challenges to Hollywood,
Steps to *The Constant Gardener*

Else R. P. Vieira

This chapter questions the notion that Latin American films can only achieve success in the international market if they emulate hegemonic models and borrow from mainstream film languages. In view of this, this chapter contests the idea that drinking from the fountain of Hollywood for genres and codes of representation will ensure international acceptance of peripheral films. This category of imitativeness is problematic; for the renowned critic Roberto Schwarz, it can be as misplaced as a Santa Claus dressed in Inuit furs in a tropical country.[1]

In this light, this chapter will initially survey the trajectories abroad of the Cinema Novo movement in the 1960s, which consolidates the personality of Brazilian cinema and brings it to international audiences and then considers the impact of *Central do Brasil* (*Central Station*) in 1998. These two landmark moments in the internationalization of Brazilian film, prior to *Cidade de Deus* (*City of God*, 2002), suggest that it is predominantly at the stage of distribution that Brazilian cinema crosses frontiers. The argument here suggests that it is mostly its capacity to renew outworn film languages and genres that has ensured Brazilian film a distinctive place in international spaces. *Cidade de Deus*, which only flowed outward at the last stage when it was eventually distributed by Miramax, shares with its Cinema Novo predecessors one of the staples of Brazilian cinema, firm roots in national reality. This film exposes major wounds in Brazilian society and focuses on the explosive, perverse process whereby drug dealers, for their own interest, attract children of the *favelas* to drugs and guns. These poor children, who also wish to have access to the goods advertised by consumerist society, feel empowered by this currency of drugs and guns. In fact, Brazilian cinema's search for autonomy and originality through the decades has entailed a focus on national issues. This chapter then focuses on Fernando Meirelles's British film *The Constant Gardener* (2005), his successful follow-up to *Cidade de Deus*, which premiered in Britain and the United States in January 2003, for the comparison offers valuable insights into the impact of Brazilian filmmaking on hegemonic codes of representation.

At the outset, it could be said that, in the case of the Brazilian production, Meirelles was not pressured by international commercial imperatives. Although not his original intent, he ended up funding the whole of *Cidade de Deus* himself. During the preproduction stage, his attention was more directed toward training the cast of 200 children and adolescents from the favela. He was thus less concerned about the continuously delayed or vague reply from Miramax to confirm its verbal agreement to invest in the film in exchange for worldwide distribution rights.[2] He further established his autonomy and challenged commercial imperatives as the basis for successful international film when, right after *Cidade de Deus*, he received sixty-four offers from Hollywood, but opted for the lower-budgeted British film, which, nonetheless, received ten nominations for the 2006 British Academy of Film and Television Arts (BAFTA) awards.

Adopting a Brazilian perspective does not imply a nonrelation with developments outside the country. For example, when *Cidade de Deus* won the annual award for best international script from the Writers' Guild of America, scriptwriter Bráulio Mantovani went to Los Angeles to receive the prize and was a guest at the home of the scriptwriter and director Alexander Payne (*About Schmidt*), who had been an enthusiastic and supportive consultant at the workshop.[3] Meirelles's dialogue with Hollywood film is apparent in his recent account of his film-related childhood experiences:

> My father . . . had an 8 mm camera and would make some amateur films with colleagues in Medicine School. They were always parodies of American genres. He went on doing this after he married, using the family as cast. I grew up projecting these small films on the walls of the house.[4]

This notion of parody (etymologically, "parallel canto") is important as it can shed light on the ways in which Meirelles has engaged in dialogue with U.S. cultural forms. A parody acknowledges the existence of another text but establishes its critical difference from it, exploring both possibilities and limitations in the text being parodied. In this light, this chapter shifts to Homi Bhabha's concept of mimicry, which also questions simplistic notions of imitation, and develops a previous insight that there is a certain blurring of the Western image in *Cidade de Deus*, as well as cracks that disclose important social dimensions.[5] The critical approach of this chapter is to highlight differences that in various degrees challenge hegemonic codes of representation.

It stands to reason that today's changing circumstances of film production and consumption determine that genres cannot exist by mere repetition and recycling of past models but have to engage with difference and change. Christine Gledhill develops this idea, arguing that the use of convention in Hollywood films, associated with industrial mass production as a source of plot formulae, stereotypes, and clichés, may have taken on an inherently conservative function of reinforcing normative meanings and values.[6] *Cidade de Deus* and the more recent *Brokeback Mountain* can be paramount examples of how other visions, discourses, and incoming cinemas break with the predictability of Hollywood genres and respective codes of representation.[7] In this connection, this chapter explores critics' views on the ways *Cidade de Deus* absorbs and transforms the gangster genre. The discussion then focuses on ways the film quotes the Western but also disturbs it, locating cracks in "the richest and most enduring genre of Hollywood's repertoire,"[8] particularly with regard to its racism and prevailing ideology of triumphant capitalist expansion.

The chapter finally suggests that there is a process of to-and-fro negotiation taking place in the transnational film circuit between competing incoming social, political, and ideological forces, which revitalize hegemonic film languages.[9] *Cidade de Deus'* great experimentalism, particularly its de-interpretation, use of little artificial lighting, and its approach to rehearsing and filming, will be seen to have become actual filmmaking methods in *The Constant Gardener*.

Over three decades ago, the Latin American critique of development theory highlighted the reductionism of the correlation between artistic creativity and economic progress. "Independency Theory," understood as the process of generating resistance to the specific phenomenon of economic dependency, is Robert Young's inspiring expression to highlight a major theoretical intervention made by Latin America outside its own terrain.[10] "Independency Filmmaking" can be an eloquent expression to sum up Meirelles's own intervention in hegemonic film language, not as a dependent partner, but as one who engages in dialogue with and contributes to mainstream cinema.

Brazilian Film in the International Market: Predecessors

Cinema Novo is a movement that started in the 1950s in Brazil and came to prominence in the 1960s. The director Glauber Rocha, in his manifesto "A *estética da fome*" ("*The Aesthetics of Hunger*") expresses the agenda of this first generation of Cinema Novo in terms of Brazilian cultural identity, external influences, and dependence. Attempting to make decolonized films by debunking the dominant American and European models, the manifesto advances the view that hunger is the distinctive trait of the social experience of underdeveloped and peripheral countries, so Cinema Novo represented "Latin hunger" and its cultural manifestation, violence. Underdevelopment is thus the stuff of Cinema Novo.[11] An *estética da fome* further turns the precariousness of Third World film technology at the time into a strategy and a weapon, capitalizing on form to oppose mainstream cinema, particularly the artifice and alienation of Hollywood's industrial film culture. It thus transformed scarcity into a creative politicized film language of contestation. Glauber Rocha, in "The Tricontinental Filmmaker: That Is Called the Dawn" states:

> These films from Asia, Africa, and Latin America are films of discomfort. The discomfort begins with the basic material: inferior cameras and laboratories, and therefore crude images and muffled dialogue, unwanted noise on the soundtrack, editing accidents, and unclear credits and titles. And on the screen a desperate body writhes, advances jerkily only to hunch over in the rain, its blood confounded.[12]

Cinema Novo was anchored in Brazil's social and cultural reality, and its perspective was of those integrated into that reality, in tune with the project of social transformation advanced by left-oriented filmmakers and artists in a prerevolutionary country.[13] It created new icons and heroes, rebellious characters ever on the alert to spot and avenge any injustice contrasting with the previous melancholic, passive, and conciliatory image of rural man. This tendency culminated in 1964 with Rocha's masterpiece *Deus e o diabo na terra do sol* (*Black God, White Devil*).

Originality of themes and of film language, rather than imitation, seems to be what has secured a favorable reception for Cinema Novo, particularly in Italy and France, associated respectively with the Italian Institute Columbianum and *Cahiers du Cinéma* and *Positif*.[14] At the time, those sites shared with Cinema Novo an ethos of resistance to patterns of domination, as analyzed respectively by Miguel Serpa and Figueiroa.

One could also posit a fusion of horizons of expectations as its radical otherness found an echo in the left-oriented intellectual circles and also had an impact on major directors, who absorbed some of its language. Converging forces, in Sylvie Pierre's view, account for a marked presence of Brazilian cinema in Italy in the 1960s. Groups or movements open to the ideas developed by Cinema Novo included: communist or socialist-oriented cinephiles, such as Moravia, Pasolini, and the young Bertolucci, the Neorealist movements in Italy and France, and Third World Catholic thinking greatly responsible for the rise of serious preoccupation with Latin America.[15]

Serpa has investigated the initiative of the Columbianum (the prestigious cultural Institute based in Genova, created by the Jesuit priest Angelo Arpa, a personal friend of Federico Fellini) in the presentation of Cinema Novo not only to an Italian but to an international audience. He has in fact highlighted the intellectual adventure of the Columbianum as perhaps the first space of cultural resistance to the process of globalization advanced by the United States after World War II.[16] Cinema Novo's vigorous contestation of Hollywood thus found a fertile soil in the Columbianum's ethos of cultural resistance. In the Cold War context in Europe, this institute further developed special attention to other people, which was channeled to Latin America, and had a major role in the dissemination of Latin American film, particularly from Argentina, Brazil, and Mexico. In the Columbianum, the films were seen not as individual productions, but as a set, and their aesthetic innovations and thematic contributions were discussed by a high-caliber audience. In their congresses, awards were given to a number of Cinema Novo's films, but it was in the historical *Terzo Mondo e Comunità Mondiale* (Third World and World Community) Congress (January 21–30, 1965) that one of its masterpieces, *Vidas Secas* (*Barren Lives*, 1963) by Nelson Pereira dos Santos, triumphed; this congress was also the site for Glauber Rocha's presentation of his groundbreaking theorization *Cinema Novo e cinema mundial*, later published as "A estética da fome."[17]

Alexandre Figueiroa has demonstrated how this explicitly anti-Hollywoodian development also finds congenial soil in the film culture of France, where it was "discovered," supported, disseminated, and analyzed by *Cahiers du Cinéma* and *Positif*. In fact, Rocha's "The Tricontinental Filmmaker" was first published by *Cahiers du Cinéma* in November 1967. In his view, Cinema Novo answers the need felt in some French circles to establish new dialogues to erase the traces of the cultural and economic colonialism that had existed for decades. The films were screened in festivals, art houses, and film clubs. Cinema Novo's film language later became an active influence on talented

European and American directors including Jean-Luc Godard, Jean-Marie Straub, and Pier Paolo Pasolini[18]

Walter Salles's Academy Award–winning *Central do Brasil*, associated with the later new Cinema Novo or the so-called "recovery of Brazilian cinema" in the 1990s, is informed by a strong sense of Brazilian identity and signals a second important moment in the conquest of international territory by Brazilian-produced films through international distributors. André Gatti, in fact, considers it a seminal film for the establishment of a new cinematography in terms of responses from national and international critics and audiences. France offers a particular example of the success of the film: it was projected in sixty-two different cinemas, fourteen of which were in Paris. The impact of this success was immediately visible in the director's career, seen in the international coproduction *Behind the Sun* (2001) and two international ones, *Diários de motocicleta* (*Motorcycle Diaries*, 2004) and *Dark Water* (2005).[19]

Salles himself has established the connection between *Central do Brasil* and *Cidade de Deus*: their small production house (Videofilmes) had the opportunity to help upcoming Brazilian directors, and his decision to be the producer of *Cidade de Deus* was taken, among other reasons, "because few films could shed more light on the social apartheid of Brazil."[20] Videofilmes' distribution agreement with Lumière was broadened when the latter, which also functions as a coproducer of Brazilian films, set up a distribution agreement with Miramax.

Cidade de Deus departs radically from Cinema Novo in its "boldness of execution," seen in the use of all available aesthetic resources to throw light on a serious blind spot of contemporary Brazilian cinema.[21] But it shares the social ethos of and a destiny with Cinema Novo: It is a cinema that is Brazilian in terms of theme, cast, location, and director, yet is international in terms of distribution and influence.

Allusion in *Cidade de Deus* as a Critical Operation

Marxist views for decades have illuminated the perception of Hollywood's mass production and domination of the world market through vertical integration, whereby it controlled the means of production, distribution, and exhibition. As pointed out by Thomas Guback, the commercial aspects associated with American cinema have in fact established certain patterns of fast and wide distribution nationally and internationally for the recouping of investments; this process, vigorously assisted by the government for political reasons, resulted in American distributors gaining control of the foreign field without competition.[22] As the doors open to foreign imports, a question arises as to how peripheral productions in the commercial transnational circuit relate to hegemonic ones and vice versa. Today's transnationalized film market offers a congenial terrain for hegemonic genres and aesthetics not only to be emulated but also to be renovated.

Cidade de Deus and the Gangster Genre: An Overview

A few critics have noted the presence of some features of the gangster genre in *Cidade de Deus*. The film shares with the gangster genre images of violence and the centrality of guns and drugs as staples of illegitimate business. This, of course, is intrinsic to the novel on which the film is based and in turn to the problem the novel addresses: the transformation of the favela into the neo-favela under the pressure of the narcotic traffic gangs that settled there, as well as parallel developments in police violence and corruption.[23] But, as Gledhill pointedly remarks, what defines the genre is not the specific convention itself, but its being placed in a particular relationship with other elements—a relationship that generates different meanings and narrative possibilities according to the genre—for example, the gun wielded against society in the gangster film.[24]

Schwarz, the major Brazilian critic who advised Paulo Lins, the author of the book that gave rise to *Cidade de Deus*, brings out what for the purposes here would be a major difference from the dominant genre of the gangster film: Even though the drug dealers exercise control over the favela, the opulence that the trade generates is not there.[25] His description of the lifeless Little Joe (equivalent to Li'l Zé in the film), the once-powerful gang leader in the favela, suggests how the class-race intersection in *Cidade de Deus* marks its distance from Hollywood's gangster genre: The "violent lord of life and death" is "a gap-toothed youngster, [undernourished] and illiterate, often barefoot and in shorts, invariably dark-skinned in [color]." With a social note, he concludes that this is "the point on which all injustices of Brazilian society converge."[26]

Miranda Shaw has thoroughly analyzed the problematic framing of *Cidade de Deus* as a gangster film and the way reviewers in the United Kingdom and United States prepared the audience for a film so deeply rooted in Brazilian reality. In contrast to the recurrent categorization of the film as a gangster film in the English-speaking countries, Brazilian counterparts stressed the film's social agenda and its connections with the ethos of Cinema Novo.[27] Framings breed expectations, arising from familiarity with the conventions of each genre. Shaw thus brings the British and American critics to task for their simplistic categorization of the film in terms of violence, the currency of bootlegging and drug trafficking, while leaving out the crucial differences of settings, themes, characters, and casting:

> It has made the film into an international commodity, and this has led to the neglect of some of its most important aspects. These are: its national relevance, its social agenda, and its link to the historically [politicized] Brazilian cinematic tradition. Such [categorization] may also give those already unwilling to look at Brazil's social problems a further excuse to misunderstand the country and fall into the paternalistic trap of the First World's image of violence and social problems in the Third World.[28]

Juliet Line has explored the ideological implications of the use of elements of a conformist cinema combined with a radical agenda. Her emphasis falls on the character Buscapé (Rocket), the photographer, who embodies some Brazilian ideals of the *malandro* in his ability to straddle two worlds but whose character also corresponds with Hollywood's "success hero" model.[29] In her critique, Line carries the argument further, suggesting that the film's international success replicates Buscapé's achievement in *negotiating* rather than challenging otherwise limiting boundaries. *Cidade de Deus*, she concludes, must respect the implications of "sitting uncomfortably between two cinematic traditions, the Brazilian social cinema and Hollywood."[30]

This chapter contends that Meirelles innovates, through his capacity to absorb elements from both the Brazilian tradition and hegemonic genres,

The favela *kids with guns.* Cidade de Deus/City of God *(2002). Photo: British Film Institute.*

Rocket (Alexandre Rodriguez) with his camera. Cidade de Deus/City of God *(2002).*
Photo: British Film Institute.

without being submissive to any. By absorbing and at the same time breaking the codes of representation of both traditions, he produces new meanings and generic innovations, thereby pushing at the boundaries of Brazil's and the world's filmmaking.

The Good, The Bad, and The Photographer

The allusiveness practiced in *Cidade de Deus* entails a certain blurring of familiar images, which make the non-Brazilian codes of representation recognizable but at the same time disturbs them. This approximates what Bhabha calls mimicry, a subversive process akin to camouflage, which permits identification of images but locates a crack that may disclose other dimensions.[31]

Meirelles debunks the formulaic aspect of the Hollywood Western, with which the Brazilian film shares images of violence and the centrality of the gun, through such a process of mimicry. This is seen in one of the initial flashback scenes that illustrates the older slum order, namely the Tenderness Trio's assault on the gas truck. The mimicry of the Western is seen in the images of the isolated community, in the clouds of yellow dust raised by the gas truck, and in the armed boys firing while they run alongside the truck.[32] The cinematographer, Charlone, has brought out this dialogue with the Western:

'Fernando and I watched a lot of Westerns,' recalls Charlone with a laugh. 'We wanted the assault on the gas truck to be like a stagecoach hold-up, with the boys and the camera running alongside the vehicle like gunmen on horseback. The boys even wore kerchiefs across their faces the way stage robbers did.'[33]

But the favela boys, black and poor, do not have the power of the horse to compete with the vehicle. Such a crack discloses a major social message. Crucially, these 1960s boys rob the gas containers to provide for the poor population, and the money is given out to them, too. This social message added to the Western scene casts it within the Brazilian tradition of the *cangaceiros*, roughly, the Brazilian development of what the historian Eric Hobsbawm has described as social banditry.[34] The *cangaceiros* were "honorable" armed bandits who roamed the Northeast of Brazil from 1870 to 1940, taking over landed estates or goods to exercise social justice and a more equitable distribution of wealth on behalf of the poor on the other side of an economically polarized region.

The traditional Western never offers the perspective of the excluded—the Mexicans and the Indians—who are defined in relation to Caucasians and often represented as killers and abductors. No attempt is made to understand them; instead, they are merely and invariably eliminated.[35] Even though there is a tragic dimension, in the classical sense of tragedy, in the Western hero who sacrifices himself for the community's sake,[36] there is an open racism in the Western's maintenance of order, in its assertion of white male supremacy.[37] The audience's eyes are directed to the deportment of the hero, a single man who wears a gun on his thigh:

> the 'point' of the Western movie is but a certain image of man, a style, which expresses itself clearly in violence . . . what interests him is . . . how a man might look when he shoots or is shot. A hero is one who looks like a hero.[38]

In contrast with the deportment of the Western hero, *Cidade de Deus's* ragged trafficker is a symptom of social exclusion which, rather than restoring order, sets in motion an inversion of order and values in the community. Cinematographer Charlone has suggested this inversion of order by the positioning of the camera, always shooting the gangsters from low angles, to convey through images the small children's perception of the gangsters as idols.[39] This area of difference invites an analysis of the infernal logic of consumer capitalism for ragged children, excluded from society but exposed to television and on whose world of misery cocaine dumped money. The gun in *Cidade de Deus* is not the prime tool of territorial expansion, wielded against the wilderness in the Western.[40] This mimicry of the Western enables a major critical updating of the agenda of the violence of capitalism so present in the Western's ethos of expansionism through exclusion.

Meirelles in fact radicalizes the insider's point of view of the novel by Lins, who was himself brought up in the favela *Cidade de Deus* and contributed to the anthropological study of drug trafficking in the favelas that paved the way for the novel. The action of the film, accordingly, is centered on the workings of the misfits *within* this excluded community. Meirelles also focuses on a perverse hierarchy in the drug business, built on the exploitation of small children who begin as delivery boys in their preadolescence and are later promoted to lookouts, then to soldiers, and finally to managers, the boss's right hand.[41]

Race is a major limitation of the Western, which *Cidade de Deus* directly challenges. In contrast with the predictability of Hollywood genres, Meirelles is constantly updating the social agenda of his films. This may be related to his trajectory in Brazilian television, which, in general, keeps a close eye on ongoing debates and social movements. There is, for example, an evident intersection with social discourses and debates on race circulating outside in *Cidade de homens* (*City of Men*), a follow-up television series to *Cidade de Deus*. Not only is *Cidade de Deus* updated in terms of the racial debate in Brazil,[42] it has also been a catalyst for important debates and interventions in the underrepresentation of blacks in the media. The insufficient number of black actors in Brazil led the film director to organize workshops for the preparation of a black cast, which succeeded in allowing these adolescents from Rio's favelas to break through the polarized class-race system of Brazil. The development of their untapped talent opened several doors for them and for others from the favela. The original cast's engagement with film production after *Cidade de Deus*, in turn, has been producing social and political action through projects that offer disadvantaged communities the empowering experience of film and positive representations.[43] This, indeed, has been the aim of the *We in Cinema* group, a media-arts nongovernmental organization formed by the original cast. The actors from *Cidade de Deus* became national stars in a number of films. However, instead of subscribing to stardom as a Hollywood-defined road to success, having learned that film can be empowering, they used the experience to create an area of intervention in the country's social and racial imbalances. This construction of a black space has additional implications in an interrogation of the racialized images of the Western. Authenticity of expression is another dimension of *Cidade de Deus* related to its strategy of improvisation, which casts it at a further remove from the Western's "white-invented babble" for the excluded.[44]

Buscapé humanizes the dramatic social situation by pointing to a way out of the violence of murder and involvement in drug trafficking, thus also moving beyond the Western's binary structure of good and evil, as is noted by Ismail Xavier. *Cidade de Deus*, he states, highlights an example of liberation. Buscapé, like the chicken in the opening scenes, is caught between two fires—the gangsters' and the police's. Twice he has the opportunity to kill Li'l Zé, but he does not want to fall into the web of violence and does not yield to the lure of fame as a criminal, also opposing the social visibility of the photographer.[45]

The Experimentalism of *Cidade de Deus* as a Method in *The Constant Gardener*

As a conclusion to this chapter, it is worth signposting ways in which the experimentalism of the Brazilian film has filtered into innovative features of *The Constant Gardener*. This international film, Meirelles points out, had a much larger structure but in the end the processes were similar.[46] *Cidade de Deus*, a landmark in Brazilian film, could hardly have been made by more traditional filmmakers, according to André Gatti; he also stresses the team's competent experimentalism derived from their experience in producing commercials and their exploration into the infinite possibilities of digital postproduction technology.[47] The weekly description of *Cidade de Deus* in the British paper the *Guardian's* influential Guide section throughout the months of screening in 2003 also suggests what can be interpreted as a fusion of horizon of expectations in terms of the international market being ready for innovative film languages. In its description of this box-office success (the film outperformed *Goodfellas*, 1990), it stresses that this Brazilian thriller brought freshness and energy to what is essentially a familiar story shifted to an unfamiliar location. *The Constant Gardener*, in turn, may perhaps consolidate the view that mainstream cinema has been modified by the interaction and interplay with other incoming cinemas.

The effect achieved by *Cidade de Deus* has been referred to as "controlled spontaneity," which derives mostly from the technique of improvisation and all the filming methods devised by Meirelles to enhance the performance of amateur actors who lacked formal training. Through improvisation, the actors grasped the mechanism of developing a situation out of a proposed conflict, without being given the dialogue. Meirelles would jot down the good ideas and interesting sentences that were incorporated into the script, the new draft of which they would start to go through. Sometimes they would say that such a situation would not happen that way, in which case the scene would be cut.

Conversely, de-performing was a technique developed in the workshops for the professional actors in *Cidade de Deus*. Meirelles explains the rationale of de-performing:

> There is nothing worse than to notice an actor is acting. Not only the many amateur actors but also the few professional ones had to learn how to enter the game of improvisation, to give life to their characters as naturally as possible. The professional ones had to learn to de-perform, doing 'non-interpretation' preparation exercises and to learn to become part of that world.[48]

In *The Constant Gardener*, even though the actors were professional ones, the same methods were used and improvisation was particularly stimulated. Rehearsal on location, still allowing for improvisation, was another carryover from *Cidade de Deus*. Even when working with stars, Meirelles also carried on rehearsals on almost all locations, which included northern Kenya, the country's slums, the Jubilee Line in London, and so forth. "Nonphotography" was another technique developed in *Cidade de Deus* to enhance the performance of nonprofessional actors, rather than, for example, limit their available area; the camera was also always handheld so as not to miss a scene. This method was also used in *The Constant Gardener*.

The lead actor, Ralph Fiennes, in an interview with Diego Lerer for the Argentine daily *Clarín*, playfully said that he is no longer the English Patient and draws attention to the actual nurse in the hospital scene in *The Constant Gardener*. He sums up Meirelles's intervention in international filmmaking arising from his spontaneous way of directing carried over from *Cidade de Deus* to the British film. There is nothing traditional about it, he says; "the actors would set up the scene and the same cinematographer Charlone would follow the actors round; the camera people would improvise with the light and the actors would do the same."[49] Crucially, Meirelles's redesigning of cinematic methods in *The Constant Gardener* has shifted the focus from the British and their cricket matches in Africa to the perspective of the powerless exploited in the global network.

Notes

1. Roberto Schwarz, *Misplaced Ideas*, edited and with an Introduction by John Gledson (London: Verso, 1992).

2. Fernando Meirelles, "Writing the Script, Finding and Preparing the Cast", in *City of God in Several Voices: Brazilian Social Cinema as Action*, ed. Else R. P. Vieira, (Nottingham: Critical, Cultural and Communication Press—CCC Press, 2005): 13–25.

3. Fernando Meirelles, "Writing the Script", 13, 14, 18.

4. Fernando Meirelles, "Fernando Meirelles (entrevista)," in Daniel Caetano (org.), *Cinema Brasileiro 1995–2005: revisão de uma década* (Rio de Janeiro: Azougue Editorial, 2005): 203–05.

5. Vieira, "Is the Camera Mightier than the Sword?" in City of God *in Several Voices*, v–xxviii.

6. Christine Gledhill, "Genre and Gender: The Case of Soap Opera," in *Representation: Cultural Representations and Signifying Practices*, ed. Stuart Hall (London: Sage Publications, 1997): 337–86, 352–53; 364.

7. The reactionary heterosexual normativeness of the Western has been disturbed by Ang Lee. This director has particularly targeted what Gledhill has referred to as the gendered codes of the Western, in which action is masculine and represents unexpressed and often inexpressible male emotion, even though a shared area is established with the genre through the immensity of landscape and the presence of the cowboy (see Gledhill, "Genre and Gender," 380). Action in *Cidade de Deus* remains masculine, perhaps reflecting the concrete fact that drug trafficking is a predominantly male activity. Its characters, particularly Li'l Zé, as in the Western and the gangster film, are as monosyllabic as ever, and project their antagonisms into violent conflict.

8. Thomas Schatz, "The Western," in *Hollywood Genres: Formulas, Filmmaking, and the Studio System* (New York: McGraw-Hill, 1981): 45–80, 45.

9. Gledhill, "Genre and Gender," 348.

10. Robert Young, "Postcolonialism and Dependency Theory," lecture presented at the conference "On Transcreation: Literary Invention, Translation and Culture (in honour of Haroldo de Campos)," Oxford University: Centre for Brazilian Studies, October 13–14, 1999.

11. Heloísa Buarque de Hollanda and Marcos A. Gonçalves, *Cultura e participação nos anos 60* (São Paulo: Brasiliense, 1989): 44–45.

12. Glauber Rocha, "The Tricontinental Filmmaker: That is Called the Dawn," in *Brazilian Cinema* (Expanded Edition), eds. Randal Johnson and Robert Stam (New York: Columbia University Press, 1995): 77–80, 78.

13. Alexandre Figueirôa, *Cinema Novo: A onda do jovem cinema e sua recepção na França* (Campinas, S.P.: Papirus Editora, 2004): 17.

14. My thanks to Maria Rosário Caetano for information on materials related to the reception of Cinema Novo.

15. Sylvie Pierre, *Glauber Rocha: textos e entrevistas com Glauber Rocha*, trans. by Eleonora Bottmann (Campinas S.P.: Papyrus Editora, 1996): 21.

16. Miguel Serpa, "O Columbianum e o Cinema Novo," in *O Cinema Novo na Revista Civilização Brasileira* (PhD diss., University of São Paulo, 2002), 146–59, 156.

17. Miguel Serpa, "O Columbianum", 146–59.

18. Figueirôa, "Cinema Novo," 17–19.

19. André Gatti, *Distribuição e exibição na indústria cinematográfica brasileira (1993–2003)* (PhD diss., Campinas: Universidade Estadual de Campinas, 2005), 259–63.

20. Walter Salles, "A Traumatised Chicken in a Crossfire," in Vieira, *City of God in Several Voices*, 3–4, 3.

21. Salles, "A Traumatised Chicken," 3.

22. Thomas H. Guback, "Hollywood's International Market," in *The American Film Industry*, ed. Tino Balio (Madison: The University of Wisconsin Press, 1976): 387–409.

23. Roberto Schwarz, "City of God," *New Left Review* 12 (Nov–Dec 2001): 102–112; reprinted as "Paulo Lins's Novel *Cidade de Deus*," in Vieira, City of God *in Several Voices*, 5–12, 5.

24. Gledhill, "Race and Gender," 357.

25. Schwarz, "*City of God*," in Vieira, City of God *in Several Voices*, 8.

26. Schwarz, "*City of God*," 8.

27. Miranda Shaw, "The Brazilian *Goodfellas: City of God* as a Gangster Film?" in Vieira, City of God *in Several Voices*, 58–70.

28. Shaw, "The Brazilian *Goodfellas*," 63–76, 59.

29. Juliet Line, "Trajectories of *Malandragem* in F. Meirelles's *City of God*," in Vieira, City of God *in Several Voices*, 72–79.

30. Line, "Trajectories of *Malandragem*, 77–88. With reference to the *malandro*, John Gledson, in his annotated translation of Roberto Schwarz's article on the book *Cidade de Deus*, clarifies that this Brazilian type is "an example of a dialectics between order and disorder profoundly characteristic of Brazilian popular existence." The Princeton editors decline to translate *malandragem*—roughly, "roguery"—which refers to the specifically Brazilian figure of the *malandro*, a layabout and trickster, living on the edge of legality. He is often portrayed as Zé Pelintra, Joe the Rogue—a black man, whose skin color in the Western and the gangster film denotes poverty but who wears a natty white suit, two-tone shoes, and a slouched hat (in Schwarz, "*City of God*," in Vieira, City of God *in Several Voices*, 6).

31. Homi Bhabha, "Of Mimicry and Man: The Ambivalence of Colonial Discourse," in *The Location of Culture*, (London: Routledge, 1994), 85–92, 86.

32. For parallels in the Western, see Schwatz, "The Western," 67–70.

33. Jean Oppenheimer, "Boyz from Brazil," *The American Cinematographer*; reprinted as "Shooting the Real: Boys from Brazil," in Vieira, City of God *in Several Voices*, 27.

34. Eric Hobsbawm, *Primitive Rebels: Studies in Archaic Forms of Social Movement in the 19th and 20th centuries* (New York: Norton Library, 1959).

35. Richard Abel, "'Our Country'/Whose Country? The "Americanization" Project of Early Westerns," *Back in the Saddle Again*, eds. Edward Buscombe and Roberta Pearson (London: BFI, 1998): 77–95, 81–82.

36. Ismail Xavier, "Humanisers of the Inevitable: Brazilian Film against Barbarism," in Vieira, City of God *in Several Voices*, 97–112, 101.

37. See Abel, "'Our Country'/Whose Country?," 81–84.

38. Robert Warshow, "Movie Chronicle: The Westerner," in *Film Theory and Criticism: Introductory Readings*, eds. Leo Braudy and Marshall Cohen (New York: Oxford University Press, 1999): 654–67, 667.

39. Quoted by Oppenheimer, "Boyz from Brazil," 27.

40. Gledhill, "Genre and Gender," 356.

41. Vieira, "Is the book," in City of God *in Several Voices*, xvi.

42. This examination of the participation of actors from the favela in *Cidade de Deus* parallels another major debate in Brazil, namely the assignment of quotas for black people who also lack social competitiveness to give them greater access to university.

43. See Vieira, City of God *in Several Voices*, v–vi; 135–39.

44. Rick Worland and Edward Countryman, "The New Western American: Historiography and the Emergence of the New American Westerns," in Buscombe and Pearson, *Back in the Saddle Again*, 182–97, 188.

45. Xavier, "Humanizers," 96–98.

46. Information provided in this section was obtained through correspondence with Fernando Meirelles.

47. Gatti, *Distribuição e exibição na indústria cinematográfica brasileira*, 49.

48. Meirelles, "Writing," 24.

49. Ralph Fiennes, "Ya no soy más el paciente inglés." Interview with Diego Lerer (*Clarín, Espectáculos*, October 11, 2005): 8.

CHAPTER FOUR

Playing Hollywood at Its Own Game?
Bielenski's *Nueve reinas*
Deborah Shaw

Nueve reinas and the Question of National Cinema

Agentinean cinema has come to the attention of the international filmgoing community because of the works of Lucrecia Martel, Daniel Burman, and Pablo Trapero, directors associated with new Argentine cinema.[1] Yet, it was an atypical film, *Nueve reinas* (*Nine Queens*) belonging to the genre of the scam movie, written and directed by a director not associated with this movement, Fabián Bielinski, that has been the most commercially successful Argentine film of recent times and has been the only Argentine film to be remade in Hollywood.[2] The remake *Criminal* (2004), directed by Gregory Jacobs and produced by George Clooney and Stephen Soderbergh, led to renewed interest in the Argentine original. This chapter explores the reasons behind this success both in Argentina and on the international circuit and uses this specific text to raise issues relating to the contemporary relationship between Argentine and Hollywood films. This chapter asks whether Argentine cinema has been forced to adopt a "Hollywood" form of filmmaking to make an impact in the international market or whether notions of national cinema need to be reconsidered and extended. It explores the way in which the film's success can be used to question certain globalization theorists' claims of the threats to national cinemas due to U.S. hegemony. Through readings of contemporary Latin American theorists, this chapter questions notions of originality and copying and challenges the belief that Hollywood has exclusive claims to specific genres. It also examines questions of marketing strategies and the critical reception of the film in a range of national contexts. The chapter focuses on the way in which transnational generic elements are highlighted while "foreign" national signifiers are edited out of the trailers for international audiences. It argues that different meanings of the film are produced depending on whether the film is read from within a national or a transnational framework.

Debates dominating writings on Argentine cinema are frequently formulated in terms of dichotomies; critics have written of the battle between commercial and artistic production,[3] of the clash between a cinema that has national political and social concerns and creates its own cinematic language,[4] and cinema that is little more than a copy of action/adventure Hollywood models.[5] The films of Martel, Burman, and Trapero are seen as belonging to the first "artistic" category, while the second category, to use the words of Tamara Falicov, is made up of "Hollywood-style movie(s) spoken in Spanish."[6] She succinctly explains the negative response to this type of movie from within critical circles, writing:

> The question of commercialization irks those who visualize Argentine cinema as a medium to tell local stories that affirm a sense of identity, and not one that replicates the language of Hollywood.[7]

There is here a clear sense that commercial cinema rejects local stories; however, a number of recent films that have achieved international commercial success (albeit within the limited space of the art-house movie theater) have told stories rooted in a national culture.[8] *Nueve reinas* may appear to be an exception to this, as a narrow surface reading divorced from an Argentine context could see the film categorized as a Hollywood-style movie spoken in Spanish. Nevertheless, *Nueve reinas* can be seen to also address national concerns. It is a film that provides an example of how the previously mentioned dichotomies can be transcended: It has achieved critical praise and commercial success; and it is concerned with local issues that have resonance in the social-political landscape of contemporary Argentina, while also being a film rooted in the internationally recognizable genre of the scam movie or crime thriller, with a plot-driven narrative and an ingenious twist that viewers can enjoy without any knowledge of Argentina. The fast pace of the action, the use of suspense, the focus on plot, strong characterization, and the concept of the final twist may all be familiar ingredients in Hollywood crime thrillers, yet, to suggest that *Nueve reinas* is little more than an Argentine version of an American genre is to grant Hollywood exclusive rights to these ingredients and to ignore the film's roots in Argentine culture and society.

Anglo-American readings of the film perhaps inevitably focus on what they see as Hollywood ingredients, with a number of critics comparing *Nueve reinas* to David Mamet's *House of Games* (1987) and seeing it as an example of the scam movie.[9] Argentine critics and Latin Americanists have acknowledged the similarity in terms of genre but have also commented on the ways in which the film fits into an Argentine tradition. Several link Bielinki's film to the thrillers of Adolfo Aristarain,[10] while Geoffrey Kantaris traces the figures of the thief, trickster, and forger back to the works of the well-known Argentine writer Roberto Arlt.[11] In addition, a number of Borgesian conceits are employed in the construction of the narrative. A variation of the revelation that the man being conned is actually the one setting the trap is played out in the "detective" story "Death and the Compass," in which the criminal lays a trap for the detective.[12] As with Borges's stories, the film places great emphasis on fiction and artifice in which coincidence is utilized as a main narrative component, and characters are not who they seem to be. Bielinski shows an implicit awareness of the influence of the Argentine writer, who titled one of his collections of short stories *Artificios* (1944), when in an interview he uses Borgesian language to refer to his film. He says that *Nueve reinas* is a story "of artifice added to more artifice."[13]

Borges as both a "universal" and an Argentine writer can shed light on the questions of national identity in relation to *Nueve reinas*, as it, too, can be read as both a "transnational" and an Argentine cultural text. Borges argued that Argentine culture was rooted in a universal tradition, which he equated with Western culture, and through his readings and writings he claimed his place within it.[14] In a frequently cited extract he outlines his position:

> I believe our tradition is all of Western culture, and I also believe we have a right to this tradition, greater than that which the inhabitants of one or other Western nation might have. . . . We should feel that our patrimony is the universe; we should essay all themes, and we cannot limit ourselves to purely Argentine subjects in order to be Argentine.[15]

While Borges looked to the classics and Arabic culture as translated by Western sources, Bielinski's film, despite its grounding in Argentine culture, is informed by Hollywood films, a fact that the director has acknowledged in interviews.[16] *Nueve reinas* then belongs to both an Argentine and a Hollywood tradition and demonstrates how films can retain their national identity, have a certain originality, and possess a generic familiarity, all of which ensures an appeal to national and international audiences.

The transnational success of *Nueve reinas* relates to theories and debates surrounding globalization and the state of national cultures. This is not the place to rehearse these debates in any depth, but it is worth exploring a few important points. Some cultural theorists, in their assessments of the effects of globalization and Hollywood domination on national film industries, have rather pessimistically talked of the dangers of extinction for national cinemas. For Frederic Jameson, "the free movement of American movies in the world spells the death knell of national cinemas everywhere, perhaps of all other national cinemas as distinct species."[17] In a similar vein Tony Fitzmaurice states: "The increasing world domination by an expensive, highly produced and technologically sophisticated American cinema raises questions about the future viability of national cinemas."[18] While U.S. domination of film in terms of production, distribution, and exhibition is clearly a fact, these writers have overstated the ability of the U.S. film industry to destroy national film production all over the world. Other theorists have argued that globalization is an uneven process, which can even open up spaces for neglected cultural expression.[19] *Nueve reinas*, among other recent Latin American films, demonstrates that the traffic in film distribution and exhibition, while unequal, is not unidirectional.[20]

This is not a new phenomenon, and Argentine films have long looked to foreign markets, as they would not be able to survive economically if they depended solely on the national market.[21] Nevertheless, this has been a good spell in commercial terms with an increase in Argentine films seen nationally and internationally. While U.S. films have been dominant in Argentina, as is the case in most theaters across the world, in 2000 there were fifty-three Argentine films shown, and *Nueve reinas* topped the list for the box-office gross, with 1,259,602 viewers recorded.[22] The film took in $1,221,261 in the United States and also did well in France, Spain, and the United Kingdom, all from a budget of $1,500,000.[23] Clearly these figures are small when compared to the production costs and profits for Hollywood blockbusters, but this comparative success demonstrates that there is a small share of international and domestic markets for non-Hollywood films, and works like *Nueve reinas* keep distributors and exhibitors interested in "foreign-language" movies.[24]

The fact that the film has been remade in Hollywood also disrupts certain traditional understandings of the relationship between Latin American and U.S. dominated cultures. As the Chilean cultural theorist Nelly Richard has argued, the paradigm of model or copy has been seen to define that relationship, with Latin American cultures felt to be reduced to copying the cultural products of hegemonic nations.[25] Richard, critiquing this position, prefers to talk of a Latin American "cultural pastiche."[26] She also explores the shift in critical terms away from the anti-imperialist discourse that has a notion of a pure Latin American culture that risks contamination from any exposure to "foreign influences."[27] Richard's ideas also find an echo in Nestor García Canclini's well-known concept of hybrid cultures. For García Canclini, popular Latin American culture cannot be reduced to traditional, indigenous forms,[28] and popular culture is not suppressed by modernity and globalization but takes new hybrid forms.[29] *Nueve reinas* provides a good illustration of these ideas in that it demonstrates how the model or copy formula and the notion of a pure cultural form cannot be used to categorize this film.

The Global and Local Appeal of *Nueve reinas*: Transnational Readings

What is it about *Nueve reinas* that has made it the most commercially successful Argentine film of recent times, while being the most popular domestic film in Argentina in 2000 and providing a rare example of a Latin American film remade by Hollywood? This section of the chapter focuses on the reasons for the global and local appeal of *Nueve reinas* by examining the transnational aspects of the film and the way these were used in the marketing process, before turning to specific national cultural references that may go unnoticed by viewers unfamiliar with Argentine culture.

Transnational qualities include an emphasis on plot from within the familiar genre of the scam movie. *Nueve reinas* tells the story of two con artists, Juan, played by Gastón Pauls, and Marcos, played by Ricardo Darín, who team up to work the streets of Buenos Aires. They successfully carry out a number of small tricks on innocent members of the public, including old ladies and café employees. Through an old swindler associate of Marcos they stumble across a large job at the hotel in which Marcos's sister works. This job involves selling a forged copy of extremely valuable stamps, the Nine Queens, to a wealthy, crooked Spanish businessman (Gandolfo, played by Ignasi Abadal), who is a keen rare-stamp collector. There are a number of complications, including the theft of the stamps before Marcos and Juan have a chance to sell them and their purchase of the "real" stamps. The final twist reveals that a large-scale con has been played on Marcos, who has throughout his career swindled most of his associates. They have taken their revenge by staging an elaborate plan in which Marcos is tricked into buying the real Nine Queens, believing he will make a large profit from their sale to Gandolfo. The plan is encouraged by the fact that a member of the group has received a tip-off from one of the main banks telling them that the board has stripped the bank of its funds and have taken all of the money out, resulting in the customers' loss of their savings. This is the information they use to trick Marcos; Gandolfo pays him with a banker's draft, which turns out to be worthless, and the final scene reveals that all the cast of characters involved with the Nine Queens, who appear to be victims of Marcos, have actually all been working to ensnare him. The master conman has been conned.

In fact, it was the plot that ensured that the film was made: Bielinski won a screenplay competition in 1998 organized by the biggest Argentine production company, Patagonik, which provided funding for the film.[30] It is highly likely that the film's potential on the international market was one of the main reasons for awarding it the prize. This potential is also exploited through the use of a contemporary, urban setting, with much of the action taking place in the international space of the ultramodern Hilton hotel in Buenos Aires, which ensures that the national context is easily transferable for audiences.[31] This helps to dilute the "foreignness" of the images, and it is no coincidence that other Spanish language films with contemporary urban settings, such as Open Your Eyes (1997), and Amores perros (Love's a Bitch) (2000), have also had international success. There are, in fact, parallels between Open Your Eyes and Nueve reinas in that the easily translatable locations and plot-driven genre based narratives can help to explain the Hollywood remakes.[32]

There is an absence of identifiably Argentine images from two of the main settings of the film: the garage and the hotel. Theories of hotels and hotel lobbies have stressed the anonymity of the location and the dissociation of the hotel space from its neighboring environment,[33] and the same point can be made for the use of multinational garage shops. Yet, both spaces can also contribute to the traveler (and international audiences) feeling comfortable and in familiar territory when outside their national environment.

The opening scene of the film takes place in the Esso garage in which the two protagonists (Juan and Marcos) meet. As Juan plans his con on the sales assistant, Marcos watches while eating the most recognizable of North American foods: a hot dog.[34] They are surrounded by recognizable grocery products of a gobalized consumer culture, typical garage fare in many modern cities: crisps, biscuits, tinned food, and sweets. While the brands are largely indistinguishable, packets of Pringles are highlighted by the promotion in the garage, and once outside, Marcos draws attention to the chocolate bar he has stolen, with the English name of Crunchy, which he notes is made in Greece. Ironically, he adds, this country "se va a la mierda" ("is going to hell"), allowing the film to make a gentle critique of the lack of national products on the market, while paradoxically this helps to sell the film abroad.

There are a number of street scenes used to show the audience the tricks of the con trade, but these scenes could again be translated to any urban center, as the locations are apartment blocks, cafés, and the street. The majority of the rest of the action takes place in the state-of-the-art hotel, which would not be out of place in an exclusive district of any modern metropolis. This emphasis on the interior shots of the Esso service station and the hotel identifies the film as a contemporary, stylish crime movie that can be transported to many urban locations with little sense of cultural displacement.[35]

While these images may not conform to Eurocentric expectations, for which Latin America should be exotic, colonial, poor, or underdeveloped, it is wrong to suggest that *Nueve reinas* deliberately distorts images of the city to fit a foreign vision. A foreign vision, in fact, has always paradoxically been at the root of a national project for the city's design. As Beatriz Sarlo notes, Buenos Aires has looked to foreign European models since becoming a modern metropolis from the beginning of the twentieth century.[36] In her words:

> As with Argentine culture its originality lies in the elements which enter into the mix, trapped, transformed and deformed by a gigantic system of translation.[37]

Large multinational chains, such as the Hilton hotel and Esso garages, while foreign owned, are as much a part of Buenos Aires's landscape as they are of those of so many cities.

It is also worth noting that while the use of transnational locations and high production values may again appear to follow conventions dominated by Hollywood, the film, in fact, cultivates its own look and does not imitate a popular and familiar style associated with the Hollywood crime thriller. Instead, it takes a naturalistic aesthetic approach and relies on an understated acting style, which ensures that there is a match between form and content. This underpins the relationship between artifice and reality, two of the central themes of the film. As Walter Chaw observes to Bielinski, "there's an ironic balance in your film between the artifice of your screenplay and the naturalism of your visual structure."[38] Bielinski agrees, telling his interviewer that this "was the substance of my idea."[39]

The director of photography, Marcelo Camarino, was instructed by Bielinski to use natural lighting where possible, and hidden cameras were used for a number of the street scenes to heighten the naturalistic effect.[40] With regard to the understated acting style, the director insisted that his actors tone down their performances.[41] Also, in terms of action, and in contrast to standard Hollywood fare, there are no dramatic fight scenes and no need for stunt

Juan (Gastón Pauls) and Marcos (Ricardo Darín). Nueve reinas/Nine Queens *(Bielinski, 2000). Photo: British Film Institute.*

Marcos confronts Valeria (Leticia Brédice) while Juan watches. Nueve reinas/Nine Queens *(Bielinski, 2000). Photo: British Film Institute.*

performers or special effects. The naturalism achieved through the understated acting styles, the location shooting, and the natural lighting are intended to make the highly contrived plot believable and to set the audience up for the trap revealed in the ending.[42]

National Readings

On the surface, then, the plot appears to be unrelated to any national context, and the setting of Buenos Aires seems to be entirely incidental. Even the prescient anticipation of the economic crash of 2001, on which the final twist of the film depends, could be read as an isolated case of bankruptcy of a single bank, something that has affected more apparently stable countries in the capitalist banking system.[43] Viewers unfamiliar with Argentine current affairs are unlikely to consider the wider socioeconomic implications of this use of national economic instability.[44] Yet this constitutes an integral element of the narrative and is more than a simple plot device. As Kantaris notes, monetary value in a country long plagued by hyperinflation and currency crises becomes a fiction and an unstable concept.[45] National audiences are thus easily able to relate to the concept of a banker's draft that has no value and to a set of forged collector's stamps that are worthless, apart from their use as a means of entrapping Marcos.

Likewise, Marcos may seem to be an isolated character; a great filmic conman and devious swindler, who, unlike his fellow conmen, is entirely selfish and always on the take. Yet, he will have hit a particular nerve in Argentina at a time of increased disillusionment with a society seen to be characterized by corruption and moral (and literal) bankruptcy. Although Marcos is not a politician, he also touches on the lack of faith that citizens had in the political classes before and after the economic crisis of 2001. At one point in the film the parallel is made; Juan, when discussing his plans as a young man, tells Marcos that he asked himself what he could do with his vocation for street cons, to which Marcos replies that he could have been a politician.[46] Yet, the film shows a society in which corruption is not limited to the political classes but is endemic. *Nueve reinas* illustrates this through a range of characters, including the numerous swindlers who populate the streets of Buenos Aires, the judge who demands $70,000 to let Juan's incarcerated father free, and the fictitious Spaniard Gandolfo Vidal, who represents the corrupt multimillionaire capitalist, profiting from the Argentine business classes who so enjoy shady dealings.[47] At one point Gandolfo says that he will miss the country as he has never seen such *"buena disposición"* ("willingness") to do business.[48] Indeed, Marcos, who dedicates himself to swindling, appears to see himself as a businessman; he wears a suit, talks of his office (a table in a local café/restaurant), and is openly dismissive of "*chorros*" ("thieves"), clearly believing that he belongs to a different class.

Thus, within the moral universe of the film, there is little difference between street conmen and judges, businessmen, and politicians because their victims are the common man and woman in the street or those without power. The film is then, in addition to being an exciting scam movie, an attack on a culture of corruption in Argentine society. Of this Bielinski has stated:

> What you see in the film, the animosity and the deception—all of that just deepened and exploded. I was just observing the zeitgeist. . . . A mood that everybody's a liar, everybody's cheating you.[49]

This widespread national dishonesty is highlighted in a scene in which Marcos points out to Juan the secret world of crime taking place on the streets of Buenos Aires. The scene takes the mistrustful point of view of Marcos, as the images appear to confirm his diagnosis of the capital's street life. A documentary style is cultivated for authenticity, as fragmented, detailed shots reveal a woman shoplifting, men on a motorbike planning to steal a briefcase, car thieves, pickpockets, and people generally looking shifty. These images accompany Marcos's categorization of them; he rejects the simple *lunfardo* slang word for thief and instead provides seventeen slang terms, the range of which suggests the richness of this culture. He is clearly an expert, and here documents this culture, while maintaining a sense that he is above it, in his notion that what he does is just "business."

Yet, the film challenges this through its strong moral code and represents another national characteristic: the desire to take action against the corrupt and greedy (embodied in Marcos) in the absence of a reliable justice system. This finds an echo in the street demonstrations in Argentina held to protest politicians and bankers who were seen as corrupt and blamed for the 2001 economic crash.[50] The message of *Nueve reinas* is then dramatically reversed in the final frames, when the film acquires its full moral meaning; a movie that appears to speak of individualism where no one can be trusted reveals itself as a celebration of retribution, in which a community of honorable thieves (and Marcos's sister) work together to take revenge against one amoral individual. The sting on Marcos would have been particularly satisfying for Argentine audiences, who may see in him the representation of a national type.

National (and international) audiences would also have taken pleasure in Juan's victory over Marcos. Although he is established as the good-hearted rogue, he is on the side of those who have been conned and abused by those in power; he is motivated principally by a desire to help his father and his girlfriend, the sister that Marcos has cheated out of her inheritance. Audiences see Juan hand over the money he secures through the scam played on Marcos to Valeria and assume that anything he gains is used to pay off the judge to bring about the release of his reformed father, also making him a victim of national corruption that Marcos comes to symbolize. His "*cara de buen tipo*" ("good guy face"), which Marcos thinks will be such an asset in their scams is thus revealed to be genuine and is ironically put to good use in the conning of Marcos himself.

Marcos, in contrast, is the amoral antihero motivated purely by self-interest. Through the twist that establishes the theme of retribution, the film sets up a distinction between those petty criminals who seek to con wealthy businessmen (Gandolfo) and steal from large multinational concerns (Esso) and those who swindle old ladies out of their savings and deceive and trick their fellow conmen, a distinction that Marcos is unable to see.[51] The audience's moral guide here is Juan, who is shown to be upset at the treatment of the old lady and has to leave the room in frustration that he is forced to hide when Marcos insists on a 90 percent cut of the scam that a seemingly sick, elderly Sandler (Oscar Núñez) has planned, leaving him with only 10 percent. Marco's most shocking act comes when he is prepared to prostitute his sister to Gandolfo when he insists that he will only complete the deal if he can have sex with her. Marcos even agrees to tell his younger brother, Federico (Tomás Fonzi), the truth about stealing their part of their grandparents' inheritance if Valeria agrees to sex with Gandolfo, thus destroying the relationship he has with Federico in the process, the only emotional bond he has with anyone.

The film thus speaks out against a culture in which everything is measured in terms of profit and human relationships are seen only in regard to monetary value; this is a message with global and local significance. When attempting to justify his actions regarding his sister to Juan, Marcos reveals how people are reduced to commodities in his moral universe. He says of his sister, "there are no saints; there are only different prices."[52]

One of the final scenes of the film also acts as a metaphor for the need for Argentina to rethink its value system. Juan, on the way to meeting his friends after successfully carrying out his sting on Marcos, comes across a young boy begging on the metro by distributing a picture of a dragonslayer on a horse.

Juan places a toy car on one knee and money on the other. The boy hesitates before picking up the note, suggesting he cannot afford the luxury of a childhood. Juan then gives the boy the car in addition to the money. In a symbolic moment of the film, it is suggested that Marcos is the dragon that Juan has slain. While this critique of material greed is a topic relevant to all capitalist consumer cultures, it is also specific to national concerns in the light of the aforementioned contemporary economic and political climate of Argentina. Interestingly, this attack on individual greed at the expense of more humane concerns is a common theme in a number of recent Argentine films: *The Son of the Bride* (2001), also starring Darín, focuses on a restaurateur who has a heart attack, which forces him to place more value on personal relationships and become less obsessed with his business; Fernando Solanas's *The Voyage* (1992) also attacks, through political satire, an Argentina that is selling off all the assets of the country while the people struggle to survive.[53]

The specific references to national corruption are clearly lost in the U.S. remake of *Nueve reinas*, *Criminal*. In this film, the context is transferred to Los Angeles, and amorality is reserved for the character of Richard, based on Marcos. Thus, a negative character trait is an individual, rather than a national, problem. Likewise, the device to allow the plot twist to be revealed—the fact that Richard is unable to cash the check he is given in his dealings with the wealthy businessman—also focuses on his flaws.[54] Before he can cash the check, he is arrested after Rodrigo/Bryan (based on Juan) has presumably tipped off the police that Richard, a wanted man, is there. This is an ending that affects Richard alone, unlike Marcos, who is caught up in a national crisis that affects many.

Marketing Strategies

All of the specific national references in *Nueve reinas*, which in many ways distinguish the film from Hollywood models, do not make the film inaccessible for non-Argentine audiences. Ella Shohat and Robert Stam have argued that the reception of films varies according to national and social context. For them: "Perception itself is embedded in history. The same filmic images or sounds provoke distinct reverberations for different communities."[55]

The production of the trailers for *Nueve reinas* for domestic and foreign audiences play on the different ways in which films are viewed according to national contexts. The trailers projected outside Argentina highlight the transnational ingredients of the film.[56] In these, specific national references are ignored to dilute any idea of foreignness for non-Argentine audiences.

Both the U.S. and the international trailers promote *Nueve reinas* as a genre film, not as a foreign-language art-house movie. The focus in the U.S. trailer is on the film as a scam movie with a twist, with fast editing highlighting the few action scenes. This is "a story," according to the voice-over, "that will keep you guessing until the last con is played." This focus on the scam links *Nueve reinas* in the audience's imagination to nationally successful films in this genre, such as *House of Games* and *The Grifters* (1990). Along with a familiar genre, the trailer offers audiences unchallenging characters who are represented as types familiar to American audiences; the voice-over informs the audience that, before the protagonists succeed in their aim of making money from the Nine Queens, "first they must fool a forger, outfox a brilliant beauty, charm a sweet old lady, deal in a dirty cop, cheat a millionaire."

The American-accented voice-over gives an outline of the plot matching the images. This is intercut with extracts of rave reviews from such familiar North American sources as *The New York Times* and *Entertainment Weekly*, which emphasize the scam movie aspects of the film, and none that mention that *Nueve reinas* is not an English-language movie. The images used are transnational, with the focus on a slap for Marcos from his sister, Valeria, (Leticia Brédice), the "forged" stamps that Marcos and Juan plan to sell, interior shots of the luxury hotel, and theft of the stamps by men on motorbikes followed by the chase scene. To reinforce this lack of specific national identity, none of the characters are ever heard to speak, something that would be unusual in a trailer for an English-language movie. The only diegetic vocal sounds by the characters are laughter and interjections such as "aha," and "no," which are not distinguishable as foreign to American audiences; thus there is no indication that this is a film with subtitles. The actors' dress style and their ethnicity also do not mark them out as foreign, and a North American watching the trailer would be given no indication that this was not a U.S. movie; a ploy taken presumably to get round North American audiences' reluctance to watch art-house films with subtitles. This approach is also taken in the international trailer, with the main difference being that text replaces the voice-over, and the music and images are more prominent, but, as with the U.S. version, there is no indication that this is a non–English-language film, as no Spanish is heard.

It is interesting to compare this sales pitch with the trailer screened in Argentine cinemas. Here the emphasis is immediately on the actors, dialogue, and rapidly edited images. The snippets of conversation focus on money and on the negotiations taking place between the conmen and their victims. These elements, the familiar actors, the language, and the themes outlined immediately mark the film as a national product.[57] The emphasis on money, corruption, greed, and deception are all national preoccupations, as will be discussed. The images themselves are similar to those used in the U.S. and international trailers; however, there are more shots of money being gained and lost: money changing hands, suitcases being filled with money, wads of money being counted, and money dropped on the floor, all hinting at the volatile financial climate that has long affected Argentina. Money is at the center of another image not highlighted in other trailers: customers, filmed from an aerial shot, are shown desperate to get into a bank to take out their savings, which we subsequently discover have been taken by the bank's board. These are images that would become familiar in Argentina as bank clients lost much of their savings during the crisis of 2001.

As well as the three trailers, the extras section of the DVD also includes short television spots made to promote the film in Argentina. Here, too, the focus is on the familiar actors, and Argentine Spanish, with the use of street language, is highlighted. The line "*un día de laboro, dos cientas lucas de ganancia*" ("one day of work to make two thousand pesos") is repeated in all of the television advertisements.[58] The audience comments by smiling filmgoers leaving the theaters chosen to promote the film also highlight the national nature of the film, obviously important in a market dominated by U.S. movies. One man comments, "I think it's Argentina," with no further explanation given, and another is heard enthusing that it's the best Argentine film ever made. The Argentine trailer and television advertisements indicate that, despite the overseas marketing of the film, it has many national resonances. It could even be said that the scam movie is perfectly suited to represent a culture of mistrust and dishonesty within contemporary Argentine society.

Nueve reinas is an individual film text that cannot be seen to single-handedly represent Argentine film either in its approach to filmmaking or in its critical and commercial success. Yet, it is a text that can shed light on a number of contemporary debates regarding the future of Argentine cinema and the position of national cinema in the international market. It demonstrates that films do not have to choose between aiming for commercial appeal and addressing local issues to achieve critical credibility. It shows that a film can be rooted in a national culture while falling within generic conventions associated with Hollywood. It demonstrates that there is a space within the international film market for non-Hollywood films, helped when these do not underestimate the importance of plot.

The different trailers produced to promote the film in Argentina and abroad also reveal the importance of perception and expectation in the marketing process. Domestic audiences are sold a cultural product that emphasizes the national characteristics of the film. Foreign audiences are sold a genre film of indistinguishable national origin, with all trailers focusing on the international appeal of the plot-driven narrative. While some films will want to highlight the national origin of the film when that film is marketed abroad, as a foreign experience is what is being "sold" to audiences, as seen with *Cidade de Deus* (*City of God*, 2002), this was clearly not relevant to *Nueve reinas*. While each film project should and will have its own artistic vision, *Nueve reinas* will provide Latin American filmmakers with certain guidelines if they wish to break into the international film market.

Notes

1. I would like to thank Petra Rau for her helpful comments on the draft chapter.

2. Sadly Fabián Bielinski died on June 29, 2006, of a heart attack at the age of 49. He had made one other film, *El aura* (*The Aura*, 2005), and national obituaries referred to the loss of a filmmaker with great promise.

3. Tamara L. Falicov, "Argentina's Blockbuster Movies and the Politics of Culture Under Neoliberalism, 1989–98," *Media, Culture and Society*, 22–23 (2000): 327–342; Gustavo J. Castagna "*Nueve reinas:* Un milagro argentine," *El amante cine*, elamante.com.ar/nota/0/0576.shtml (May 4, 2005).

4. Deborah Shaw, *Contemporary Latin American Cinema: Ten Key Films* (London: Continuum, 2000), 105–109.

5. Falicov, "Argentina's Blockbuster Movies," 328.

6. Falicov, "Argentina's Blockbuster Movies," 328.

7. Falicov, "Argentina's Blockbuster Movies," 328. The film she focuses on to illustrate this trend is *Comodines* (1997), an action movie that was advertised as the "first Hollywood movie spoken in Spanish" and did extremely well at the Argentine box office but was not distributed abroad.

8. Some examples of these are *The Son of the Bride* (Campanella, 2001), *Kamchatka*, (Piñyero, 2002), *Valentín* (Agresti, 2001), and *La niña santa* (Martel, 2004).

9. Todd Mccarthy "*Nueve Reinas*," *Variety*, September 9, 2001, www.variety .com/index.asp?layout=bio&peopleID=1010 (accessed May 10, 2005); Ryan Gilbey, "Nine Queens," *The Observer*, July 14 2002, film.guardian.co.uk/News_Story/ Critic_Review/Observer_review/0,4267,754835,00.html (accessed October 5, 2005); Joe Queenan "Stamp of Approval," *The Guardian*, July 10, 2002, film.guardian .co.uk/features/featurepages/0,4120,754388,00.html (accessed May 10, 2005).

10. Gustavo J.Castagna, "*Nueve reinas: Un milagro argentine*"; Quintín, "*Ahora y entonces*," *el amante cine*, October 9, 2000, elamante.com.ar/nota/0/0577.shtml (accessed May 11, 2005).

11. Geoffrey Kantaris, "Simulation and Dissimulation in the City: Nueve Reinas," October 25, 2003, www.mml.cam.ac.uk/spanish/sp12/cine/nuevereinas/ (accessed May 11, 2005).

12. Jorge Luis Borges, "Death and the Compass," in *Collected Fictions*, translated by Andrew Hurley (New York: Viking, 1998), 147–156.

13. Castagna, Quintín, Wolf, "Entrevista a Fabián Bielinsky, Los inconvenientes del éxito," *el amante cine* October 16, 2000, elamante.com.ar/nota/0/0539.shtml (accessed May 11, 2005, my translation).The Sony official Web site of *Nueve reinas* also informs that the director had previously made a short film based on Borges's short story, "La Espera," which won an award at the short film international film festival in Huesca, Spain.

14. See Gerald Martin, *Journeys Through the Labyrinth: Latin American Fiction in the Twentieth Century* (London: Verso, 1989), 155–169 and Beatriz Sarlo, *Jorge Luis Borges: A Writer on the Edge* (London: Verso, 1993), 26–30.

15. Jorge Luis Borges, "The Argentine Writer and Tradition" in *Labyrinths, Selected Stories and Other Writings* (1962; repr., New York: Harmondsworth, 1970), 217–18. For a critique of this position, see Martin, *Journeys Through the Labyrinth*, 156. He argues that Borges's was "a classicist and an imperialist," and his views were based on a notion of a barbarous Latin America compared to a civilized Europe.

16. In one example Bielinski said: "I spend a lot of time watching films—mainly American films. The 1970s in the United States were possibly the best period of filmmaking in any place or time in the world. I was a teenager then and these movies awakened feelings in me at a period in life when you are most vulnerable to passionate feelings," Walter Chaw, "Heavy Hitters of the New Argentine Cinema," www.filmfreakcentral.net/notes/argentinecinema.htm, April 15, 2002 (accessed May 11, 2005).

17. Frederic Jameson, "Notes on Globalization as a Philosophical Issue," in *The Cultures of Globalization*, eds. Frederic Jameson and Masao Miyoshi (Durham, N.C.: Duke University Press, 1998), 54–80.

18. Tony Fitzmaurice, "Film and Urban Contexts in a Global Context," in *Cinema and the City: Film and Urban Societies in a Global Context*, eds. Mark Shiel and Tony Fitzmaurice (Oxford, Mass: Blackwell Publishers, 2001), 23.

19. Néstor García Canclini, *Culturas híbridas: estrategias para entrar y salir de la modernidad* (Mexico: Grijalbo, 1989); Jesús Martin-Barbero, *Communication, Culture and Hegemony* (Newbury Park, Calif.: Sage 1993); Ella Shohat and Robert Stam, *Unthinking Eurocentrism: Multiculturalism and the Media* (London: Routledge, 1994).

20. Other films that have been particularly successful on the international market since 2000 include *Amores perros* (2000), *Y Tu Mamá También* (2001), *Cidade de Deus* (2002), and *Los diarios de motocicleta* (2004). For a related discussion of the way in which Latin American *Telenovelas* represent a contra-flow of cultural production from South to North in a way that disrupts paradigms of some globalization theorists, see Daniel Biltereyst and Philippe Meers, "The International Telenovela Debate and the Contra-flow Argument: a Reappraisal," *Media, Culture and Society* 22 (2000), 393–413.

21. Falicov, "Argentina's Blockbuster Movies," 336.

22. For more information about Argentine box-office figures, see www.sicacine .com.ar/. The film continued to be screened in 2001 and was seen by 35,445 spectators. The biggest national hit of that year was *The Son of the Bride*, a film that also did well internationally. See www.sicacine.com.ar/datos01est%20arg.htm (accessed September 13, 2004).

23. "*Business Data for Nine Queens*," www.imdb.com/title/tt0247586/business (accessed June 10, 2005).

24. The film was distributed in the United States by Sony Pictures Classics.

25. Nelly Richard, "*Latinoamérica y la postmodernidad: la crisis de los originales y la revancha de la copia*" in *La Estratificación de los Márgenes: Sobre Arte, Cultura y Política/s* (Santiago de Chile: Francisco Zegers, 1989), 53.

26. Richard, "*Latinoamérica y la postmodernidad*," 56.

27. Richard, "*Latinoamérica y la postmodernidad*," 54.

28. García Canclini, *Culturas híbridas*, 203–205.

29. García Canclini, *Culturas híbridas*, 200.

30. Patagonik is co-owned by Buena Vista International, the Argentine publishing group Clarin and Spain's Admira. The Argentine producer Bossi owns the remaining 10 percent. John Hopewell, "Patagonik Eyes Funds: Argentine Film Outfit Seeking US Coin," *Variety* (21 May 2002) www.variety.com/index.asp?layout= cannes2002_page&internal=cannes2002_story&articleid=VR1117867330&dept= News (accessed May 20, 2005).

31. The hotel itself is never named, yet is clearly part of a large successful chain. The actual Hilton hotel featured is located in Puerto Madero in Buenos Aires and opened in 2000, the same year the film was released. It is clearly out of the price range of most Argentines, with the rooms in 2004 costing from $150 for a double room. "*Frommer's Accommodations: The Hilton Hotel*," www.frommers.com/destinations/more accom.cfm?h_id=41745 (accessed May 25, 2005).

32. *Open Your Eyes* was remade as *Vanilla Sky* (2001), directed by Cameron Crowe and starring Tom Cruise and Penelope Cruz.

33. Siegried Kracauer "The Hotel Lobby," in *The City Cultures Reader*, eds. Malcolm Miles and Tim Hall with Iain Borden (1927; repr., London: Routledge, 2000) 33–39; Fredric Jameson, "Postmodernism, or the Cultural Logic of Late Capitalism," in *Postmodernism: A Reader*, ed. Thomas Docherty (Hemel Hempstead: Harvester Wheatsheaf, 1993), 81–83.

34. It is revealed at the end of the film that Juan's "real" name is Sebastián, however, for the purposes of clarity I refer to him throughout as Juan.

35. This contrasts with images of poor urban or rural Latin America, such as those seen in recently internationally successful films, such as the Brazilian *Central do Brasil* (1998) and *Cidade de Deus* (2002), demonstrating that, provided there is a good story, many images of Latin America can be accepted by foreign audiences.

36. Beatriz Sarlo, *Tiempo presente: notas sobre el cambio de una cultura*, (Buenos Aires: Siglo XXI, 2001), 29. For further discussion of the European influence on the

design of Buenos Aires, see Ana Betancour and Peter Hasdell, "Tango; A Choreography of Urban Displacement," in Lesley Naa Norle Lokko, ed. *White Papers, Black Masks* (Minneapolis: University of Minnesota Press, 2000), 277–290.

37. Beatriz Sarlo, *Tiempo presente*, 29 (my translation).

38. Chaw, "Heavy Hitters of the New Argentine Cinema."

39. Chaw, "Heavy Hitters of the New Argentine Cinema."

40. Chaw, "Heavy Hitters of the New Argentine Cinema."

41. Castagna, Quintín, Wolf, "Entrevista a Fabián Bielinsky."

42. In this approach there are also parallels with the approach of Borges, who uses a concise, realist language to write his highly contrived "fictions."

43. One well-known example is the collapse of Barings Bank in 1995, caused in large part by the rogue trader Nick Leeson.

44. Some key points of Argentina's economic troubles include hyperinflation in the late 1980s, a currency crisis between 1997 and 1999, an economic collapse in 2001, and currency devaluation, which left many people stripped of their savings and facing poverty, and an extremely large debt to the International Monetary Fund (IMF).

45. Kantaris, "Simulation and Dissimulation in the City."

46. The ideas for the street cons were adapted by Bielinski from stories told to him by local shopkeepers, Castagna, Quintín, Wolf, "Entrevista a Fabián Bielinsky."

47. While he has been created to con Marcos, the important point is that he is believable and succeeds in fooling Marcos and the audience as he represents a type that does exist. His fictional nature is hinted at in his name, Gandolfo, which resembles that of J. R. R. Tolkein's wizard Gandalf.

48. For an analysis of the film's critique of capitalism through the character of Vidal, see Kantaris, "Simulation and Dissimulation in the City."

49. Chaw, "Heavy Hitters of the New Argentine Cinema."

50. Fernando Solanas has made a documentary detailing the causes of Argentina's economic collapse and popular action taken against the government, *Memorias del saqueo/Social Genocide* (2004). See also Naomi Klein and Avi Lewis, *The Take* (2004), which looks at how a group of factory workers take on the running of their factory after it goes bust in the 2001 economic crash. For an English-language news story about the riots of 2002, see, "Protests Mark Argentine Anniversary," BBC News Online, December 20, 2002, news.bbc.co.uk/1/hi/world/americas/2592661.stm (accessed June 1, 2005). The article tells us that "protesters defaced the facades of banks with slogans such as 'Thieves! Robbers! Murderers!'" For an analysis of the riots, see Naomi Klein, "Argentina: A New Kind of Revolution," *The Guardian*, January 25, 2003, 14–24.

51. One of Marcos's favorite scams is stealing from old ladies by claiming to be their nephew who needs some money to get his car out of impoundment.

52. *"No hay santos, lo que hay son tarifas diferentes."*

53. See also his *Memorias del saqueo/Social Genocide* (2004), mentioned in endnote 49.

54. He is paid by Hannigan (based on Gandolfo), who is a Scot in this version, for a forgery of an original extremely rare antique banknote.

55. Shohat and Stam, *Unthinking Eurocentrism*, 163.

56. Fabián Bielinski, *Nueve reinas*, DVD extras (Sony Pictures, 2002).

57. Of all the actors, the best known is Ricardo Darín, who had worked in films and television before *Nueve reinas*; since the film he has appeared in a number of successful Argentine films including *Son of the Bride* (2001) and *Kamchatka* (2002)

58. "Luca" and "laboro" are from *lunfardo*, Buenos Aires slang, initially associated with immigrant communities and tango lyrics, but now common in Argentine street language.

CHAPTER FIVE

Afro-Brazilian Identity
Malandragem and Homosexuality
in *Madame Satã*
Lisa Shaw

The Brazilian-French coproduction *Madame Satã* (Madame Satan, 2002) was the first feature-length film directed by Karim Ainouz, who hails from Brazil's northeastern state of Ceará. It was awarded a Gold Hugo for best film at the 38th Chicago International Film Festival and the Audience Award at the Toronto Inside Out Lesbian and Gay Film and Video Festival in 2003, among other accolades.[1] Based on the life story of João Francisco dos Santos (1900–1976), a legendary figure in the bohemian circles of Rio de Janeiro, the film is set in the early 1930s. It focuses on a brief but key period in the life of dos Santos (better known as Madame Satã), a black homosexual who enjoyed celebrity status among the demimonde of Rio's red-light district, Lapa.

Rather than a conventional biography, Ainouz set out to paint what he terms a "human portrait" of dos Santos, to counterbalance the mythology that has grown up around this character.[2] The film thus rejects a linear narrative in favor of a series of imaginary vignettes based on the protagonist's life. The opening credits are immediately followed by an arresting, frontal close-up of the battered and bruised face of a young black male in a police cell in 1932. This point-of-view shot has been described by the director as akin to a mug shot (an effect that is reinforced by the sound of a camera shutter and a momentarily white screen to evoke the effect of a flash bulb), intended to strip the character bare before the audience learns anything about his life,[3] yet dos Santos defiantly avoids his interlocutor's direct gaze. The latter's words, in voice-over, are taken from a literal transcription of a court case, one of many in which dos Santos was the defendant:

> The accused, a.k.a. Benedito Emtabajá da Silva, is a mischief maker well known to the police. He frequents the district of Lapa and its vicinities. He is a passive pederast who shaves his eyebrows and imitates women, even changing his own voice. He has no religion. He smokes, gambles, and is addicted to alcohol. He has no education. He speaks crudely, in the language of the gutter. He is of little intelligence. He hates society, which rejects him because of his vices, and associates with pederasts, whores, procurers and other misfits. He boasts about his wealth, but has no regular work. His money can come only from degenerate criminal activities. He has numerous prior convictions. When in custody, he is often disruptive and attacks police officers. He is cunning, vicious, a habitual lawbreaker. For all these reasons, he poses a great threat to society. Rio de Janeiro, Capital City, May 12, 1932.

The film returns to this scene at its close, and the intervening action focuses on the unorthodox lifestyle that ultimately led to the protagonist's incarceration for murder. In a visual epilogue, we see images of a Rio carnival parade, dated 1942, in which dos Santos emerges triumphant. Dressed extravagantly in drag, in a costume for which he earned first prize in that year's parade, he finally appears as his alter ego, Madame Satã, a name taken from Cecil B. de Mille's 1930 camp movie, *Madam Satan*. Ainouz described his motivation in interview as follows:

> I wanted to show João Francisco's daily life and that of his "family," inhabitants of the "Republic of Lapa." These characters lived at the beginning of the 1930s in a world on the margins of the official Brazil, in a separate universe, with its own laws, codes, and rituals, a universe in which João Francisco was both king and queen, male and female, saint and Satan. One of my intentions was to capture, through an intimate cinematography, the enthusiasm and contradictions of the experiences of a *malandro* hustler, a black and a homosexual in Brazil at the beginning of the last century.[4]

This chapter will consider how the film sets out to convey these three integral aspects of dos Santos' life—his ethnic, cultural, and sexual identities—that conspired to create his threefold marginalization. It will also suggest possible reasons for the critical and popular success of *Madame Satã* among foreign audiences.

Afro-Brazilian Identity

Brazil was the last country in the Americas to abolish slavery in 1888, a traumatic event that gave way to mass migration of free blacks from rural plantations and interior mining areas to the cities of the coast, particularly the then-capital, Rio de Janeiro, well into the twentieth century. We know from his biography that dos Santos was the child of former slaves and made this same journey from the Northeast to the capital in the hope of a better life.[5] Like millions of others, he found his employment options drastically reduced by the prevailing ideology of *branqueamento*, or whitening, which favored white, European emigrants as a labor force and a "civilizing" influence on the largely mixed-race population. Furthermore, the press stirred up racial prejudice in the first decades of the century, with the result that Afro-Brazilians and their culture were seen as a polluting menace to be feared. Laws on vagrancy dictated that unemployed blacks could be arrested for simply being in the streets, and thus many had little option but to retreat to the shadows, to a life of petty crime. The film shows dos Santos earning a living as a pimp, an activity that was a common solution for poor black men. We see him initially trying to support himself in a more respectable way by working as an assistant and dresser for a white female cabaret star, to whom he is uncharacteristically submissive as a result of the abusive, racist relationship to which she subjects him. When his rage at his ill-treatment eventually boils over, he is forced to steal the wages that are owed to him, for which he later serves time in prison.

The film makes the audience aware of the racial context of the protagonist's life, not least in its mise-en-scène. One of the main concerns of Ainouz, and the film's director of photography, the highly acclaimed Walter Carvalho, centered on the depiction of black skin on screen. In a film in which low-key lighting and nocturnal scenes predominate, they sought to create a wide range of shades of brown and beige, to convey the full spectrum of the skin tone of the characters by applying the bleach bypass technique to the processing of the negative.[6] The darkest skin on screen is usually that of dos Santos himself (played by Lázaro Ramos), who lived by night, yet the cinematography succeeds in evoking his inner luminescence via lighting techniques. Ainouz has said that throughout the film the landscape or establishing shot is, in fact, dos Santos's body, which is the means through which he negotiates life, whether as a means of self-defense or attack or to express his sexuality. His body is thus privileged cinematically, with the texture of his skin highlighted by the processing of the negative, and a succession of extreme close-ups of individual parts of his body, such as his back or armpits, forcing the audience to identify with him as a human being rather than a mythical figure.[7] Throughout the film, the contrasts between the skin tones of different characters are emphasized by the lighting, not least during the sex scene between dos Santos and his white lover, Renatinho, again characterized by extreme close-ups designed to "lick the characters' bodies."[8] The stark contrasts between light and shade in the film equally connote the marginal, underground lifestyle that many Afro-Brazilian men were forced into at the beginning of the twentieth century in Rio de Janeiro.

Afro-Brazilian cultural production enjoys a privileged space in *Madame Satã*, evoking the creative effervescence of Rio's poorer, stigmatized quarters in the 1920s and early 1930s.[9] Dos Santos is a skilled *capoeirista*, or practitioner, of the martial art *capoeira*, which was devised and disguised as a dance by plantation slaves. In the film he puts this skill to effective use in street fights. He also incorporates elements of the Afro-Brazilian religion *candomblé* into his stage and carnival performances, not least in his costumes and dance moves. The film's soundtrack also draws heavily on samba, based on an African rhythm, the *batuque*, performed on rural sugar plantations and created by the descendants of slaves in Rio at the beginning of the twentieth century. The arrival in power of President Getúlio Vargas in 1930 led to a major transformation of official attitudes to Afro-Brazilian culture in general. Samba was poised for reformulation to suit the demands of the nascent music industry and the wider cultural policies of the Vargas regime. Likewise, in the early to mid-1930s, Vargas began to embrace other expressions of Afro-Brazilian culture, such as capoeira and candomblé, in his drive to forge a sense of national as opposed to ethnic identity and to attenuate the power of such ethnically marked practices.[10] The film's setting in 1932 thus aligns the protagonist with Afro-Brazilian culture as a whole, since by that juncture both were reaching a turning point in their ethnically marked trajectory and were about to emerge from their marginalized and stigmatized status.

Malandragem and Samba

In his book *Memórias do Café Nice*, Nestor de Holanda mentions two of the most famous Rio malandros of the 1920s and 1930s, Madame Satã and Meia-Noite (Midnight).[11] Dos Santos, as we hear him say to Laurita in the film, explicitly identified himself with the ethnically marked archetype of the malandro, a hustler or delinquent who spurned poorly paid manual labor in favor of a lifestyle of idleness, pleasure-seeking, and petty crime, a countercultural lifestyle known as *malandragem*. The cultural anthropologist Robert DaMatta writes that:

> the malandros prefer to keep for themselves their labor force and qualifications. The lay-about, thus, is the one who does not enter the system with his labor force, and hovers around the social structure, being able to enter or leave it, or even transcend it. His craftiness, in turn, can be seen as the equivalent of *jeito* (or *jeitinho*), as a structurally defined way of using the established rules of society for his own benefit, but without destroying them or calling them into question.[12]

With its close associations with slave labor, manual work was spurned by the malandro antiheroes of the Afro-Brazilian community in favor of the quest for pleasure. Labor was viewed as the negation of pleasure, and the malandro's "toil" took the form of his efforts to explore all the hedonistic avenues open to him. In *Madame Satã* we see dos Santos enjoying carnal pleasure with his lover, Renatinho, to the full, and witness the joy that he derives from his artistic performances. So that tiring manual labor did not lessen his aptitude for pleasure, the malandro often looked to women for material support, whether by living off several unwitting girlfriends or pimping for prostitutes in Lapa or the Rio district known as Mangue.

Although it is known that dos Santos earned his living as a pimp, in Ainouz's film his indirect involvement in prostitution is favorably depicted as an economic necessity within a caring yet unconventional domestic arrangement. He lives with a female prostitute, Laurita (played by Marcélia Cartaxo), fulfilling the role of father to her illegitimate child,[13] but nevertheless benefiting from her presence in the home. Furthermore, a homosexual male prostitute, Tabú (Taboo, played by Flávio Bauraqui) also lives with them as a "female" household member who tends to the domestic chores and is obliged to share his illicit income with dos Santos, forming the fourth element in this unorthodox "family." Although he often directs his anger and frustrations with his life at Tabú, whose open femininity he both admires and despises, dos Santos is his surrogate father.[14] In one of the few daylight scenes in the film, we see the four family members enjoying a day at the beach. Similarly, dos Santos fulfils the role of caring husband to Laurita, as is evoked by the Super-8/home movie–style shots of them spending time in a park with Laurita's young daughter, complete with 360-degree axis of action and the kind of technical errors typically made by an amateur filmmaker. Rather than providing a questionable endorsement of exploitative relationships, Ainouz reinforces an unconventional, nuanced portrayal of dos Santos's polyvalent character and societal role.

The malandros of Rio in the 1920s and 1930s were synonymous with the first Afro-Brazilian samba composers or *sambistas*. As Gilberto Vasconcelos has written, samba composers in the 1930s were well aware that malandragem was the only possible alternative lifestyle in a society whose structure turned working men into economic outsiders who became poorer with every day that passed.[15] As Ainouz has acknowledged, "Brazilian popular music of the '20s and '30s was . . . very important in order to understand the era,"[16] and the setting of *Madame Satã* is authenticated by the frequent incorporation of popular samba songs from the 1930s that are intimately bound up with the ethos of malandragem. The samba "Se você jurar" ("If you swear," 1931), in its original recording in duet by Francisco Alves and Mário Reis, features in the film's diegetic soundtrack at several key moments. The function of this particular choice of song goes far beyond simply adding local color and realism to the scenes in question. Rather, this iconic samba is used to situate the eponymous protagonist of the film within a community of socially stigmatized yet defiantly proud Afro-Brazilian men, who were obliged to adopt the persona of the mythical malandro to give dignity to their economic marginalization.

"Se você jurar" ("If you swear," 1931)
by Ismael Silva, Nilton Bastos and Francisco Alves
Se você jurar/If you swear
Que me tem amor/That you love me
Eu posso me regenerar/I can reform myself
Mas se é/But if
Para fingir, mulher/You're pretending, woman
A orgia assim não vou deixar/I'm not going to give up malandragem

A mulher é um jogo/Women are a game
Difícil de acertar/Difficult to win
E o homem como um bobo/And men, like fools
Não se cansa de jogar/Never tire of playing
O que eu posso fazer/All I can do
É se você jurar/Is if you swear
Arriscar a perder/Risk losing
Ou desta vez então ganhar/Or this time win

Muito tenho sofrido/I've suffered a lot
Por minha lealdade/For my loyalty
Agora sou sabido/Now I'm wise
Não vou atrás de amizade/I don't look for friendship

A minha vida é boa/My life is good
Não tenho o que pensar/I've no worries
Por uma coisa à-toa/For something so pointless
Não vou me regenerar/I'm not going to clean up my act

This samba is first heard in an early scene in which dos Santos and Laurita dance and sing along to it in a bar, where it is playing on presumably either the radio or a gramophone. This samba is subsequently the preferred choice of gramophone record at the small gathering held when dos Santos is released from jail, where he had been held for theft. The song also plays over the film's final credits.

First recorded by the crooners Francisco Alves and Mário Reis for Odeon records (10745-B) in 1931, this samba is credited to three composers, namely Francisco Alves, Nilton Bastos, and Ismael Silva. In a classic case of what was known as *falsa parceria* (literally, false partnership), all the evidence suggests that Alves, the most popular white-skinned singer of the era, simply bought the right to put his name to this record from the other two struggling Afro-Brazilian songwriters. The song became closely associated with Silva, its lyrics endorsing the malandro lifestyle that he came to embody. He took part in the traditional, improvised *rodas de samba* (informal, impromptu samba) in the *morro*, or shantytown, of São Carlos, but drawing on his streetwise *jeitinho*, he also had access to the music industry in the form of *parcerias* with the most famous singer of the era, Alves. Silva, along with three other Afro-Brazilian sambistas, Bide (Alcebíades Barcellos), Bastos, and Armando Marçal, was responsible for creating a new type of samba by accentuating the rhythm and adapting it for percussion instruments. This group thus distanced this new music from the traditional *maxixe*-inspired rhythm, which placed a heavy emphasis on the downbeat and had a piano accompaniment.[17] These semiliterate composers from the poor Rio district of Estácio de Sá, with no formal musical training or knowledge, were sometimes referred to disparagingly as *maestros de assobio* (maestros of whistling). However, the new rhythm that they created to provide a suitable accompaniment for the carnival processions of "Deixa Falar," the first *escola de samba*, or neighborhood carnival group, which they established, appealed to the tastes of the popular masses. They were the pioneers of carnival samba and responsible for establishing the rhythm that would characterize this brand of music until the present day.

The iconic figure of Silva and his undeniable associations with an emerging Afro-Brazilian cultural identity and nonconformity inform the representation of dos Santos in Ainouz's film. Like dos Santos, Silva was a homosexual who also clearly lived by the malandro ethos and acquired a prison record.[18] A photograph of him was tellingly chosen to illustrate the front cover of Carlos Sandroni's book about samba, *Feitiço decente* (literally, *Respectable Magic Spell*,[19] 2001), and he was the dapper, streetwise malandro incarnate, with his sharp white suits ironically contrasting with his dark skin, in a visual comic swipe at respectable, middle-class white office workers. (As Claudia Matos says, the malandro parodies the bourgeois male by always being well dressed.)[20]

By the beginning of the 1930s social mobility was available to Afro-Brazilians in Rio de Janeiro for the first time via the nascent music industry and particularly the composing of samba. Silva was one of this first generation of Afro-Brazilian popular composers able to make the transition from amateur music-making and solely live performances in Rio's poorer quarters, to participating on the fringes of the record industry by selling his compositions to famous frontmen, such as Alves, the most notorious so-called *comprositor* of the era (a pun on the Portuguese words *compositor*—composer, and *comprar*—to buy). In this respect Silva was a classic representative of the exploited Afro-Brazilian (a real-life precursor of Grande Otelo's character in Nelson Pereira dos Santos's social realist film, *Rio, Zona Norte*, 1957).[21] The association between dos Santos and arguably Silva's most famous samba, "Se você jurar," in *Madame Satã* consequently connotes not only assertion of a proud ethnically marked identity but also a reality of prejudice and discrimination. Both Silva and dos Santos were obliged to live by the rules of malandragem to survive by living off their wits. Both were forced to pursue a livelihood and a sexual existence on the fringes of respectable society. As Claudia Matos argues, the malandro traditionally belongs to the border or the margins.[22]

The Body, Gender Performativity, and Homosexuality

Despite his liminal status and aptitude for transgressing conventional social boundaries, the mythical malandro was characterized, particularly in the lyrics of samba, as an inveterate womanizer and philanderer. In apparent contradiction of his malandro persona, however, dos Santos never tried to hide the fact that he liked sex with other men.[23] The cinematic depiction of his body in Ainouz's film captures the ambivalence of the character's physicality, emphasizing the muscular strength and attractiveness of his body via lighting techniques and close-up shots of his bare chest and back. Tatiana Heise has argued that his body plays a dual role in the film: It is not only the object on which power is exerted by authority but also his instrument of power. It is made appealing to both the female and male gaze, using the cinematic techniques described by Yvonne Tasker in her book *Spectacular Bodies*.[24]

As James N. Green has shown, many young homosexual men in Rio de Janeiro between 1920 and 1945 not only accepted their sexuality "but were rather self-affirming about it."[25] Green explains that the pervasive notion in this period was that same-sex relationships could only develop by playing out the strictly mutually exclusive roles of "active" manly men and "passive" feminine men, although there is ample evidence to suggest that the sexual practice of many men was more complex than this prescribed binary model.[26] Dos Santos is a case in point; as the transcription from the court case that provides the voice-over for the opening scene of *Madame Satã* states: "He is a passive pederast who shaves his eyebrows and imitates women, even changing his own voice," and yet his reputation as a fearsome malandro street fighter and criminal stridently contradict this self-conscious effeminate identity. On screen, however, we see only a macho and virile active man who anally penetrates his lover, Renatinho, and yet can confidently adopt an alternative feminized identity, thus representing a fluid notion of sexual identity that transcends the contemporary "real" man/*fresco* (fairy) paradigm. As Green says:

> Madame Satã . . . openly admitted that he liked to be anally penetrated, a sexual desire that was socially stigmatized and the antithesis of manliness represented by the penetrating knife blade. While the popular respect usually afforded a malandro was linked to his potency, masculinity, and his willingness to die for his honor, Madame Satã simply contradicted the stereotype.[27]

In the film, a main turning point in dos Santos' existence occurs when he is released from prison and learns of his white lover Renatinho's death. He resists the urge to self-destruct, and to survive the trauma he channels his energies into finally reinventing himself by performing a cabaret act in the Danúbio Azul (Blue Danube) bar in Lapa. (As Heise has noted, self-reinvention is one of his strategies of resistance, the other is through his body).[28] He draws his inspiration from Vitória dos Anjos, the white female cabaret artist for whom he worked and whose identity he has always coveted, creating a collage from memory of the lines of her performance of the Arabian Nights. The amateurish nature of his performance in the film is intentional, reflecting how dos Santos succeeded in stamping his unique signature on such exuberant displays.[29] In real life he voraciously consumed new ideas from his immediate surroundings and experiences, and in the film, after a visit to the cinema with Laurita in which he sees Josephine Baker dancing frenetically on-screen, he appears for the second time on stage. His costume of a close-fitting sequined headdress, strings of beads, and a sarong-style skirt clearly takes its lead from Baker's mix of flapper girl and African tribal princess, but it is also evocative of the costumes worn by the priestesses of candomblé, an effect that is reinforced by his spinning dance moves, which also characterize the rituals of this religion. His muscular chest is bare however, Ainouz having rejected an earlier version of this costume, which featured a feminine, midriff-revealing top of the type favored by Carmen Miranda in her musicals made by Twentieth Century Fox.[30] The director's desired effect was that of an "enigmatic figure that plays with masculinity and femininity," and not a drag queen or a transvestite. He sought to depict a man whose identity could not be defined in conventional terms.[31]

One of the songs that dos Santos performs during this stage act is the samba "Mulato bamba" ("Cool Mulatto"), written by Noel Rosa in 1931.[32] Again, he improvises his own version of the lyrics, which are translated in the film's English subtitles as follows:

> The big mulatto now turns tricks
> And writes samba for kicks
> Since a kid
> Goes for the glitz
> Never works
> Lives on his wits
> Always knows the latest songs
> Society's where he belongs
> All the girls
> He makes them cry
> Because they know
> He prefers the guys

This samba, in keeping with a deep-rooted lyrical tradition that characterized the genre in the 1920s and early 1930s, portrays a typical malandro but with the ironic twist that the tough guy in question is gay. In fact, this samba was allegedly inspired by Madame Satã, as Rosa's biographers, João Máximo and Carlos Didier, suggest, although this is not explicitly referenced in the film.[33] The inclusion of this song in the film's soundtrack thus serves to underscore the ambivalent sexuality of dos Santos. Similarly, the samba "Se você jurar," quoted in full previously, touches on the idea of pretense and playacting within heterosexual relationships, in an ironic nod to the performative aspects of the fluid gendered identities assumed by the protagonist.[34]

In the film dos Santos creates self-conscious performances both onstage and off. One such spectacle takes place in the backyard of his rundown home in Lapa; when dressed up for an evening out in a striking red shirt he parades up and down along one of the walls, singing another of Rosa's sambas, "Fita Amarela" ("Yellow Ribbon," 1932). Written from the standpoint of the irreverent malandro, these lyrics take pride in Afro-Brazilian identity: "When I die/I don't want tears or candles . . . I want a mulatto girl/To dance on my coffin."

The film's setting, Lapa, was not only a popular hangout for bohemian popular musicians and the city's major red-light district but also a central location in Rio's homoerotic topography. The area did not necessarily protect gay men from social hostility, but the homosexual artists and writers who frequented Lapa achieved a relative acceptance within this social milieu, albeit one tempered by light-hearted ridicule, while still keeping their sexual secrets from a wider audience.[35] There is ample evidence that many effeminate gay men worked as maids and cleaners in brothels and boardinghouses in this district of the city, just like the character of Taboo in *Madame Satã*. In common with many of his gay contemporaries, dos Santos was hired at the age of eighteen to work as a waiter in a brothel in Lapa, and in the film we see him and Taboo staging a so-called *conto do suador* (literally, "the story of one who sweats"). This was a common exploit among pairs of male prostitutes in Rio, one of whom engaged in homosexual practice with a client while the other removed the contents of the latter's wallet.[36] But dos Santos was unique in the circles in which he mixed for his defiant pride in his sexuality and active, sometimes aggressive, defense of his rights. As he says in his memoirs:

> I thought that there was nothing wrong with being a *bicha* [fairy]. I was one because I wanted to be, but that didn't make me any less a man because of it. And I became a bicha willingly, and was not forced by anyone else. I had my first sexual experience when I was 13 years old when the women of Lapa organized orgies in which men, women and bichas took part. When I was 13 I was invited to take part as both a man and a bicha and I preferred being a bicha and that is why I became one.[37]

He refused to accept the humiliation and abuse routinely meted out to homosexuals by the police, who arrested them for vagrancy or assaults on decency just so that they could be commandeered into carrying out domestic chores in police stations.[38] At the climax of the film we witness his ultimate defense of his sexuality. After performing his second show at the Blue Danube he is insulted by a drunk bystander with a range of racial and homophobic slurs: "Queer," "Nigger," "Nigger faggot," and "Pervert." This is a pivotal moment in his life and in the film and for this reason this incident is recounted on the opening pages of his biography.[39] Initially he restrains himself, with uncharacteristic control, and proudly declares in the film: "I'm a queen by choice! It doesn't make me less of a man!" After returning home he tries to forget this aggressive act by washing off his stage makeup, but the sight of blood from his injured face forces him to react and seek revenge. He turns his back on all his previous values by using a gun, rather than his body, to attack, and shoots his aggressor, an off-duty policeman, dead in a dark alley from behind. This is the point at which his identity is transformed into that of a criminal outlaw. As Green says, this legendary crime committed by dos Santos "challenged his masculinity and created a myth around him, a myth that subverted the popular image of the passive and helpless homosexual."[40]

The cinematography of *Madame Satã* foregrounds dos Santos's body as a strategy of resistance to authority and social conventions. As Ainouz says, "His body is his fortress. Objectively, it is the only thing he has. Everything he creates is through his body, his voice, his way of dressing [and] moving. . . . To me, the landscape of this film is his body, and this is why Walter Carvalho and I decided to work the negative in such a way as to enhance the texture of the skin and the presence of the body."[41]

Dos Santos's active assertion of his sexual identity in real life is all the more surprising given the color of his skin. By the 1930s theories of eugenics that emphasized the degenerate nature of certain races and close links between skin color and the propensity for deviance were gaining credence and popularity in Brazil. In this context, dos Santos was doubly stigmatized and doubly marginalized. What is even more fascinating about his self-affirming sexual orientation is how he succeeded in preserving his malandro status while taking pride in his sexuality and reconciled these two apparently paradoxical aspects of his identity. As Green writes, "Although he projected a tough-guy image, his assumed name, Madame Satã, undercut the traditional association of malandro with manliness, evoking a figure at once mysterious, androgynous and sinister."[42] He claimed that the role and reputation of malandro had been forced on him as a result of his fatal shooting of the policeman. Although he only spent two years of the sixteen-year sentence in prison, because of a successful appeal that he had fired in self-defense, the incident and his infamy defined him as a malandro cop killer who went on to offer "protection" for bars in Lapa. Both also led to continual harassment by the police, and between 1928 and 1965 he spent more than twenty-seven years in jail. In the film, we see him sharing a prison cell with various other inmates, and accepting the existing power relations. Unlike outside the prison walls, here he could free himself of his malandro persona and enjoy a relative peace and safety, an idea that is reinforced in the mise-en-scène by the uncharacteristically high-key lighting.

Within the macho posturing required to survive in Lapa, dos Santos's ambivalent masculinity was seen as provocative, leading many to challenge him to a fight. As he stated in his memoirs, "They couldn't get used to my bravery because I was a known homosexual. . . . On the other hand, the newspapers always emphasized my exploits precisely because I was a homosexual."[43] In an interview with the tabloid O Pasquim in 1971 he described himself as a viado (faggot), taking pride in a term that has traditionally had pejorative connotations, preempting the recent phenomenon of gay and lesbian activists adopting the term "queer" as a political identity to subvert the term and give it a positive meaning.[44]

Conclusions

No longer one-dimensional slaves or demeaned manual workers at the bottom of the economic heap, Afro-Brazilians could benefit from the context of growing interest in their culture to explore their own polyvalent identity at the dawn of the 1930s. The ethnically marked evolution of the samba, which predominates in the diegetic soundtrack of Madame Satã, provides an important point of comparison with the protagonist's personal trajectory and negotiation of identity. The incorporation of Silva's samba "Se você jurar," for example, a metonym for the new breed of samba intimately linked to Silva, aligns this other gay malandro with dos Santos, but perhaps more importantly points to the shifting status of Afro-Brazilian identity in the early 1930s. Dos Santos was arguably the most extreme representative of the quest for new possibilities for multiple black identities. As a review of the film by Gary Morris in the online Bright Lights Film Journal perceptively commented: "João's story is seductive indeed, both as a personal biography and as a history of the ascendance of Afro-Brazilian slum society from disrepute into visibility."[45] Indeed, the film celebrates dos Santos's disregard for and thus ultimate victory over constraints of class, race, and sexuality. As its director, Ainouz explains: "Poor, black, homosexual. How do you deal with this man who is stigmatized three times over? By de-stigmatizing him. In his daily life João Francisco imploded these definitions."[46] His transgression of contemporary assumptions about homosexuality, femininity, and passivity is perhaps the most remarkable aspect of his life, and something that evidently created social anxiety. As Green notes, "His rebellious attitude outraged his enemies and the police and made good copy in the press precisely because he did not conform to the standard stereotype of the homosexual."[47] Neither did he conform to the standard stereotype of the exploited poor black man or that of the womanizing malandro, remaining proud and defiant into his old age, as is evidenced in his memoirs.[48]

Madame Satã's commercial and critical success outside Brazil can partially, at least, be attributed to the appeal of a true-to-life tale of courageous assertion of ethnic and sexual identity against the odds. The film naturally struck a chord with gay audiences, as evidenced by some of the awards that it garnered. Its Rio de Janeiro setting during the ascendance of Afro-Brazilian culture, aspects of which, especially samba capoeira and candomblé, authenticate the cultural specificity of the context, also tapped into a current vogue for what is seen as a typically Brazilian brand of marginality, as depicted in *Cidade de Deus* (Fernando Meirelles and Kátia Lund, 2003) and *Carandiru* (Hector Babenco, 2004). There is also ample evidence of the enduring appeal of an apocryphal Brazilian "exotic" spiced with stereotypical hedonism. Certainly this is true of the United Kingdom, where in 2003 the BBC used a short sequence of capoeira to entertain viewers in the brief time slot between its television programs, and in 2004 when the luxury department store Selfridges staged the "Brazil 40°" promotional event at its London and Manchester flagship stores, complete with "tropical" Brazilian products, such as *caipirinha* cocktail kits and skimpy bikinis.

Notes

1. These included the Cinema Brazil Grand Prize for Best Actor (Lázaro Ramos), Best Actress (Marcélia Cartaxo), and Best Art Direction (Marcos Pedroso); the ADF Cinematography Award—Special Mention at the Buenos Aires International Festival of Independent Cinema (for Walter Carvalho); a Golden Colón at the Huelva Latin American Film Festival (for the director, Karim Ainouz); Best Art Direction (Marcos Pedroso) and the Special Jury Prize (Best First Work, Karim Ainouz) at the Havana Film Festival; and a nomination for a GLAAD Media Award in the category of Outstanding Film with Limited Release. Data courtesy of Internet Movie Database, www.imdb.com.html, (accessed April 8, 2005).

2. Karim Ainouz, *Madame Satã*, commentary on the DVD of the film (Fox Lerber, 2004).

3. Ainzou's commentary on the DVD.

4. Karim Ainouz, "Macabea com raiva," *Cinemais* 33 (2003): 178. This and all other translations from Portuguese-language sources are my own.

5. Sylvan Paezzo, *Memórias de Madame Satã* (Rio de Janeiro: Lidador, 1972).

6. Ainzou's commentary on the DVD.

7. Ainzou's commentary on the DVD.

8. Ainzou's commentary on the DVD. Ainouz even describes this love scene as a ménage à trois in which the camera is the third party.

9. Ainzou's commentary on the DVD. Ainouz likens this period in Rio to the Harlem Renaissance in New York.

10. In 1935 the *escolas de samba*, or neighborhood carnival, groups were officially recognized by the state, having previously been repressed as manifestations of Afro-Brazilian culture.

11. Nestor de Holanda, *Memórias do Café Nice: subterrâneos da música popular e da vida boêmia do Rio de Janeiro* (Rio de Janeiro: Conquista, 1970). Meia-Noite is also briefly referenced in the film, in the form of a shot of a newspaper headline and accompanying photograph.

12. Roberto DaMatta, *Carnavais, malandros e heróis: para uma sociologia do dilema brasileiro* (Rio de Janeiro: Zahar, 1979), 226. *Jeito* or *jeitinho* refers in Brazilian Portuguese to a way of getting around the law or bureaucracy by means of a slightly shady or underhand act. People who have *jeito* (or "have the knack") are particularly good at pulling off such acts.

13. In reality this was the first of seven children that dos Santos adopted.

14. Tatiana Heise describes dos Santos as "a charismatic but authoritarian patriarch." "The (Re)configuration of power in *Madame Satã*," paper given at the conference New Latin American Cinemas: Contemporary Cinema and Filmmaking, University of Leeds, June 28–30, 2005.

15. Gilberto Vasconcelos, *Música popular: de olho na fresta* (Rio, Graal, 1977), 161.

16. Ainouz, "*Macabea com raiva*," 179.

17. The *maxixe* was an urban dance form and its instrumental accompaniment that emerged in the city of Rio de Janeiro between 1870 and 1880 and drew on elements of the polka, the habanera, and African rhythms brought to Brazil by slaves.

18. Silva was convicted of attempted murder after shooting a fellow malandro, and spent half of his five-year sentence in prison. Coincidentally, Alves, also known as Chico da Viola, Silva's musical partner and interpreter, was also a practicing homosexual, unbeknownst to his legions of female fans. As the popular singer of the time Jorge Goulart recalled: "In our group Chico's sexual habits were openly discussed, they said that he was a *fanchono* [slang term for a homosexual], that he liked to have sex with boys. I mentioned this fact to some people; the subject is taboo. They wouldn't allow the myth to be touched, or rather the myth couldn't stand information like that, as if it were the worst thing imaginable." Quoted in Alcir Lenharo, *Cantores do rádio: a trajetória de Nora Ley e Jorge Goulart e o meio artístico de seu tempo* (Campinas: UNICAMP, 1995), 28.

19. This title is taken from a line in a samba by Noel Rosa, *Feitiço da Vila* (Vila Isabel's Magic Spell, 1934).

20. Claudia Matos, *Acertei no milhar: malandragem e samba no tempo de Getúlio* (Rio de Janeiro: Paz e Terra, 1982), 56.

21. Bryan McCann elaborates on the racism and exploitation that existed in the world of popular music in Brazil in this era: "Through much of the Vargas period, radio stations and record labels shied away from featuring black performers, allowing

white professionals to become rich and famous while Afro-Brazilian composers often remained relatively poor. Rhetorical praise of African influence served to mask this ongoing racism. Thus, charges that Afro-Brazilians were often exploited by the popular music industry hold weight. Given Brazil's economic stratification, with Afro-Brazilians concentrated heavily in the lower range, this could hardly fail to be the case." Bryan McCann, *Hello, Hello Brazil: Popular Music in the Making of Modern Brazil* (Durham, N.C.: Duke University Press, 2004), 12.

22. Matos, *Acertei no milhar*, 54.

23. Green, *Beyond Carnival: Male Homosexuality in Twentieth-Century Brazil* (Chicago: The University of Chicago Press, 1999), 86.

24. Heise, "The (Re)configuration of power in *Madame Satã.*" See also Yvonne Tasker, *Spectacular Bodies: Gender, Genre and the Action Film* (London: Routledge, 1993).

25. Green, *Beyond Carnival*, 66.

26. Green, *Beyond Carnival*, 75–76. Green shows how men made sense of their attractions to other men in this rigidly gendered system. Many thought of themselves as having an essence, soul, spirit, or mind that was feminine and wrongly incarcerated in a man's body.

27. I Green, *Beyond Carnival*, 90.

28. Heise, "The (Re)configuration of power in *Madame Satã.*"

29. Ainouz explains that the opening and initial closing credits of the film were laboriously made from hand-embroidered sequins to echo this improvised yet highly colorful aspect of Madame Satã's artistic persona.

30. These include *Down Argentine Way* (1940) and *That Night in Rio* (1941).

31. Ainzou's commentary on the DVD.

32. The original lyrics of this samba are as follows:

> Este mulato forte/This strong mulatto
> É do Salgueiro/Is from Salgueiro
> Passear no tintureiro/Hanging around in the dry cleaner's
> Era seu esporte/Was his favorite sport
> Já nasceu com sorte/He was born lucky
> E desde pirralho/And since he was a kid
> Vive à custa do baralho/He's lived from a pack of cards
> Nunca viu trabalho/He's never seen a day's work
>
> E quando tira samba/And when he plays a samba
> É novidade/It's news
> Quer no morro ou na cidade/Both on the hillside and down in the city
> Ele sempre foi o bamba./He's always been the coolest dude.
> As morenas do lugar/The local dark girls
> Vivem a se lamentar/Are always complaining
> Por saber que ele não quer/That he doesn't want
> Se apaixonar por mulher./To fall in love with a woman.

(The word *tintureiro* [literally, dry cleaner's] was also contemporary Rio slang for the police van used to round up malandros.)

22. João Máximo and Carlos Didier, *Noel Rosa: uma biografia* (Brasília: Linha Gráfica, 1990), 220. In his memoirs, dos Santos refers to his friendship with Noel Rosa and other popular composers and singers who frequented the bars of Lapa, such as Heitor dos Prazeres, Cartola, Nelson do Cavaquinho, Benedito Lacerda, the duo Jararaca and Ratinho, and Aracy de Almeida. Paezzo, *Memórias de Madame Satã*, 17.

34. All the evidence suggests that this samba's creator, Ismael Silva, took pains to conceal his homosexuality. In her biography of Silva, Maria Thereza Mello Soares makes no mention of his homosexuality, concentrating instead on his encounter with his alleged illegitimate daughter. Maria Thereza Mello Soares, *São Ismael do Estácio: o sambista que foi rei* (Rio de Janeiro: Funarte, 1985), 35–36.

35. Green, *Beyond Carnival*, 84–85.

36. Green, *Beyond Carnival*, 101–2. As Green writes, "Difficulties in finding employment led some [homosexuals] to prostitution and petty theft. Getting paid to have sex with a man and then stealing his wallet was, for at least a few, part and parcel of scraping together a living, particularly in the 1930s, when the Brazilian economy was still suffering the effects of the worldwide depression."

37. Paezzo, *Memórias de Madame Satã*, 115–16. It is interesting to note in this quotation that dos Santos saw men and *bichas* as being separate sexual categories. He thus tacitly abides by the prevalent active/passive binary in his choice of terms, although blatantly flouting such essentializing in his own sexual behavior.

38. Green, *Beyond Carnival*, 91.

39. Paezzo, *Memórias de Madame Satã*.

40. Green, *Beyond Carnival*, 88.

41. Ainzou's commentary on the DVD.

42. Green, *Beyond Carnival*, 89.

43. Paezzo, *Memórias de Madame Satã*, 115.

44. Green, *Beyond Carnival*, 330.

45. Gary Morris, "Fists and Feathers: Madame Satã Reviewed," *Bright Lights Film Journal*, Issue 41, www.brightlightsfilm.com/41/madame.htm (accessed April 8, 2005).

46. Ainouz, "Macabea com raiva," 181.

47. Green, *Beyond Carnival*, 91. The tabloid newspaper *O Pasquim* fostered a cult image of Madame Satã, whom it described as a *bicha brava* (brave faggot), and thus someone who did not threaten established gender roles.

48. Paezzo, *Memórias de Madame Sata*.

CHAPTER SIX

Family Romance and Pathetic Rhetoric in Marcelo Piñeyro's *Kamchatka*

David William Foster

Marcelo Piñeyro's *Kamchatka* (2002), featuring the two Argentine megastars Cecilia Roth and Ricardo Darín, was a critical and commercial success both in Argentina and in its foreign venues.[1] This chapter examines the family romance and the use of a rhetoric of pathos to explore how an excellent example of commercial filmmaking like *Kamchatka* nevertheless undercuts its own effectiveness by the appeal to bourgeois norms and a universal idealization of human experience. Unquestionably Hollywoodish in its style, execution, and plot development, Piñeyro's film nevertheless demonstrates the continuing need in Argentina to process the experiences of the long period of neofascist tyranny and military dictatorship (1966–1973 and 1976–1983), particularly as regards to the so-called disappeared people.

Much like the Jewish Holocaust at the hands of the Nazis during World War II, the Argentine Holocaust at the hands of the Argentine armed forces, which manifested inspiration by fascist movements of the first half of the twentieth century in Europe, involved the systematic extermination of individuals. In the case of Argentina, it has been estimated that approximately 30,000 individuals (it may be impossible ever to establish an exact number) were arrested, incarcerated, tortured, murdered, and disappeared through mass burials and dumping in the broad estuary that borders the capital city of Buenos Aires. These individuals were alleged to be (because none were ever brought to formal judicial trial) subversives and terrorists or accomplices and fellow travelers of subversives and terrorists, committed to overthrowing the de facto military regime, and it was further alleged, establishing a socialist/

communist state in Argentina. Certainly, there were terrorists and subversives committed to violent resistance to government by the armed forces. And certainly there were individuals who made it clear that they were committed to supporting a government in the style of the one that had resulted from the 1959 Fidel Castro revolution in Cuba, but because no legal trials were ever held, it is important to underscore how there was never any constitutional, judicial basis for their persecution and extermination. The so-called Dirty War from approximately 1976 (in reality it began before the actual military coup in March of that year) to about 1980, nevertheless, did effectively destroy virtually all armed resistance to the military regime. However, it is now abundantly clear (as it was even at the time) that those detained and eventually disappeared (some were released along the way after incarceration and in some cases, torture) included a larger number of individuals who could never have been reasonably brought to a fully legal justice. One must acknowledge that many, many innocent people were caught up in the machinations of the Dirty War who were either the victims of mistaken identity or whose only crime was to be at the wrong place at the wrong time or to count among friends, family, and acquaintances individuals who were, in fact, engaged in acts of guerrilla warfare against the government and established society.[2]

Since the return to constitutional democracy in 1983, Argentine society has struggled on many fronts to come to terms with its own Holocaust. Efforts have ranged from programs focusing on the redemocratization of Argentine society—both public and educational programs—and the investment in the production of an entire range of cultural texts (novels, the visual arts, essays, and plays) that explore the origins, nature, and consequences of this historical event. The newly elected democratic government put the leaders of the military regime on trial in 1984 (the first time such a Nuremberg-like process had ever been applied to dictators in Latin America), and a number were convicted and sentenced to various terms of imprisonment. Most, however, were pardoned in the early 1990s by the succeeding democratic government, with the assertion that Argentina needed to put the Dirty War behind it and heal its social and historical wounds.[3] However, many Argentines disagreed with this position, believing that full and formal justice, not presidential pardons of the principal agents of tyranny, is the only thing that can truly solidify democratic institutions in Argentina and render effective the rallying cry of "*nunca más*" ("never again"). This latter conviction is what drives the continuing production of cultural texts that examine the Argentine Holocaust, inspired in large measure by the widely respected 1985 film by Luis Puenzo, *La historia oficial* (*The Official Story*), the only Latin American film ever to have won the Oscar for best foreign film.[4]

A certain amount of current debate underscores the degree to which the citizenry as a whole, exhausted by years of political and, more significantly, economic instability, supported the military. This support cut across class boundaries, although there was a more unanimous support among the oligarchy, the industrial capitalists, traditional Catholics, and the historical allies of the armed forces, such as nationalists; some members of the working class supported the coup because of economic chaos and disenchantment with the Peronists. Most of the intellectual/artistic/academic community were opposed to the coup from the outset. The level of initial general public support for the need for a coup and of the need for a strong hand to sort things out is a fact that in no way legitimized the coup by the armed forces, but rather served, at least at first, to attenuate resistance to it. Yet the general feeling among many was inevitably an attitude of We versus They: We the citizenry at large held hostage to a foreign-supported (i.e., U.S. invested) military regime and the They of the armed forces. As a consequence, in some of the productions (*La historia oficial* would be an example), there is an investigation of the complicity and acquiescence of parts of the citizenry with the military regime: "There must be a good reason why they are arresting" people. By contrast, other works emphasized the disjunction between a clear-cut monstrous enemy, a military regime pretty much disposed to ignore any and all human rights to maintain its hold on the government, and a harassed citizenry that never knew when an individual—a friend, a neighbor, a loved one, a colleague, or even oneself—might fall into the often unnamed and unknown dungeons of the apparatus of persecution and oppression (one of the best films to capture the dynamics of this apparatus is Marco Bechis's 1999 *Garage Olimpo*; the title is the name of one of the clandestine detention and torture centers).

Although the detainees were in general characterized globally as subversives and terrorists, there were three groups of prisoners who received especially harsh treatment: Jews, because of their presumed repudiation of the fundamentalist Christianity that was one of the underpinnings of the regime; homosexuals, because of their presumed repudiation of the rigorously heterosexist masculinity of the regime; and women, because of their presumed repudiation of the proper Christian role of women in their assumed refusal to refrain from political involvement (in part, activist women were seen as the return of the phantom of Eva Duarte de Peron, "Evita"). Of special interest were women who were pregnant, because they were kept alive long enough to give birth. While they were then disposed of, their newborn children were placed with supporters of the military, to be given a proper Christian upbringing. The main plot issue of *La historia oficial* involves such a newborn child. It is in the context of this practice that the question of the protection by the regime of children in general, which is central to *Kamchatka*, takes on added resonance. Thus, the disappearance of individuals and most importantly this theft of children, who, from another point of view, were given as prizes for their support to defenders of the military and its dictatorship, continue to have enormous repercussions in the national mind of the country and certainly among the many families affected by this history.

The plot of Piñeyro's movie is uncomplicated. During the early years of the dictatorship, a father and mother (they are never given names) become concerned for their safety and the possibility that, as a consequence of their own political convictions and the activities of friends and associates in resisting the dictatorship—perhaps even being involved in acts that could be characterized as terrorist—they might be picked up by the police. Accompanied by their two young male children, Harry (not his real name, but the pseudonym he chooses, because of his fascination with Harry Houdini), and his younger brother, who is only called *El enano* (or *El enanito* [dwarf; little dwarf]), they take refuge in the country home of a friend. Because most of the immediate persecution is taking place within the cities, their assumption is that they will, in the country, be essentially out of view; that is, they chose to "disappear" themselves from their everyday society before they are disappeared by the security apparatus. Mom is a research physician and dad is a lawyer, and they are able to commute back and forth to the city in a sporadic fashion. However, their actual employment activities are never really clarified, and there is a certain amount of suspension of disbelief in their ability to pull off this change in living conditions. They enroll their children in a parochial school nearby, under assumed names, and they attempt to live new daily lives as though they were somehow refugees in a foreign land.

The title of the film refers to the board game, known in English as *Risk* and in the film as *T.E.G.* (*Táctica y Estrategia de Guerra* [Tactics and Strategy of War]).[5] In the game, which Harry plays with his father, opposing players attempt to engage in geopolitical conquest based on how many countries they can conquer through the throw of the dice, with Kamchatka somehow being the greatest jewel in the crown of empire. With a phonology and orthography totally alien to Spanish, "Kamchatka" apparently stands for the absolute political "other," the antipodes of one's own global positioning. As an icon of the circumstances of tyranny and uncertain personal security, Kamchatka seems to stand for the Argentina this family now inhabits, a society that is now alien to them, one in which they are at great personal risk as undesirable within its borders. But at the same time, Kamchatka (which, of course, is not a country, but a peninsula of Russia) is the one territory Harry's father is left with the last time they play the game. As the father leaves his son in the hands of the latter's grandfather, he hands Harry the game, and the son receives it with the understanding that one realm is their refuge, the bond between them, what they will have symbolically to remember each other by, and also the private realm of self that the alien forces can never take from them, individually and as a pair of bonded human individuals.

Eventually, the parents realize that they must leave. Entrusting their children to their paternal grandparents, the film closes with the parents driving away alone, with the implication being that they will either go into deeper hiding within the country or that they will, like so many fellow countrymen at the time, seek asylum elsewhere in Latin America (Mexico was often a successful destination), in the United States, or in Europe. Spain, which had recently returned to constitutional democracy with the 1975 death of the dictator Francisco Franco, was a frequent destination, along with other Western European countries, including Sweden, which was particularly generous to Latin American political refugees. Because Harry's voice-over says he never saw his parents again, it is reasonable to assume that they are eventually discovered wherever they have gone to hide and end up among the disappeared.[6]

Piñeyro's film is particularly effective in capturing the tension, fear, and anxiety of the period of tyranny, because it works with the family nucleus. Actual events of arrest, torture, incarceration, and death are only referred to obliquely in the film, and its particular impact derives from the way in which it is told from a child's (Harry's) point of view. Thus, the confusion, disorientation, and consternation of the adults is magnified in the experience of the child, who has only enough lived experience to sense that terrible things are happening and that there is an impending doom hanging over the family (El enano, meanwhile, is too young to sense any threat), without being able really to fathom the monstrous dimensions of the Dirty War. The film relies on the fact that its immediate Argentine audience knows enough to fill in the gaps of Harry's perceptions, while a foreign audience must rely on the way in which the film evokes the familiar narrative of the flight from political persecution.

This focus on the family is significant. While the military dictatorship made much of defending the traditional Catholic, Argentine family, it was doing much to undermine actual families through various forms of oppression and persecution. The term "family romance" usually refers to Freudian theories of how the individual psyche is forged in the crucible of the dynamics of family relationships, between parents, between children, and between parents and children; this is the so-called Oedipal struggle or complex. However, here the concept of family romance is used in a different way, to refer to the way in which the family acts as a microcosm of society and the way in which conflicts within the family may mirror directly or in an inverted fashion the conflicts of society as a whole. Moreover, family romance refers both to the way in which individual aspirations are played out within the microcosm of the family and the ways in which the family, as a microcosm of larger societal institutions, may both abet and foil the realization of those aspirations.[7]

Undoubtedly, part of the resonance of Piñeyro's film as a family romance derives from its relationship to the *Diary of Anne Frank* model. That is, readers have been repeatedly moved by how Anne Frank's diary alludes to the circumstances of her family having had to hide themselves from society. Yet the family is never really ever able to represent the historical process that made it necessary for them to go into hiding because the *Diary* is too contemporary to the events being described; readers are, however, likely to know enough about the Holocaust to provide for themselves this information. Thus what is most emotionally moving about Frank's diary is the way in which we read it with the full knowledge that she will die in a concentration camp, something she can never have known as she was writing it. In the case of Piñeyro's film, there is no firm evidence that either the parents or their children will fall victims to the Argentine tyranny, but that likelihood is there, and the real historical fact, as in the case of the *Diary*, colors the way in which we view the film and provides part of the compelling engagement the viewer has with the story: that is the full historical reality beyond the limited perception of the ten-year-old child.

One of the driving principles of the film is the family dynamic: that is, the way in which the film adheres to certain principles relating to the modern, bourgeois family and the interactions among its members. Much of the plot is driven by the position of authority of the parents, as they are empowered to make decisions for the family as a whole; part of the way in which this is a modern Argentine professional family is that the decision making is shared between mom and dad (and it is important to note that, by the 1970s, Argentina is progressive enough to have a research physician mom as an unremarkable fact). Another aspect of the family dynamic is the pecking order between the two sons, with the older son lording it over his young brother, with the right to called him a dwarf taken for granted. Additionally, there is the feature of male bonding, sealed by embraces given each other by strong and silent men in lieu of any meaningful verbal communication, which establishes a particularly strong relationship between the father and his two sons. There is also the evocation of the strong relationship (but also nonverbal) between the father and his own father, who will become the children's surrogate paternal parent. Moreover, one notes the privileging of a greater bond between the father and his older son, which is symbolized in the board game that they alone share. Mom may be a research scientist, but she is never represented as more than an anxious housewife, and the only other significant woman in the film, the children's grandmother, is little more than a cartoon figure. One particular moment in the film is unintentionally eloquent in this regard: Harry praises fulsomely the mother of a friend of his for her superb *milanesas* (the Argentine version of Wienerschnitzels).

There is considerable evidence to the effect that the film wishes the audience to understand that this particular family is a model of the Argentine family. This is true in a first instance as a historically established fact, the consequence of a network of social, political, and economic processes that has made such a family possible in mid-twentieth century Argentina. An icon of their status is the family car, a Citroën 3CV, the French equivalent of the Volkswagen, and the accustomed vehicle of the Argentine middle class during the period.[8] But more importantly, this model family is also an allegory of the destruction of Argentina that is threatened by the military regime. While the propaganda of the dictatorship was making the promise of saving the Fatherland from subversion and terrorism and the Communist threat, its apparatus of persecution was systematically destroying the family unit by causing people to disappear and driving individuals into exile. More specifically, the trade in newborns in which the regime engaged was the result of destroying a family (that of the parents) and the potential destruction of another by placing a newborn with it. The justification was that the child was being removed from an allegedly Communist environment to be raised in a putatively Christian one. But the subsequent knowledge of that practice became, in fact, another basis for the destruction of families because of the way in which that knowledge impacts deleteriously on the adoptive families. Reference to the film *La historia oficial*, in which this destructive effect is directly represented at the end of the film, has already been made, and the documentary *Malajunta '76* (Eduardo Aliverti, 1996) devotes considerable time to the psychological impact on the now-adult children when they discover who their real parents were and what the circumstances of their previously unknown adoption were.

Piñeyro has used the image of the family in numerous prior films as an allegory of Argentine society, in the sense that the internal misfortunes of the family are direct representations of the sociohistorical misfortunes of Argentine society: *Caballos salvajes* (*Wild Horses*, 1995), *Cenizas en el paraíso* (*Ashes From Paradise*, 1997), and one could even include the homosexual "family" of thieves in *Plata Quemada* (*Burnt Money*, 2000). Nevertheless, the focus on the middle-class family in *Kamchatka* and the *Caballos salvajes* and *Cenizas en el paraíso* is not without its ideological problems.

The chapter now focuses on three major problematic issues in *Kamchatka*. The first involves the decision to make use of a pathetic rhetoric to make the film's point. *Kamchatka* is basically an excellent film and rather effective in its use of pathos, that which evokes pity and sadness. Piñeyro repeatedly underscores the tremendous dislocation that is produced in the family by the need to pull up roots, first to take refuge in the country, and then, most dramatically, to leave their children behind as they go into a different type of hiding. By focusing the film's narrative from the perspective of a child, not yet an adolescent, but nevertheless old enough to have some measure of comprehension of impending doom, the film is able to raise the anxiety of unknowing to a higher power: If mom and dad have no idea of what will happen to them, Harry is left in an even greater confusion as to why his parents are so fearful and what this will ultimately mean in terms of the survival of the family. In one sense, this uncertainty is raised to an even higher level by the way in which the viewers are left with still more unknowing, in that they are unable to know what will happen to the parents and what will happen to Harry and El enano. This is all a way of capturing the terrible stress of daily life in Argentina during the early years of the neofascist dictatorship, when, to put it in highly pathetic terms, one never knew when military agents would break the door down and invade the household (they rarely bothered to knock). Unquestionably, we are talking here about "tactics and strategy of war" (the so-called Dirty War), but they are no longer the features of a board game, but rather the everyday procedures of the military or militarized police. It is a significant aspect, however, of *Kamchatka* that such violence is never represented directly; rather it is unseen and implied, a detail than makes this film easier to take, so to speak, than more explicit portrayals of arrest, incarceration, and torture, such as the aforementioned *Garage Olimpo* or Héctor Olivera's *La noche de las lápices* (*The Night of the Pencils*, 1986).

Pathos is ever-present in the interactions among the members of the family. It is there in the hushed and anguished conversations mom and dad hold over their uncertain future; it is there in the interactions between the parents and their children, where every encounter is played out as though it were the last. This is especially evident in the idyllic moments the characters spend together exploring the grounds of the country house where they are staying, as though this were some sort of lush paradise they were about to lose at any moment—which is, certainly, quite literally true. Every separation, leading up to the final one, which uses the tried-and-true cliché of a car disappearing down a road as the person left behind stares achingly after its diminishing image, is played out as though there were no return. This is worked out with enormous and pathos-drenched suspense one day when Harry decides to go back into town alone on the train to visit his best friend, only to be turned away at the door by his friend's mother, petrified that there is something sinister about his family's sudden disappearance. Meanwhile, Harry's mother grows more and more frantic as the hours pass without him showing up at home. Clearly, she is afraid that he has been picked up by the police, with all of the consequences such a possibility would evoke, and when he does make it back to the country house, her emotions overflow in a mixture of happiness and the fear that his and their individual and collective disappearance might become a horrible reality.

Finally, an ambience of pathos, tinged with melancholy (the yearning over what has been lost) is at work when the family visits the children's grandparents. Not only does this visit evoke a lost paradise of youth (that of the father, but also that of an Argentina before the neofascist terror), but it depends on strong family ties that could be destroyed by the terror and will, inevitably, be disrupted and damaged by the tensions of the uncertainty provoked by the parents' subsequent abandonment of their children to the care of their grandparents.

All of the publicity images of the film, which suggest those moments of the film spectators will or ought to most remember, involve the happy middle-class family unit. Now, it is unquestionably important that a film with a potential international distribution disengage from the U.S. or First World stereotype of the crime-ridden ghettos of Latin America as one vast slum. Yet at the same time, *Kamchatka*, by focusing so insistently on the Argentine professional bourgeoisie, gives the impression to the (preponderantly middle-class) spectator that it was that class that was most affected by the terror of the dictatorship. Of course, many middle-class families experienced the tragedy of the disappearance of individuals occasioned by the practices of the apparatus of persecution. Many families were, quite literally, destroyed. But segments of the middle class benefited from the dictatorship and were complicit with it. After all, most of the military command was also made up of children of immigrants who had made it within the opportunities offered by the Argentine version of middle-class social mobility. Those that were most implacably impacted, however, were the working class. The military dictatorship was unquestionably the enemy of the working class, seeing many of the ills of the country as the consequence of the unionism, social engineering, and class warfare attributed to the populist reforms of Peronism during the 1940s and 1950s. The dictatorship was intransigently reactionary, wishing to return the country to a time in which the working class "knew its place." Thus, the working class not only suffered far greater direct persecution than did doctors and lawyers (except for those committed to human rights), but the economic policies of the military also provoked a material misery that was its own form of everyday torment. By contrast, *Kamchatka* relies on a decidedly pastoral image of Argentina, one in which, while there may not have been the high gloss of prosperity of equivalent U.S. professional families, Harry and his brother and their parents occupy a world of considerable comfort and leisure, one that includes hearty meals, books, television, first-rate schools, private bedrooms, and while comical, a family car that runs and that they can afford to buy gasoline for.

These features of the film contribute, from one point of view, to its Hollywoodish texture; not only is the photography highly professional and executed with full technical control (this being a long way from the so-called "imperfect cinema" of Latin America of the 1960s and 1970s), but such technical and stylistic attainments underscore the well-arranged world that is the reality, or the ideal for such a reality, of the Western middle class. Moreover, such Hollywood clichés as autumn leaves, children playing happily, poetic sunsets, and soothing country settings punctuated by birds singing and frogs croaking may be viewed as solidifying the privileged fabric of comfortable bourgeois existence, while yet also contributing to framing what will be destroyed by neofascist tyranny. And at the same time, the film unintentionally echoes the way in which the military regime, in its official versions,[9] privileged bourgeois values and attempted to project within the country and abroad the notion that Argentina, under the dictatorship, would achieve an ever greater level of bourgeois stability and prosperity. Of course, one would also want to argue that *Kamchatka* is certainly being ironic in this regard: middle-class well-being, which the dictatorship wishes to insist it is defending, is precisely a part of what it is destroying. But yet one cannot escape the impression that Piñeyro's film monumentalizes a sector of society that is not the one that suffered most under the generals.

Finally, the working out of the pathos of the film in terms of the family unit, a family unit that, at least before the terror, appears to be a highly functional one, underscores the myth of the middle-class family. Myth is used advisedly here, because there is no implication that there is no such thing as a highly functional family. However, part of the bourgeois ethos is to maintain the façade of a happy family, although part of the problem lies in the way that "happy" in these myths is never satisfactorily defined. Be that as it may,

Harry's family is, apparently, before the disruptions, a decidedly happy one. It is a family in which the children are protected from the ugliness of life, including, at the moment of the film, the horror of the neofascist persecution of alleged subversives and terrorists. Santiago Kovadloff has a famous essay in which he writes about children during the repression: on the one hand, parents felt they needed to protect them from the growing evidence of violence (no parent wanted his or her children to witness, much less be the victim of the invading agents of the dictatorship);[10] on the other hand, no parent wished his or her child to put the family in danger through a slip of the tongue at school or in any other place where information about the discussions within the family, its political opinions and affiliations, and its friends and associates might jeopardize the safety of family members. Thus, the middle-class principle of never arguing in front of one's children, never engaging in the discussion of the serious matters of life in their presence, took on a sinister dimension that showed how exposed the family was to danger from without the family unit. It was not just that family business might leak out the front door, but that information uttered carelessly, thoughtlessly might occasion real peril. This explains in part why Harry's parents wish to remove the family from most social contact, but it is a detail that resonates with the criterion of middle-class privacy: It is a criterion that is hardly operant or observable in the working-class neighborhood, the ghetto, or the slum, where privacy is virtually a nonexistent concept.

In conclusion, *Kamchatka* is an effective film in portraying the enormous anguish and suffering provoked by the neofascist tyranny in Argentina between 1976 and 1983. By contrast with other films that are more graphic in detailing the dynamics of the terror, here it is more in evidence in psychological terms than in material or physical ones. Because the terror, or the impending threat of it, is more psychological than directly explicit, Piñeyro's use of emotions in the characters, in their interactions, and in the essentially pathetic rhetorical effects directed at the spectator, which are essentially pathetic in nature, mostly works. Yet by narrowing the film to engage the myth of the happy middle-class family threatened by evil forces it cannot know and fully calculate, *Kamchatka* runs the risk of idealizing the victims of neofascism.

Notes

1. I wish to acknowledge the contributions to this study by my research associate Eduardo Muslip.

2. For a survey of the cultural production relating to the period of the neofascist tyranny, see David William Foster, *Violence in Argentine Literature: Cultural Responses to Tyranny* (Columbia: University of Missouri Press, 1995); see also Marguerite Feitlowitz, *A Lexicon of Terror; Argentina and the Legacies of Torture* (New York: Oxford University Press, 1998) and Marcos Novaro and Vicente Palermo, *La dictadura militar (1976–1983); del golpe de estado a la restauración democrática* (Buenos Aires: Paidós, 2003)

3. This was the position of President Carlos Saúl Menem (1989–1999), who early in his term successfully defended the need for a law of the *punto final* (final period), in the sense that it was necessary at some point to end the trials against agents of the military regimes and the *obediencia debida* (due obedience), in the sense that most members of the military regime could be excused as only obeying the orders of their superiors; the latter could be held legally accountable, but the former could not. Both laws were declared unconstitutional in 2004 by the Argentine Supreme Court.

4. See David William Foster, *Contemporary Argentine Cinema*, (Columbia: University of Missouri Press, 1992).

5. The film is based on a script by Marcelo Figueras, in collaboration with Piñeyro; subsequently, Figueras published a novel by the same name. The screenplay was published in book form in 2002, the same year the film was released; the novel was first published in 2003.

6. Although the parents' original intent may have been to go into hiding outside Argentina, this would not necessarily have kept them from being part of the disappeared: Some exiles were hunted down and killed abroad, while others were forcibly returned to Argentina, where they then disappeared. There was even collaboration in this regard among the countries with neofascist dictatorships in the 1970s.

7. My use of family romance in this sense is based in particular on Djelal Kadir's examination of such narratives in Latin American literature, *Questing Fictions; Latin America's Family Romance* (Minneapolis: University of Minnesota Press, 1986). I am fully aware, however, that Kadir is less interested in the dynamics of individual families in the fiction he examines than he is in the use of the metaphor of the family to describe a network of Latin American narratives. However, I have found suggestive his decision to "twist" the Freudian ground to provide a new and more productive meaning for the phrase.

8. Anyone who knows Joaquin Salvador Lavado's internationally famous comic strip *Mafalda* (drawn under the pseudonym Quino), which is from the same period as the action of the film, will recall the recurring motif of the family car—also, to be sure, a Citroën 3CV—in numerous panels of the strip.

9. For example, as in the photography of Pedro Luis Raota, a favored photographer of the military regime whose sentimentalized photography depoliticizes and sugarcoats social reality.

10. Santiago Kovadloff, "Los niños y el proceso," in *Argentina, oscuro país; ensayos sobre un tiempo de quebranto* (Buenos Aires: Torres Agüero, 1983), 39–47.

CHAPTER SEVEN

Soapsuds and Histrionics
Media, History, and Nation
in *Bolívar soy yo*

Geoffrey Kantaris

Reflections on the power of the "society of the spectacle"[1] are not new in Latin American culture. One only has to think of the novels of Manuel Puig, Luis Zapata, Alberto Fuguet, and Jaime Bayly to see that literature has been dealing reflexively with the power and influence of mass culture since at least the 1960s. Yet there has been a curious lack of sustained filmic reflection on such phenomena, apart from a few self-reflexive, *Cinema Paradiso*–style reviews of the rise and influence (and sometimes the nostalgic decline) of cinema in the subcontinent.[2] Main postmodern themes, such as the role of the media in the production of national and geopolitical simulacra, the massive influence of soap operas in the Latin American social imaginary, and the "production" of history as a placeholder for the loss of foundational narratives, have hardly been touched on in the region's cinematography despite the presence of such debates in Latin American sociological and communication theory.

This chapter examines the rise of media self-reflexivity in postmodern Latin American cinema through an analysis of the internationally successful Colombian film *Bolívar soy yo* (*Bolívar is Me*).[3] This film—the third feature of director Jorge Alí Triana—is a comic reflection on the historical and social drama that is contemporary Colombia and by extension, Latin America.[4] It concerns a soap-opera dramatization of the life and love affairs of the great nineteenth-century liberator of Latin America, Simón Bolívar, whose deluded actor, Santiago Miranda, comes to believe that he *is* Bolívar and sets about trying to reestablish the dream of a united Greater Colombia.[5] This chapter will show that the film provides acute commentary on the role of the mass media in the construction and mediation of the Latin American political and historical imaginary, while at the same time cleverly critiquing, through its insistent self-reflexivity, the discourses of visual culture, from the television soap opera to the daily news bulletin, and the role of those discourses in articulating the "histrionics" of the contemporary state.

Anachronous Performances

The film begins in the style of a *dramatizado*, or television costume drama, with a sequence portraying the execution by firing squad of Simón Bolívar at the Quinta de San Pedro Alejandrino near Santa Marta (the place where the real Bolívar died from illness in 1830) preceded by the farewell between his mistress Manuelita Saenz and himself. The standard visual rhetoric of made-for-TV historical drama is employed, such as establishing crane shots that provide the illusion of omniscience, extensive use of tracking or steadycam shots to follow characters, close-up and two-shot for dialogue (in preference to reverse shot), and confined angles that focus primarily on actors and their dialogues. However, even at this early stage in the film, the attentive viewer will notice some anachronistic aspects to the mise-en-scène, which already signal the parodic dimension of the visual rhetoric employed in this sequence, e.g., the appearance of mass-produced cutlery and glassware on a table early on in the sequence, a tracking shot of Bolívar being taken to the firing squad, which has him walking on a tarmac path, and a brief glimpse of a modern-day clipboard at the edge of the frame. Because most local spectators would know that Bolívar did not die by firing squad and that Manuelita Saenz was not with him when he died, these apparent flaws in verisimilitude, together with the inappropriate reaction of some of the characters (e.g., a shot of Manuelita and a maidservant smiling happily during his dramatic final speech before the firing squad) act as estranging devices that puncture the film's mode of representation.[6] They also act as a meta-commentary on the fusion of temporalities—the fundamental *anachrony*—which, it has been suggested, is constitutive of the Latin American soap opera as a genre. This is a point to which the chapter will return.

The words of the final speech are taken textually from Bolívar's last (written) proclamation on December 10, 1830, a week before his death:

> Colombians: You have witnessed my struggle to implant freedom where tyranny once reigned. I have worked selflessly, sacrificing my fortune and even my tranquillity. . . . As I depart from your midst, my affection for you dictates

that I must impart my final wishes. I aspire to no greater glory than to the consolidation of Colombia.[7]

Just as the firing squad is preparing to shoot, Bolívar raises his hands and, gesticulating wildly, shouts "Cut, cut, CUT! Bolívar didn't die this way. Bolívar didn't die this way! I refuse to kill Bolívar in this or any other way!"[8] The viewer then sees a shot of him through a television camera's viewfinder as he angrily reaches out his hand to cover the camera lens and prevent himself being filmed. Cut to a furious director who had been watching the filming on a monitor and his assistant who laments: "But the scene was going so well. I was almost crying."[9]

The literal interruption of continuity and of the illusionistic narrative mode propels the film into the dimension of self-reflexivity, as its referent is no longer history, the life and death of Bolívar, but the discursive process, the modes and procedures of filming.[10] Self-reflexivity in film can of course have many different meanings, from a narrow fetishization of the processes and vagaries of film production, including obsession with celebrity personalities and their relationships, to meditation on the ethics of filmic representation or even on the social role of visual culture more broadly. This film seems to examine knowingly the full spectrum of such self-reflexivity, placing the mass media's obsession with its own signifying system of stars and celebrities, ratings and romance, into the broader context of the precarious underpinning of the contemporary state in the compulsive manufacture of simulacra.[11]

The film appears to begin in the former mode, as "actor" Santiago Miranda, played by Robinson Díaz, becomes so obsessed with his role as Bolívar that he is unable to kill off his character, while "actress" Alejandra Bernardini, played by real-life soap-opera star Amparo Grisales (*La sombra del deseo*, *Bésame mucho*), sees herself as the real attraction of the show in her role as Manuelita Sáenz: "In case you haven't understood, the real star of this show is me. Did you get that? Me! Me! Me!!"[12] While this is a source of some humor in the opening sequences, the film rapidly moves into a more complex use of self-reflexivity, aided by the foundational role of the historical Bolívar in the formation of Colombia and his continued importance for the self-image of the state and its various institutions. The willingness of the producers of the *telenovela* to rewrite history to make it more dramatic ("this ending has more dramatic impact"),[13] emphasizing the primacy of representation in unwittingly postmodern fashion, is matched by the absurd way in which the president's office exploits the charisma of Santiago in his role as Bolívar, inviting him to take part in a military parade in Bolívar's honor and asking him to give a speech in full nineteenth-century military uniform at an international summit of Bolivarian presidents. Triana has commented on this aspect of the portrayal of Bolívar in discussing the source of inspiration for the film:

> For several years I directed a television series called *Relive Our History* and as part of the series I did a life of Bolívar from cradle to grave called *Bolívar, a Man of Difficulties*, with an actor called Pedro Montoya. The actor ended up identifying very strongly with the character, the character pursued him and from then on he never removed his uniform. He would go to the Quinta de Bolívar [Bolívar's estate in Bogotá], to San Pedro Alejandrino and in general to places identified with Bolívar. But that was not the worst of it. The really worrying thing was that the country also went along with it: he was invited to political campaigns with demagogical intent, he was asked to crown the winners of beauty contests, to attend military parades, and people in the street would ask him for favours, and no-one knew whether it was the popular actor or Bolívar whom they were addressing.[14]

The film thus plays skillfully with the performative dimensions of the social (in general) and of politics (in particular), with the histrionics of everyday life and of the state. Virtually everyone is complicit in the delusion that Santiago Miranda is Bolívar, from the airplane pilot who lets Bolívar ride in his cabin, claiming that it will be an honor for his crew and for the firm, through his mother, who talks of historical battles as if she remembers her son partaking in them, to the president of the republic, who addresses him as "Simón" and discusses aspects of his biography with him. Yet Santiago is racked with doubt regarding the truthfulness and authenticity of his representation of Bolívar, both on- and off-screen, condemning the distortion of the "real" Bolívar's political program and aspirations despite his awareness that "each person has their own image of Bolívar."[15]

This focus on performativity is linked to astute and often highly amusing commentary on the soap-opera genre. For example, one particular sequence has Santiago in bed with a prostitute (albeit showing more interest in eating and drinking than in sex) when the latter notices that it is time for the latest episode of the series *Los amores del Libertador*. She turns on the television, and we are shown a close-up of the screen dramatizing a well-known historical episode when Manuelita saved the sleeping Bolívar from a plot against his life. The style is blatant melodrama, and Santiago groans as Bolívar declares of a highly trussed-up Manuelita, her breasts virtually bursting out of the top of her dress, "You have more balls than any of my generals. You are . . . (*drum roll*) the Liberator of the Liberator!"[16] Santiago is so embarrassed by his own performance in the telenovela that he reaches for the remote and turns off the television, much to the prostitute's annoyance: "Oh, but I always watch this series. I always watch it, I like it. Even when I've got a customer."[17] The film is here commenting on the fusion of narrative pleasure with the (over-)performance of generic conventions that characterizes soap opera, as well as its ability (the ability of the televisual medium) to insert itself within the fabric of everyday life. Two types of pleasure and two types of artifice are here cleverly juxtaposed: the sexual pleasure of the clients created and maintained by the artifice of the prostitute, interrupted (presumably) by the prostitute's pleasure in viewing maintained by the artifice of televisual narrative. Santiago, rejecting both modes of pleasure, declares that he is fed up with the falsity of the show and wants to give up acting, whereupon the prostitute launches into an astute commentary on the necessity—and pleasure—of artifice:

> False? But that's the whole point. I also have to act, you know. . . . In each role I moan in a different way (*imitating different moans of pleasure*) . . . so that the customers believe it. And if they are satisfied, they return. . . . When you're a prostitute, if you don't enjoy it, you're in purgatory, and if you enjoy it, you're a complete loser, nothing but a floozy. (*Changing tone*) I'm doing it for my child.[18]

This somewhat postmodern prostitute, with her advanced understanding of the workings of libidinal economy, is, like the film itself, operating in self-reflexive mode, revealing her own artifice even as she is aware that nothing can escape from the realm of artifice. Her final comment appears to puncture the artifice, but it is of course a stock-in-trade cliché (the good prostitute who sacrifices herself for the future of her child) and so its "naturalness" is revealed to be an effect of the performance.

The parodic style of the mock soap episode seems designed to illustrate the analysis undertaken by Colombian media theorist Jesús Martín-Barbero of the fundamental anachrony of the Latin American telenovela. This temporal heterogeneity arises from the fusion of the modernity of the medium with all the narrative devices of the nineteenth-century *folletín* (serialized novel) and becomes an almost perfect representation of the hybrid temporalities that arise from the intense cultural layering that is considered to be constitutive of Latin American culture and society:

> [Television links] the discourse of modernization to the employment of narrative devices and forms of recognition which are shamelessly anachronistic. Anachrony—not contemporaneity—that in the case of Latin America fits hand in glove with the untimeliness which forms a constitutive part of the

cultural dynamics of its peoples. And amongst the genres which constitute the
weave and the weft, the text(ure), of television, in none is the interweaving of
modernity and anachrony so visible as it is in soap opera: that modality of
melodrama in Latin America in which popular narrative and the seriality of
television are reconciled and hybridized.[19]

The telenovela therefore, in its fundamental anachrony, hybridizes different
modes of (cultural) production (e.g., the televisual and the literary), would-
be autonomous cultural spheres (the elite and the popular), distinct genres
(e.g. in this case historical documentary and fictional romance), conflicting
temporalities (nation-based modernity and globalizing postmodernity), and
processes of sociocultural transformation (cultural embedding and disembedding). "Disembedding" (a process theorized by Anthony Giddens and elabo-
rated in relation to Latin American culture by Renato Ortiz) describes the
way in which first national capitalism and then globalization uproot cultures
that are embedded in local community, "prise social relations free from the
hold of specific locales, recombining them across wide time-space dis-
tances."[20] The classic form of the Latin American telenovela combines cultural embeddedness (here the foundational narratives of nation formation,
elsewhere national literary adaptations or the intrigues and personal lives of
fictional local oligarchs) with the disembedding forces at work within the
medium of television, the "tremendous increase in the mediation of experience which these communication forms [bring] in their train."[21] It is precisely this dialectic that we see at work in Bolívar's anachronistic call for a
confederation of Bolivarian states of which contemporary economic globalization is both an echo and an inverted parody, as will be discussed.

History and Histrionics

That history and histrionics have a shared etymological root in the historian
or teller of tales seems particularly apt in a context in which both history and
politics (which lays foundational claims to history) are revealed to be complex simulations, mass delusions that rely on the disavowal of their constructed and artificial nature.[22] This is compounded by the postmodernization of such foundational narratives, which we might summarize as their
subjection to the logic of the commodity and of the mass media, and particularly by the role of television, which is capable of extending this logic both
upward into the mechanisms of state power and outward into the whole populace with entirely unpredictable and uncontrollable consequences. What
begins as the delusion of one actor becomes, through such mediation, a mass

delusion, which threatens to overwhelm the state and even destabilize the politics of the entire region. This acts as a comment on the power of television and the mass media to fuse the fetishistic logic of the spectacle with forms of populism, whether revolutionary, nationalistic, or demagogic, creating new political forces which threaten, at least momentarily, to bypass traditional political structures, which will be discussed later.

The traditional way in which the political classes employ representation—theatrical display and performance of ritual—to consolidate or enhance power takes on a new meaning in the era of tele-politics. This film in fact charts the tensions between the traditional notion of the nation as a performance of writing—from scripture to literature—which has been conceptualized in Latin America as the "ciudad letrada,"[23] and the new politics of mass mediatization in which the agents of the state not only use the media to manipulate their public image but are increasingly constructed by and within the self-same logic of mediatization. This point is summarized well by Martín-Barbero:

> More than substituting, the mediations of television or radio have become constitutive of, have become a part of the plots and discourses of political action itself, [because] what such mediations produce is the intensification of the symbolic, ritualistic, and theatrical dimensions which always pertained to politics.[24]

Having made what appeared to be nothing more than a clever witticism when he had told the president that he would attend the Bolivarian Summit on condition that "you take care of the theater, and I'll take care of the politics,"[25] Bolívar goes on in his speech at the summit to berate the six presidents for betraying the true spirit of Bolívar and for abusing Bolívar's name "to justify a *coup d'état*, to give grandiloquent names to mediocre schools, hospitals which do not function, constitutions which are never applied."[26] If the Colombian president's use of this soap-opera *Bolívar* can be seen as a classic case, *à la* Baudrillard, of the proliferation of media simulacra serving to camouflage and disavow the fictive nature of the state's performance of power, then it is clear that, as in Baudrillard's discussion of the impossibility of simulating a bank robbery,[27] what cannot here be tolerated is a simulation (of Bolívar, of history, and of the foundational narratives of the nation), which in turn exposes the *simulated nature* of state power:

> I have risen from the grave because the continent deserves a second chance. I have come . . . to summon you to the reintegration of Greater Colombia!

(*Applause*) The only possibility for our countries to emerge from underdevelopment is by uniting in a single great nation! (*Applause*) All the rest is lies, mere hot air for occasions such as this. Because you, gentlemen, you (*pointing at the assembled Presidents*), do not know the real Bolívar. Because you do not make politics. You only make theatre. (*Laughter*).[28]

It is no surprise that the Colombian president, appalled at this departure from the inane script he had prepared for "Bolívar," promptly orders the military police to intervene and cut short the speech. But Bolívar, grabbing the gun of the soldier who moves to arrest him, manages, in the ensuing chaos, to kidnap the president and secure a river barge to retrace, in reverse, Bolívar's last journey along the Magdalena River, together with his captive. If it is impossible to simulate a hold-up, it is similarly impossible to simulate the kidnapping of a political leader without calling in the imposition of a ferocious "reality principle," and simultaneously causing a crisis in the state's mode of (self-)representation.

Bolívar becomes a political threat once the state is no longer able to contain and exploit the proliferation of simulacra surrounding his character and his perceived political role for different sectors of the populace. The first shots of the river barge are overlain on the audio track with a proliferation of superimposed local and national radio reports (followed by a television report), indicating the "discursive" crisis occasioned by Bolívar's action. Among the general media noise, the following report is the most audible:

After suffering several bouts of dementia, Santiago Miranda has confused reality with television. What began as a prank by an eccentric actor has turned into a delusion which the country has never seen the likes of before, and which threatens to become a terrible nightmare. Santiago Miranda, believing himself to be Bolívar, is convinced that his resurrection is beneficial to the Bolivarian Republics.[29]

This apparent epistemological certainty regarding the distinction between reality and television is ironically undermined in the sequence that follows immediately after this, in which we see a television journalist in a remote fishing village reporting for Caracol TV (Colombia's principal broadcasting company) surrounded by an enthusiastic crowd of villagers awaiting the arrival of the barge and bearing a large placard reading "Bolívar Department salutes you, Bolívar."[30] The reporter refers to the actor having brought Bolívar back to life and declares that the waiting people are preparing to receive a visit from Bolívar "in person." Bolívar's popular appeal is both a historical mirage (Bolívar the revolutionary hero) and a media-induced simulacrum (the star of a television soap opera) and thus lies at the anachronistic interface of two different epistemological systems. In this way, the mass media become, literally, mediators between popular memory (of nationhood and self-determination) and the increasingly deterritorialized imaginaries (with their interlocking transnational dependencies), which the media themselves propagate.

But it is not only the elite and those connected with the media industry who are aware of the importance of such mediations. The guerrillas of the Bolshevik Front of Salamina, Simón Bolívar Division, also see an opportunity in Santiago's manipulation of his media image and storm the barge to offer their services to their namesake Bolívar and to return his sword to him: "Bolívar: your sword, ready for the fight. . . . We recovered your sword to strengthen our struggle. Now it is in your hands once more awaiting its glorious destiny."[31] Bolívar's sword (one of those claimed to have been used by the Liberator) was in fact stolen on February 17, 1974, from the museum at the Quinta de Simón Bolívar in Bogotá by members of the guerrilla movement M-19 as their inaugural symbolic act.[32] Here, on presenting Bolívar with his sword, one of the commanders informs her comrades that this "historic moment" needs to be recorded for posterity, and a camcorder is brought in. The postmodernization of social conflict, the role played by video images in kidnappings and executions, the effective if often gruesome way in which guerrillas and terrorists alike have learned to use the mass media, from the Internet to Al-Jazeera, is now a global phenomenon. If it is now the camera that is mightier than the sword, then "Bolívar" finds himself caught between the historical role of print culture and the contemporary role of visual culture in (re)constituting imagined communities,[33] and this double bind is amply dramatized in the many shots of him attempting to write ("rewrite history," as he puts it) and the repeated failure of that writing, representative of a wider symbolic crisis at the heart of lettered culture.

This particular video footage of Bolívar and his kidnap victim surrounded by guerrillas rapidly finds its way onto the main evening television news broadcast:

> Bolívar has threatened to commit suicide, and with him will die all those who accompany him, including the president of the republic, if the Bolivarian presidents do not attend a summit on board the barge. We have obtained an exclusive video of the barge, which shows the dramatic situation on board, aggravated by the unexpected presence of the guerrillas. Here we see Bolívar prepared for anything.[34]

Ironically, the image is far from dramatic, and shows a rather uncertain-looking Bolívar with guerrillas milling around trying to find the best position for the camera. More dramatic are the images that follow of mass demonstrations in Bogotá and elsewhere in support of Bolívar's demand for the reunification of a sovereign, powerful, and independent Greater Colombia, which, the newsreader says, "has caused total delirium in the country and in the other Bolivarian Republics."[35] The footage shows the Plaza Bolívar in Bogotá filled to brimming with demonstrators, many holding placards in support of Bolívar's demands. The long shots are probably taken from original news footage of peace demonstrations, because posters seen in these shots are in defense of national sovereignty and against the United States's controversial Plan Colombia, widely seen as a process of militarization of the country. The close-up shots show amusing poster titles such as "with Bolívar . . . the people will never be defeated," "The workers of the Bolivarian Insurance Company are with you, Liberator. Long live Greater Colombia!" and "Simón, do not abandon us again."[36] Bolívar's manifesto includes not only a proposal for uniting all of the congresses of the Bolivarian republics and the drawing up of a single constitution, but also that the first act of the new government shall be a refusal to service the foreign debt (one of the main demands of recent antiglobalization movements in Latin America). There is also an amusing jibe at the simplistic, black-and-white nature of U.S. foreign policy toward the region, which confuses social struggles with drug trafficking, when the news reader declares that "the government of the United States does not approve of Bolívar's proposal, stating that the proposal originates from the drug cartels who want to create a Narco Greater Colombia."[37]

Integration or Globalization?

In the scenario presented by moves toward *Latin American integration*, albeit united by language and by long and deep traditions, economic integration is fracturing regional solidarity, especially because of the forms of *exclusivity* demanded by the insertion of regional groupings (North American Free Trade Agreement [NAFTA] and Mercosur) into the macrogroupings of the North, the Pacific, and Europe.[38]

The broaching of the international dimension of Bolívar's demands projects the film's self-reflexivity onto a much wider debate about the integrative or disintegrative role that the audiovisual industries (principally television, but also cinema and even the popular music industry) play in mediating the individual's relationship to imagined communities, whether national or transnational (globalized). While at the level of content these industries (including the soap-opera genre) repeatedly signal the nation as their horizon of reference, at the levels of both form and function their allegiances lie with global networks, with the financial requirement for the industries to compete on a global stage, and with the increasing orientation of some of their products toward an international audience. Martín-Barbero comments on this ambiguity in relation to the genre of the telenovela, which enjoyed huge international success during the 1990s and became, along with dance music, Latin America's most visible tertiary export product, reaching countries as distant culturally and geographically as Greece, Poland, and Russia:

> Paradox: even as the television companies, in search of transnational competitiveness, integrate more and more frequently scripts and actors from one country with those of others, fusing in one soap series Brazilian or Venezuelan scripts, Mexican actors and Colombian or Argentine directors, the genre of the soap opera—which had become a strategic locus for the production and reproduction of the images which these countries create for themselves and by which they achieve recognition by others—is becoming cheapened both economically and culturally.[39]

More broadly, the complexities surrounding the question of Latin American integration, from Bolívar's dream of a grand federation of South American states to the largely technocratic, finance-driven "integration" of different Latin American countries into supranational trading blocks, such as the NAFTA, Mercosur, or the Andean Pact, are strongly suggested by this play on the ambiguous agency of the audiovisual industries in these processes. The guerrillas clearly see themselves as combating, through appeal to revolutionary nationalism, the finance-driven dissolution of the nation under the guise of capitalist "imperialism," and this struggle is what Bolívar represents for them, as their leader proclaims to him even while posing for the video camera:

> Parmenio: We have realized part of your dreams. We control a large part of the nation's territory. We are combating imperialism with patriotic aims, destroying its infrastructure, and we are a belligerent and self-sufficient force.
>
> Santiago: That has nothing to do with my dreams.[40]

The dialectic at work here between guns and cameras, between anti-imperialist revolutionary struggle and the technological infrastructure which generates mediatization, represents well the dialectic at the heart of the film. It is also one observed later when the guerrillas conduct a kangaroo-style prosecution of the president, reading out the death sentence they have passed on him from the screen of a laptop computer.

Yet Bolívar's popular appeal is more reminiscent of a different kind of mediated politics: that represented (in the aftermath of this film) by the rise of the new Left under the banner of neopopulism in countries such as Venezuela and Brazil (though not in Colombia, largely because of the insecurities caused by ongoing violence in the country). That such politics is thoroughly dependent on the mass media even as it finds itself in often deep conflict with the supranational class interests underlying them is well represented by Bolívar's ambiguous relationship to the media, being both a product of them, able to manipulate them by playing to their desire for spectacle, and emerging as a fundamental threat to ruling interests. There is no specific political agenda behind the film's portrayal of populism, though, and ultimately the play on the huge popular appeal of Bolívar throughout the "Bolivarian countries" is more effective as a comment on the survival of popular practices and aspirations within mass society, whether mass society is considered as an object of politics or as an object of the mass media.

Indeed, the film explicitly represents such popular enthusiasm as an appropriation and carnivalization of the signs of power, replete with creative forms of representation and contestation. The viewer sees this in the density of signs (placards and banners) in the mass demonstrations, which the camera encourages the viewer to "read," lingering over their letters, but also in the preponderance of masks, costumes, and impromptu performances that the viewer glimpses, suggesting a popular desire to appropriate modes of representation as well as to encourage media dissemination of the protest. Of particular interest is the fact that the people compose a *vallenato* in praise of Santiago Miranda and Bolívar, which we see and hear them singing at an impromptu street party in front of Santiago's house and which is used as one of the accompaniments to the film's credits at the end. Vallenatos are popular songs for listening to or for dancing, which originate from the region of Valledupar, each of which tells a distinctive story, and are thus strongly suggestive of an oral storytelling tradition. Yet the songs are marketed both nationally and internationally alongside *salsa, cumbia, merengue,* and such as part of Colombia's lucrative popular music industry, in which dance music in Spanish still has the edge over international pop. This form thus fuses oral traditions with mass distribution so that, like the telenovela and indeed the film itself, it is strongly suggestive of the survival of syncretic cultural practices within the homogenizations of the increasingly globalized media industries.

The viewer can see, then, that the film took him or her from the kind of indulgent self-reflexivity, which characterizes the media's obsession with the lives and loves of the celebrities that they have themselves created to broader reflection on the mediatization of national and supranational discourses, be it in the anachronous rewriting of historical "truth" in the *telenovela*, caught between the modes of print culture and the forms of electronic and televisual media, or in the similar incapability of the news media to separate simulacra and reality effects. One might say, following Giddens, that such reflexivity is constitutive of modern life, of the way in which knowledge about life is constructed reflexively (through the media and other reflexive institutions) for modern subjects, "the emergence of an internally referential system of knowledge and power."[41] But the film goes further to suggest the proliferation of simulacra through the entirety of the institutions of the state and even within the national discourses appealed to by oppositional revolutionary groups. Yet, as this chapter shows, it also suggests the survival of syncretic cultural practices, whether those of popular narrative or storytelling, within the homogenized formats of the mass media industries. Finally, the film makes no pretence of escaping from or standing outside the processes on which it reflects, for even after the tragic events of the dénouement the viewer is not allowed to indulge in a fantasy of the real. As Bolívar and the other protagonists of the film lie dying in the Quinta de Bolívar after the botched military operation to save the president, his final words are "cut . . . cut . . . cut. . . ," over which a clipper board cuts and freezes the final frame of the film.

Notes

1. Guy Debord, *La Société du spectacle* (Paris: Buchet-Chastel, 1967).

2. Examples would be: *Mi querido Tom Mix* (*My Dear Tom Mix*, Mexico, 1991), *El elefante y la bicicleta* (*The Elephant and the Bicycle*, Cuba, 1994), *El viento se llevó lo que* (*Wind with the Gone*, Argentina, 1998), and *Cinema do lágrimas* (*Cinema of Tears*, Brazil, 1995). Note that Sarah Barrow's chapter on *El destino no tiene favoritos* in this volume discusses the way in which that film parodies the soap opera genre.

3. *Bolívar soy yo* directed by Jorge Alí Triana, script by Jorge Alí Triana, Manuel Arias, and Alberto Quiroga (Colombia, 2002; 35mm/Color, 91 mins).

4. Other features directed by Triana are *Tiempo de morir* (*A Time to Die*), script by Gabriel García Márquez and Carlos Fuentes (Colombia, 1985; Color, 98 mins) and *Édipo alcalde* (*Oedipus Mayor*), script by Gabriel García Márquez and Stella Malagon (Colombia, 1996; Color, 100 mins), both based on scripts by Gabriel García Márquez, and both mediating literary/theatrical motifs and contemporary social issues in Colombia.

5. Gran Colombia was a confederation of the present-day territories (approximately) of Colombia, Venezuela, Ecuador, and Panama, corresponding to the Spanish colonial jurisdiction of Nueva Granada. It existed for eleven years from 1819 to

1830, but it never managed to overcome regional interests and power structures and came to be seen as a product of Bolívar's misplaced if worthy idealism. In the film, Bolívar also wants to include Peru and Bolivia in the confederation.

6. The concept of estrangement (*ostrenanie*) as a procedure that disrupts the illusion of transparency in representation is to be found in the work of the Russian formalists and in Brecht's well known *Verfremdungseffekt* (alienation effect).

7. "*Colombianos: Habéis presenciado mis esfuerzos para plantear la libertad donde reinaba antes la tiranía. He trabajado con desinterés, abandonando mi fortuna y aun mi tranquilidad. . . . . Al desaparecer de en medio de vosotros, mi cariño me dice que debo hacer la manifestación de mis últimos deseos. No aspiro a otra gloria que a la consolidación de Colombia. . . .*" (Simón Bolívar, "*Última proclama del Libertador*," *Archivo del Libertador* 1830, archivolibertador.hacer.ula.ve/documentos.htm, accessed May 7, 2005). The order of the first two paragraphs of the proclamation is reversed in the film.

8. "*¡Corten, corten, corten, cor-ten! Bolívar no murió así. ¡Bolívar no murió así! ¡Yo no mato a Bolívar así ni de ninguna otra manera!*" *Bolívar soy yo* DVD version (Venevisión, 2003, 0:08).

9. "*Tan bien que iba la escena. Estuve a punto de llorar.*"

10. Film theory of the "narratology" school makes a fundamental distinction between a film's *histoire* (its plot/story, but here also the "history" that is recounted) and its *discourse* (its mode of narration, style, and use of filmic language).

11. The concept of the simulacrum appears originally in Plato as the deceptive substitute, which feigns resemblance to an ideal but is merely the copy of a copy. It is theorized extensively in the work of Jean Baudrillard (e.g., Jean Baudrillard, "Simulacra and Simulations," in *Jean Baudrillard: Selected Writings*, ed. Mark Poster (Cambridge: Polity, 1988) as that which is produced by processes of simulation (of reality) and has become a key postmodern term signaling the collapse of the traditional order of representation: reality is no longer represented (in the mass media, etc.), it is simulated to such an extent that it is impossible to separate reality from simulation.

12. *Bolívar soy yo* DVD version, "*Si no te has enterado, el éxito de esta novela soy yo, ¿me entendiste? ¡Yo! ¡Yo! ¡¡Yo!!*" (0:10).

13. Ibid., "*Este final es más impactante*" (0:09).

14. "*Yo dirigí durante muchos años en televisión una serie que se llamaba Revivamos nuestra Historia y ahí hice una biografía de Bolívar desde la cuna hasta el sepulcro que se llama* Bolívar, el hombre de las dificultades, *con un actor cuyo nombre era Pedro Montoya. El actor [logró] un grado de identificación muy grande con el personaje, el personaje lo persiguió y él no se volvió a quitar el uniforme, iba a la Quinta de Bolívar, a San Pedro Alejandrino y en general a los espacios de Bolívar. Pero eso no era lo más grave, lo realmente grave era que el país lo tomaba como tal, lo invitaban a campañas políticas con fines demagógicos, lo llamaban a coronar reinas de belleza, a desfiles militares y la gente en la calle le pedía cosas, y no se sabía si se las pedían al actor popular o se las pedían a Bolívar*" (Orlando Mora, "Bolívar soy yo: entre la razón y la locura," *El ojo que piensa* (2002): 2, www.elojoquepiensa.udg.mx/espanol/revis_01/secciones/cinejour/artic_03.pdf (accessed June 10, 2004).

15. *Bolívar soy yo* DVD version, *"Cada uno tiene su imagen de Bolívar,"* (0:39).

16. *Bolívar soy yo* DVD version, *"Tienes más pantalones que cualquiera de mis generales. Eres . . . (tambores) ¡la Libertadora del Libertador!"* (0:33).

17. *"Ay, pero si yo siempre veo esta novela. Siempre me la veo, me gusta. Inclusive si tengo un cliente."*

18. *Bolívar soy yo* DVD version, *"¿Falso? Pero si ésa es la gracia. A mí sí me toca actuar, ¿oyó? . . . En cada papel yo grito distinto* (imita gritos de placer) *. . . para que los clientes se coman el cuento. Y si les satisface, vuelven. . . . Cuando una es puta, si no se la goza, estás en el purgatorio, y si te la gozas, lo estás haciendo de pura perdida, de pura gocetas no más. (Cambiando de tono) Yo lo estoy haciendo por mi hijo"* (0:34).

19. *"[La televisión articula] el discurso de la modernización a la explotación de unos dispositivos de narración y reconocimiento descaradamente anacrónicos. Anacronía—no contemporaneidad—que en el caso de América Latina empata con aquellos destiempos que forman parte constitutiva de la dinámica cultural de estos pueblos. Y de los géneros que hacen el tejido, el texto de la televisión, en ninguno se hace tan visible la trama de modernidad y anacronía como en la telenovela: esa modalidad latinoamericana de melodrama en la que se resuelven y mestizan la narrativa popular y la serialidad televisiva,"* Jesús Martín-Barbero, *Oficio de cartógrafo: travesías latinoamericanas de la comunicación en la cultura* (2002; repr., Bogotá: Fondo de cultura económica, 2003), 165.

20. Anthony Giddens, *Modernity and Self-Identity: Self and Society in the Late Modern Age* (Cambridge: Polity Press, 1991), 2; Renato Ortiz, *Otro territorio: ensayos sobre el mundo contemporáneo*, trans. Ada Solari, 2nd ed. (1996; repr., Bogotá: Convenio Andrés Bello, 1998).

21. Giddens, *Modernity and Self-Identity*, 24. It should be noted that Giddens implicitly refuses any separate concept of "postmodernity" and also subsumes print media and electronic media into the same causes and effects of "time-space distanciation" at the heart of a "late modernity" which has (in Northwest Europe) been late since at least 1867.

22. Disavowal is the refusal to acknowledge some (traumatic) fact or perception, and is an important term in (psychoanalytical) film theory, central to fetishistic processes, which are said to be always at work within the spectator's relationship to film.

23. Ángel Rama, *La ciudad letrada* (Hanover, N.H.: Ediciones del norte, 1984).

24. *"Más que a sustituir, la mediación televisiva o radial ha entrado a constituir, a hacer parte de la trama de los discursos y de la acción política misma, ya que lo que esa mediación produce es la densificación de las dimensiones simbólicas, rituales y teatrales que siempre tuvo la política,"* Martín-Barbero, *Oficio de cartógrafo*, 314.

25. *Bolívar soy yo* DVD version, *"Usted se encarga del teatro, yo de la política,"* (0:25).

26. *Bolívar soy yo* DVD version, *"Para justificar un golpe de estado, para ponerles nombres a colegios mediocres, hospitales que no sirven, a constituciones que no se aplican,"* (0:53).

27. This is not only because all hold-ups belong already to the order of simulation, "inscribed in advance in the decoding and orchestration rituals of the media" (Baudrillard, "Simulacra and Simulations," 157), but also because the law depends on and must at all costs maintain its powerful "reality effects."

28. *Bolívar soy yo* DVD version, *"Me levanté de la tumba porque el continente se merece una segunda oportunidad. Vine . . . para convocarlos a la reintegración de la Gran Colombia.* (Aplausos) *La única posibilidad de que nuestros países salgan del subdesarrollo es la unidad, ¡en una gran nación!* (Aplausos) *Lo demás son mentiras, simples frases para estas ocasiones. Porque ustedes, señores, ¡ustedes!* (señalando a los Presidentes), *no conocen al verdadero Bolívar. Porque ustedes no hacen política. Ustedes hacen teatro.* (Risas)," (0:53).

29. *Bolívar soy yo* DVD version, *"Luego de reiteradas crisis de demencia, Santiago Miranda confundió la realidad con la televisión. Lo que comenzó como un disparate de un actor excéntrico se ha convertido en una alucinación nunca antes vista en el país, que amenaza con convertirse en una atroz pesadilla. Santiago Miranda, creyéndose Bolívar, está convencido de que su resurrección es benéfica para los países bolivarianos,"* (0:55).

30. *"El Dpto Bolívar te saluda, Bolívar."*

31. *Bolívar soy yo* DVD version, *"Bolívar: su espada en pie de lucha. . . . Recuperamos su espada para fortalecer nuestra lucha. Ahora regresa a sus manos para llenarse de gloria"* (1:02).

32. It became the symbol of the movement and was carefully kept for nearly twenty years (some of the time in Cuba) until the movement's reintegration into civil society, when it was returned on January 31, 1991. It is now kept under lock and key in a vault at the Banco de la República. For more information, see Johannes W. de Wekker, "La espada robada de Simón Bolívar," *Simón Bolívar, el hombre* 2004, www.simon-bolivar.org/bolivar/la_espada_de_sb.html (accessed July 28, 2005).

33. The concept of the "imagined community," used to describe the imaginary relationship of the individual citizen to collective identities, such as the nation, was first introduced by Benedict Anderson, *Imagined Communities: Reflections on the Origins and Spread of Nationalism* (London: Verso, 1983).

34. *Bolívar soy yo* DVD version, *"Bolívar ha amenazado con suicidarse, y con él morirán quienes lo acompañan, incluido el Presidente de la República, si los presidentes bolivarianos no asisten a una cumbre en el barco. Hemos obtenido de manera exclusiva un video del barco que muestra la dramática situación que se vive allí, agravada por la sorpresiva presencia de la guerrilla. Observamos a un Bolívar dispuesto a todo"* (1:06).

35. *"Ha causado un verdadero delirio en el país y en el resto de los países bolivarianos."*

36. *Bolívar soy yo* DVD version, *"Con Bolívar . . . el pueblo jamás será vencido," "¡Los trabajadores de Bolivariana de Seguros estamos contigo, Libertador, viva la Gran Colombia!" and "Simón, no nos abandones otra vez"* (1:07).

37. *Bolívar soy yo* DVD version, *"El gobierno de los Estados Unidos no ve con buenos ojos la propuesta de Bolívar y considera que se trata de una propuesta del narcotráfico, para tener una Narco Gran Colombia"* (1:07).

38. "En el escenario de la integración latinoamericana, *aún estando estrechamente unida por la lengua y por largas y densas tradiciones, la integración económica está fracturando la solidaridad regional, especialmente por las modalidades de* inserción excluyente *de los grupos regionales (TLC, MERCOSUR) en los macrogrupos del Norte, del Pacífico y de Europa,"* Martín-Barbero, *Oficio de cartógrafo,* 354.

39. "*Paradoja: al mismo tiempo que, buscando competitividad transnacional, las empresas de televisión integran cada día con mayor frecuencia libretos y actores de unos países con otros, juntando en la misma telenovela libretos brasileños o venezolanos, actores mexicanos y directores colombianos o argentinos, la telenovela—que se había convertido en un terreno estratégico de la producción y reproducción de las imágenes que estos países se hacen de sí mismos y con las que se hacen reconocer de los demás—se está viendo abaratada económica y culturalmente,"* Martín-Barbero, *Oficio de cartógrafo,* 355.

40. *Bolívar soy yo DVD* version, "*Parmenio: Hemos cumplido parte de sus sueños. Controlamos gran parte del territorio nacional. Combatimos al imperialismo con criterio patriótico destruyendo su infraestructura, y somos una fuerza beligerante y autosuficiente. Santiago: Esto no tiene nada que ver con mis sueños*" (1:03).

41. Giddens, *Modernity and Self-Identity,* 144.

CHAPTER EIGHT

Killing Time in Cuba
Juan Carlos Tabío's *Lista de espera*
Rob Stone

What would happen if Luis Buñuel trapped a representative group of the Cuban proletariat in a single room instead of the Mexican middle classes? Instead of selfishness we might have solidarity, instead of cannibalism we might have a picnic, instead of hate and spite we might have love and affection, instead of nightmares we might have dreams, instead of *El ángel exterminador* (*The Exterminating Angel*, 1962) we would have Juan Carlos Tabío's *Lista de espera* (*The Waiting List*, 2000). For such is the reimagining of Buñuel's most exquisite conceit that a tumbledown coach (or bus) station in the middle of the eastern coast of Cuba becomes the stage for a multicharacter, magic-realist illustration of a country and its citizens caught in time between two worlds: the idealistic, optimistic past of a communist utopia that never was and the pragmatic, resigned acceptance of a post-Castro Cuba that is sure to be.

In *Lista de espera* a motley group of would-be travelers wash up amidst the cultural, historical, and ideological flotsam at a coastal bus station, but their initial squabbling over meaningless places in the hours-old queue gradually softens into an affectionate portrait of a community that makes the most of the little they have, which adds up to little more than each other. Neither resentful nor tragic, *Lista de espera* is an elegiac, melancholic fable that casts a wry eye on Cuban history and the parallel past of its representation on film. Unlike many Latin American films of the new millennium, it makes no attempt to redefine the national cinema it represents or even invigorate the place and reputation of this cinema in the world; rather, it is an insular work

135

in subject and theme that offers a self-diagnosis of Cuban cinema as a self-reflexive national cinema that is neither intended nor intelligible for international audiences. *Lista de espera* was not released in the United States, yet its limited distribution was perhaps fitting. In marking time between 2000 and the inevitable demise of President Fidel Castro, *Lista de espera* embodies the tensions between Cuba and the United States by shelving its ambitions for American distribution alongside any attempt at the global projection of an image of Cuba that can be anything more than fragile, isolated, temporary, and pending drastic changes. With time to kill until the end of Castro's regime, Tabío's *Lista de espera* looks inward while it waits, considering an intertextual history of Cuba and its cinema that is testament to the *auteurism* of its director and his typical mix of sarcastic and melancholic self-reflection.

Cuba and Juan Carlos Tabío: Post-Glasnost, post-Alea

The most immediate instance of intertextuality in *Lista de espera* relates to the spirited and sympathetic sparring of Vladimir Cruz and Jorge Perugorría six years after the international success of *Fresa y chocolate* (*Strawberry and Chocolate*, 1994). Tabío had worked closely with Tomás Gutiérrez Alea, the director of *Muerte de un burócrata* (*Death of a Bureaucrat*, 1966) and *Memorias del subdesarrollo* (*Memories of Underdevelopment*, 1968) on the preproduction of *Fresa y chocolate* and had assumed directorial control of that film when Titón (as Alea is nicknamed and to whom *Lista de espera* is dedicated) was hospitalized with cancer as he would on *Guantanamera* following Alea's death in 1995.

President Fidel Castro had famously rounded on *Guantanamera*, without having seen it, in his closing speech at the 1998 National Assembly, reviling it as an example of the type of Cuban cinema that encouraged the defeatism (*derrotismo*) that followed the breakup of the Soviet Union,[1] yet the black comedy of *Guantanamera*, which followed the clumsy progress of a coffin across present-day Cuba, was far less politically astute than *Fresa y chocolate*, which had diverted attacks on its own social and political criticism by a deliberately half-hearted attempt at the disguise of a period setting and arguably, its focus on the frustrated gay romance at its emotional core. *Fresa y chocolate* had been set in 1979 but filmed in 1994 without recreating the earlier period exactly, thereby effecting a timelessness that resulted from a confusion of temporal references that included the use of locations unchanged since the late seventies and references in its impassioned dialogue to the state of Cuba in the mid-nineties. Vladimir Cruz had played the fey, idealist David, whose moral, cultural, political, and sexual awakening was selflessly instigated by Perugorría's flamboyant but dignified Diego. Through Diego, Alea, Tabío, and the screenwriter Senel Paz (working from his short story *El lobo, el bosque y el hombre Nuevo* [*The Wolf, The Forest and The New Man*][2]) had criticized the Communist Party of Cuba for suppressing imagination. Diego's homosexuality also allowed for criticism of the blinkered and vindictive cult of machismo that had existed in Cuba since the revolution, while, as Reynaldo González affirms, "the anecdotal material and the focus reflected a problematic in which the marginalized and those who marginalize them were captured in the battle between tradition and the need to interrupt it."[3]

Fresa y chocolate seemed to illustrate the imminent end of Castro's Cuba in the mid-nineties, when the United States was hiding between Bushes and catching its breath between military assaults on Iraq; 1996 was also halfway through the twin tenures of Bill Clinton, and thus the presidential election year that saw his administration mired in secret talks with Cuba. These discussions led to a dramatic change in Cuban refugee policy: While the 21,000 refugees at Guantanamo would be let into the United States, all future refugees would be sent back to the island.[4] This meant that, whereas for thirty-five years the White House had treated Cuban refugees as fleeing victims of oppression akin to the West's welcoming of escapee East Germans, from now on they would be treated as undesirable immigrants and whenever possible intercepted and returned to the Cuban authorities. Four years later, as the U.S. elections of 2000 imploded around the contested ballots of Florida, where the exiled Cuban community is a vociferous social and political force, Juan Carlos Tabío made *Lista de espera*.

To attempt contextual analysis of the meaning that underpins the artistry of *Lista de espera*, however, one must first consider the career of its maker. Born in Havana in 1943, Tabío enrolled in 1961 as trainee production assistant at the Cuban Film Institute, the Instituto Cubano de Arte e Industria Cinematográficos (ICAIC) and graduated to making a wide variety of documentary shorts, including *Higiene en el ordeño* (*Milking Hygiene*, 1968), *Proceso industrial de leche* (*Industrial Milking Process*, 1969), *Ingeniería mecánica* (*Mechanical Engineering*, 1972), a biographical feature on the Catalan singer-songwriter *Joan Manuel Serrat* (1976), and *Un breve reportaje sobre Siberia* (*A Brief Report About Siberia*, 1978). He also collaborated on numerous scripts, including Alea's *Hasta cierto punto* (*Up To A Certain Point*, 1983) before debuting as director with *Se permute* (*House for Swap*, 1983), which was based on his own play. With *House for Swap*, Tabío moved to the front rank of Cuban filmmakers alongside Alea following Julio García Espinosa's ascent to the presidency of the ICAIC on a mandate of low-budget filmmaking and democratic production procedures that was exemplified by Tabío's film.

Michael Chanan declares that with *Se permuta* "Cuban cinema now discovered a new genre, the sociocritical comedy."[5] Indeed, this new production system, genre, director, and film were emblematic of a sea change in Cuban cinema from "the jagged framing and fragmented montage of the 1960s, the syncopations of camera and editing, the controlled hysteria of revolutionary agitation . . . to the composed image, the taming of the violent tropical light, a more harmonious decoupage."[6]

Tabío's follow-up was the zany, self-referential, and self-deprecating *¡Plaf!* aka. *Demasiado miedo a la vida* (*Splat!* aka *Too Afraid of Life*, 1988) in which a middle-aged woman's house is intermittently pelted with anonymously lobbed eggs. Playful, postmodern, and politically astute, *¡Plaf!* marked a clear indication of Tabío's ironic and melancholic appropriation of magic realism alongside his pointed, surgical deployment of postmodernist conceits. Scattershot and scatological, *¡Plaf!* most bitterly targeted the weighty metaphors of the postrevolution Cuban cinema that Roy Armes defines as being "structured to serve the wider needs of the state."[7] *¡Plaf!* is plagued with purposeful errors, goofs, and calamities that add up to an affectionate but brutal satire on the tensions between the limitations and the pretensions of Cuban cinema that includes sight gags, such as the entire film crew deliberately glimpsed in mirrors. Most strikingly, *¡Plaf!* gets off to a false start when the film breaks and apologies are followed by the film beginning in the second reel with the woman already on her quest to determine the origin of the lobbed eggs. Only at the film's end, when the woman resigns herself to bafflement, is the first reel declared mended and watchable and tagged on the end of the film, thereby revealing that the first person to throw an egg was the woman herself. This immensely playful narrative may have amused foreign audiences, but it struck Cubans alert to the satire of spiteful self-denial that the joke was on them.

¡Plaf! attested to what Armes describes as the "growing confidence of Cuban cinema and the gradual loss of that sense of neocolonial dependence so characteristic of Latin America."[8] In its portrait of confusion and increasing despair, it also reflected the destabilization of the Cuban economy in the post–Cold War era of Cuban *perestroika* known as *rectificación* (rectification), when the collapse of Communism saw Cuba's island mentality exacerbated by a crisis of faith in the world order that had sustained it, both literally and figuratively. It also weakened support for artists and intellectuals who had insistently expressed a belief in Communism and allowed for a return to the specifically Cuban patriotism of José Martí that was perhaps more in line with the "community of sentiments" identified by Georg Sorensen, one that is defined by the relation between citizens as a group with a common lan-

guage and a common cultural and historical identity based on myths, symbols, music, and art, rather than a community defined by the relation between citizens and the state.[9] The application of such postcolonial theories was subsequently considered by Cuban filmmakers whose works surrendered to the logic of seeing post-glasnost Cuba as a colony of Communism that was free despite itself. The gradual termination of subsidies worth four to six billion dollars annually from the moribund Soviet Union[10] provoked an economic liberalization that accelerated social changes and ushered in a period of rationing, blackouts, and black-marketeering that was bound to affect the Cuban film industry.

Integral to the deconstruction of Marxist dogma that followed the termination of the dream of a Socialist world order was the questioning and even rejection of Marx's principle that history is irreversible. The crisis prompted conflicting emotions of nostalgia for a Communist utopia that never was and doubt about Cuba's progress toward an uneasy future relationship with the United States. This investigation of the relationship between the past and the future allowed for a transformation in the critical approach to Cuban cinema by Cuban filmmakers themselves, such as Tabío, who, with his next film *El elefante y la bicicleta* (*The Elephant and the Bicycle*, 1995), effected a timely retrospective on Cuban history and, most pertinently, its cinematic representation.

The Punchline as Dead End: *El elefante y la bicicleta*

El elefante y la bicicleta begins in 1925 on an island off the coast of Cuba called La Fé (The Faith) with a classroom full of peasant children arguing over the shape of a cloud—is it an elephant or bicycle?—and ends with an argument over the meaning of the film that celebrates the imagination and suggests it can be both an elephant *and* a bicycle. The film follows a man known as The Islander, who returns from the mainland toting film reels and a projector to regale the islanders with a screening of *Robin Hood*, a silent, black-and-white melodrama. The next day in the marketplace the new-to-cinema islanders engage in a surprisingly sophisticated theoretical debate about the dramatic, thematic, and aesthetic "shape" of the film. "Life is bad enough without the cinema reminding us. Films should have a happy ending with the woman marrying the man," says one woman before she is aggressively countered by a fruit-seller who imperiously dons thick-rimmed spectacles:

> Damn it, Serafina! The cinema, like all artistic manifestations, must be a reflection of reality. The function of aesthetics is to be an enriching manifestation

of the cognitive recognition of man's own reality giving the keys to its own transformation. Art must be an instrument for the transformation of reality. Epistemologically speaking.

The debate ends in confusion when the blind schoolmistress interrupts to opine that what she liked best about the film was the music because, as all reply, there was not any. Nevertheless, with the bridge to the mainland destroyed, The Islander is exhorted to screen the film again, and this time *Robin Hood* has both audible dialogue and music. On successive nightly screenings in the open-air cinema, the film is transformed into cinematic representations of successive decades in this pseudo-Cuba's history. Tabío cuts between the reactions of his audience of islanders and the fictional characters in the film they are watching, who are played by the islanders themselves and even interact with their real selves in the audience by responding to heckling and advice. This sleight of hand effects a postmodern parody of a filmic representation of reality that invokes representative cinematic styles of passing decades in its retelling of the legend of *Robin Hood*, including a creaky melodrama of the Middle Ages in the style of cinema before the revolution when "the island was a source of cheap tropical locations for Hollywood studios,"[11] and a pompous period drama relocated to the struggle against the occupying Spanish forces at the end of the nineteenth century that recasts Hood as a rebel fighter and recalls Spanish *cine cruzada* (the so-called "crusade" cinema of the Francoist dictatorship), such as Antonio Román's *Los últimos de Filipinas* (*Last Stand in the Philippines*, 1945).

The following version is an agitprop Soviet-style account of the Cuban Revolution that recalls Mikhail Kalatasov's *Soy Cuba* (*I Am Cuba*, 1964) and duly inspires revolution in the audience, who rise up against the Lord of their island. Sprightly, inventive, and emphatically revolutionary, *El elefante y la bicicleta* then becomes a celebratory musical, with masses of synchronized revolutionary peasants dancing behind tractors in an ecstatic, musical montage depicting the postrevolution reconstruction of Cuba that shows a cinema being built as well as a hospital, a block of flats, and a spacious new school, thereby signaling the development of the cinema in Cuba as part of a cultural revolution that was linked to a literacy campaign and progress in health care; but then the film breaks and the audience is left without an ending. "It's turning into a political issue," comments one character about the agitated debate of the frustrated islanders, just as the projector is mended and the characters flock back into the cinema in contemporary Cuba that was shown being built in the previous montage. Finally, *El elefante y la bicicleta* is revealed as the type of Cuban film that, as Chanan states, "gave the feeling of being fully at home on [Havana] screens,"[12] because, most subversively, the missing last scene of the film is a shot of an audience staring back at the islanders, who, having failed to grasp the structural and episodic metaphors, do not realize it is an exact reflection of themselves. This audience fidgets and some get up and leave while others sit it out, reasoning, "let's see what they're going to do." And that's where Tabío leaves them, staring at their reflection: the audience of El elefante y la bicicleta in present-day Cuba that is staring straight back.

Clearly this punch line only works with an audience of Cubans in Havana. The gaze of any other audience, particularly a foreign one, is immune to Tabío's attack on complacency and consequently receives his postmodern volte-face as cute whimsy. In its representation of an imaginary, cinematically rendered homeland and the unveiling of same as a poignantly postmodern, open-ended narrative of itself, El elefante y la bicicleta is a prime example of Cuba's "engaged cinema, constantly revolutionary in substance as well as form"[13] that nevertheless requires a specifically Cuban audience to function. As shall be discussed, this dilemma remains unresolved in Lista de espera.

Dreaming of Home: Magic Realism

Despite the dead end of the punch line in El elefante y la bicicleta, Tabío's work may also be situated in the magic realist tradition of Latin American writers, such as Gabriel García Márquez, whose postcolonial sensibility was expressed in novels based structurally and thematically on their desire to create a reasonable sense of identity midway between long-held traditions and a progressive relationship with its past and present oppressors (i.e., Spain and the United States). Novels such as Márquez's Cien años de soledad (One Hundred Years of Solitude) and Isabel Allende's La casa de los espíritus (The House of the Spirits) reveled in typically magic-realist strategies that included the paradox of the union of opposites, like life and death, and the brokering of no conflict between a rational view of reality and a deadpan acceptance of the supernatural. In Latin American magic realist literature there exists a tension between a European rationality and a more primitive understanding of the world through the irrational elements of indigenous faiths and superstitions, such as the Cuban Santería, which, nonetheless, allows for exemplary projections of the idealized homelands that are rendered in the metanarratives of the films and dreams (which surrealism holds as analogous) that feature in El elefante y la bicicleta and Lista de espera.

Magic realists mix ordinary events and descriptive details together with fantastic and dreamlike elements, while maintaining an ironic distance from the magic so that the realism is not compromised. At the same time, magic realists respect the magic so that it does not degenerate into fairy tale and separate from reality instead of providing its counterbalance. Another characteristic of magic realism is a cyclical understanding of time and a correlative rejection of linearity, which may affect narrative development and often leads to conclusions that demonstrate how irony and paradox remain constant in recurring social and political aspirations. The cyclical narrative is typical of magic realists, because it unifies structural and thematic concerns that ally magic realism with the theories of Mikhail Bakhtin in instigating a carnivalesque celebration of the body and its senses, language, dress, dance, and music. The ultimate effect of magic realism is that life-affirming celebrations of natural and supernatural cycles culminate in optimism about revolution that, in turn, may inspire the readership or audience to engage with the struggle to realize a political ideal. The fact that magic realist authors and filmmakers employ metaphysical strategies, such as the manipulation of time and space, dream flights, and the unremarkable appearance of ghosts to explore their literary or cinematic world (all of which are also present in *Lista de espera*) allows for the ghosts of Cuba's past to appear in front of both the intrinsic audience of *El elefante y la bicicleta* (i.e., the one in the cinema on La Fé watching all those versions of *Robin Hood*) until the circle meets and the extrinsic audience (i.e., the one in the Havana cinema watching *El elefante y la bicicleta*) is made aware of its own eminently ghost-like condition.

Carnival in a Coach Station: A Bakhtinian Approach

Crucially, as Chanan indicates, the publication of the works of Bakhtin (1895–1975) in Cuba in the 1980s led to a belated philosophical evaluation in Cuba of the social and cultural issues that had been posed by the Russian Revolution and the mutation of Socialism into Stalinism.[14] As with members of Russia's Bakhtin Circle, Cuban artists, musicians, and commentators held that they were subjects of a single, authoritarian, monologic language whose centripetal force disallowed differences among languages or rhetorical modes so that this one unified and official language might rule. Instead of following this party line, however, they began to focus on the linguistic production of a dialogue that they found in social interaction and adjudged central to meaning in art and its reception, contending that language registers and represents the conflicts between social groups of the type that were increasingly polarized in postrevolution Russia and, correlatively, post–Cold War Cuba.

For those in favor of reform and liberalization, the interaction of different social values was registered in dialogic terms of the speech of others, while those who clung to the dream of a Communist utopia stayed faithful to the regime's claim of a single, exemplary, monologic discourse. The awareness of dialogic interaction signaled the resurgence of the carnivalesque in ways that brought Cuban cinema back from becoming the kind of industry that repeated the words of monolithic officialdom to one that echoed the chaotic hubbub of the streets. This, in turn, led to the emergence of Cuban films that were multilayered, with several narrative threads and a multitude of characters that represented a menagerie of colorful but realistic Cubans, of which Tabío's *Splat!*, *El elefante y la bicicleta*, and *Lista de espera* are the most representative.

What these three films by Tabío have in common is an interest in aesthetic activity as identified by Bakhtin rather than the aesthetic judgment favored by Immanuel Kant. Bakhtin expressed the belief that reciprocal, intersubjective relationships were essential to the production of an intimate, unified solidarity among individuals who did not suffer anonymity in their collectivization. Consequently, as in *Lista de espera*, a community of sentiments could be formed from a collection of the most idiosyncratic characters. In *The Dialogic Imagination*, Bakhtin uses the term carnivalization to describe this coalescing sensibility and its effect on language, literature, society, and politics.[15] In his analysis of the novel, he concentrates on the liberation of multiple characters from the monologic control of the single author through their dialogic interaction, and he celebrates the resultant reality because it subverts the monologic discourse of the novelist. In social-political terms, this suggests that a multifarious hubbub or "carnival" might represent reality far more effectively than the dictate or dogma of a hegemonic religion or party. Even so, the individual protagonists of any hubbub or carnival that takes place within a religious regime or political dictatorship must negotiate the paradox of holding two things to be true: A peasant who struggles to feed his family, for example, might also believe that his god or his government will provide. This negotiation between reality and fantasy, between faith and empiricism, among hearts, minds, and stomachs, is central to *Lista de espera*.

Lista de espera may be analyzed with reference to Bakhtin's theories of the novel, because its multicharacter dialogic effects an informative discourse without any pretension to delivering an absolutist discourse of truth such as that which might be formulated and propagated by a religious or political hegemony. In contrast, *Lista de espera* has a fractal and open-ended narrative that unifies structure and theme. It is also subversive in its disruption of authority and illustrative of alternative modes of group identification, presenting a tale of an antiauthoritarian popular cultural strategy that incorporates satire and parody to deflate the dogmatism of the official language and ideology of Castro's Cuba and institute a popular, collective, learning process in its place. The romantic irony of the paradox, however, is that although the film's discourse might be expected to be critical, Tabío manages to evoke a nostalgic reconciliation with the impossible dream of a Socialist utopia, most poignantly in the dual meaning of his film's title, where its play on the verb *esperar* (which can mean both "to wait" and "to hope") allows for both *The Waiting List* and the equally valid *The Hoping List*.

Your Place in the Queue: The Waiting List

Because Tabío sets his film in an *interprovinciales* coach station in the middle of Cuba, halfway between Havana and Santiago, from which a coach departs on alternate days to these distant destinations, the cyclical nature of events is embedded in the geographical imagining of the island. The cyclical motif is present in the notion of a single coach traveling back and forth between the two cities, a one-day trip in either direction, only stopping to pick up an occasional traveler from this midpoint coastal limbo. Such a traveler is Emilio (Vladimir Cruz), who is released from a freeze-frame of the film's title that reveals it to be written on the back of his T-shirt. He enters the coach station where each new arrival calls for *el último* (the last person in the queue) to identify himself or herself and then remembers his place in a queue that exists in the collective memory. This queue is therefore like a story in which each person holds a unique section of the tale, thereby symbolizing the multicharacter dynamic of the film, its themes of interdependence and solidarity, and its illustration of Bakhtin's theories of a complete picture being made up of the contributions of every individual rather than any overbearing statement of the way things are. The actual length of the queue should not be an issue, though squabbling does break out when Rolando (Jorge Perugorría) arrives and claims priority, because he is apparently (though only pretending to be) blind. Others rally to the debate and solidarity prevails, though Rolando is identified as separate from the compassionate group, and it is his redemptive character that will largely shape the loose, episodic narrative. Indeed, the evolution of Rolando from acting blind and being unable to see the value of the precious solidarity that he exploits, to his final condition of being both honestly sighted and able to recognize the worth of the collective effects an almost religious parable of renewable faith in Socialist ideals.

Because these travelers-in-limbo carry in their heads no greater sense of place than their imaginary position in one of two unformed but pending queues (one to Havana and the other to Santiago), the interprovincial coach station seems both geographically and philosophically estranged from the forces of cultural centralization and stabilization that function at both ends of the island. Havana and Santiago, it is supposed, exist in the territory of the "official" unitary language, whereas the coach station is an island on an island in which the destabilizing influence of popular culture is fermented. First, by queue-jumping, arguing with the station authorities, and moving benches to make beds, then by the collective ridicule of an officious party member and a Buñuelian parody of officialdom that leads to the stranded travelers resolving to celebrate the coincidence of their encounter by contributing to a banquet, the fixing of the broken coach, the painting of the coach station, and its rehabilitation with potted plants, a lending library, and even a marital suite for the rekindling of romance. These popular festivities even include anticanonic rituals, such as the burial of Avelino (Saturnino García) out back in a filing cabinet, while the collective activities are correlated with the breaking down of cultural boundaries that separate race, class, and gender and include the assimilation of homosexuals and a Cuban-Spanish couple. However, Tabío's paradox is that the negotiation of a contemporary, all-inclusive, populist identity ridicules the official culture's claims to universal validity and the ossified conventionality of canonic forms and language, while simultaneously upholding the ideals that gave rise to such dogmatism. Like a loving parent who scolds children for their reckless play, *Lista de espera* both berates Cuba and Socialism and adores them.

The conflictive romanticism of the film is also represented in the romance between Emilio and Jacqueline (Thaimí Alvariño) who is on her way to a new life in Spain with Antonio (Antonio Valero), her Spanish boyfriend, when she falls for Emilio, a handsome, revolutionary-minded engineer. Jacqueline could easily have been the one-dimensional stereotype of a Cuban whore for the Spanish master that Emilio accuses her of being, but pat symbolism and cliché are avoided by the spirited and sympathetic performances by both Alvariño and Valero, who collaborate on an honest and complex rendering of Jacqueline: "Eighty percent of directing is choosing good actors," says Tabío.[16] Other narrative threads in this tapestry of contemporary Cuba include the running gag of the old woman (Assenech Rodríguez) who finds events in the coach station reminding her of the films that she has watched alone in her apartment. Abuela's recollection of having seen Buñuel's *The Exterminating Angel* is the most poignant of these and Jacqueline and Emilio's recollections of Alea's *Fresa y chocolate* (which starred Vladimir Cruz, who here plays Emilio) are the most postmodern, while both references attest to Tabío's admission that the film was partly "a pretext to make a homage to many friends."[17]

The sting in the tale of *Lista de espera* is that the day's hard work of doing up the coach station and the evening's carousal is revealed as a midsummer night's dream. The group awake to find themselves stranded among strangers in a rundown coach station, though the suspicion of having experienced a collective dream does inspire them to a tentative reignition of the Socialist spark. With still no sign of a coach, they set about the truthfully laborious task of doing up the coach station while casting glances at those who loved and laughed and even died during the night's oneiric experience of Communism. The notion of having experienced the Socialist utopia, albeit briefly, is what powers them in their humble efforts at recreating its like in the waking world, until practicalities draw them apart. Jacqueline's boyfriend arrives to collect her, and far from resembling the stereotype of an exploitative Spaniard in the former Spanish colonies, he enthusiastically packs his Range Rover with as many of the stranded as possible. For Emilio and Rolando, meanwhile, rescue comes in the shape of a coach that takes them and other passengers on to Santiago. There, Rolando discards his white stick and dark

A bus finally arrives. Lista de espera/Waiting List *(Juan Carlos Tabío, 2000). Photo: British Film Institute.*

Emilio (Valdimir Cruz) and Rolando (Jorge Perugorría). Lista de espera/Waiting List *(Juan Carlos Tabío, 2000). Photo: British Film Institute.*

glasses in favor of solidarity with the endless queues and Emilio responds to a fellow passenger's thirst by attempting to fix a water fountain, only to be distracted by a woman offscreen calling for "*¿El último?*" ("The last in the queue?"). It might be Jacqueline, but then again, it may just be poignant wish fulfillment. "Me!" replies Emilio, and the film ends by returning him to the limbo of a freeze-frame that inevitably recalls that of Antoine Donel (Jean Pierre Leaud) in Francois Truffaut's *Les quatre cents coups* (*The Four Hundred Blows*, 1959), in which the adolescent Antoine is caught between the land and the sea, between childhood and adulthood, between the embittered, selfish, guilt-ridden postwar France of the 1950s and the rebellious, reckless, New Wave France of the 1960s, just as the characters in *Lista de espera* and its primary Cuban audience are caught in a present-day limbo between the Cuba that was and the Cuba that will be.

Practicalities: The Formation of the Subject

This bittersweet imagining of Cuba by magic realist means was arguably mirrored in Tabío's creation of the coach station set from the ruins of a building that had been a casino during the Batista regime. Tabío was attracted by the "beauty of run-down luxury"[18] evident in the arched outer walls of the abandoned casino and set his crew to its restoration in a manner that would be continued by the characters in his film. The building received electricity, water, and an asphalt road; however, any revivification of its elegance in the film is purposefully toned down by the flat, pastel lighting favored by cinematographer Hans Burman. Indeed, the warmer, more vibrant colors of the extended dream sequence are offset by the realist aesthetic of the early scenes, whose naturalism was accentuated by Tabío limiting his cast to a brief rehearsal period of read-throughs in which they were permitted to embellish and adapt. In creating his set and bringing together his cast, therefore, Tabío effected a parallel between the filmmaking process and the story of his film that constitutes a unique, multilayered representation of contemporary Cuba.

Moreover, the collaborative nature of the filmmaking process and the film's narrative focus on the collective solution to the problem of a crumbling Cuba suggests a practical response to imminent political, social, and ideological changes. This is clearly affined to the description of the relationship between the village square and the castle of the Middle Ages offered by Bakhtin, who concentrated on the collapse of strict hierarchies as a precursor of the Renaissance. In *Problems of Dostoevsky's Poetics*, Bakhtin claimed that people lived two lives: One was official, monolithic, serious, censorious and subject to a hierarchy that was maintained by fear, dogmatism, and the demand for piety.[19] The other life was lived in the village square and was carnivalesque, liberated, and unfettered, characterized by humor, satire, blasphemy, profanity and familiar contact with everyone present. Both these lives were legitimate, claimed Bakhtin, but separated by strict boundaries. Most importantly, Bakhtin claimed that the collective human experience, which is subject to the cycles and rhythms of nature, reemerged in the popular culture as a counterweight to official culture. In *Lista de espera*, wherein the coach station functions as the village square, Tabío shows that although the Communist regime of Castro may end, the Socialist ideals that emerge in the popular culture of the carnival that occurs in the coach station remain intact and retain the potential to reemerge.

Tabío's islanders may engage with the formation of the subject in relation to an ideology that is articulated through their actions rather than the dictate of the state, but there are several moments in the film when characters consider their actions in terms of possible reprisals. The carnival of the coach station includes the caricature of the party member who protests at the stranded passengers fixing the coach and decorating the station without permission and storms off to a nearby village with his family in tow to complain to the proper authorities; but the broadness of the caricature does not erase his threat. This cynical but wary response to officialdom is subsequently concluded by the return of the party member the morning after the collective dream, this time accompanied by the authorities, who naturally discover his horrified tale of civilians acting entirely on their own initiative to be false. Like Bakhtin, the islanders want to find alternatives to a strict formalist or structuralist approach to their dilemma, but such mischievous elements as their multifarious contributions to the renovation of the coach station are inhibited by their knowledge of the official language and therefore limited to the dream state. Their various actions may be equivalent to different rhetorical strategies that embody an implicit popular conception of the world that is polyphonic rather than monologic, but the revamped coach station remains a product of their imagination.

Going Nowhere: The Discreet International Distribution of *Lista de espera*

In his book on Cuban cinema published in the official Cuban Culture Collection, Reynaldo González describes *Lista de espera* as a "satire about contemporary themes [that] zig-zags between political criticism and a chronicle of customs."[20] His division of the political from the popular element is misguided, however, because it does not recognize their complex interdependence. *Lista de espera* does not zigzag as much as spin out a shaggy-dog story that goes nowhere fast on purpose, but it does manage to provide a glimpse of the Socialist utopia that was promised Cubans. Chanan is somewhat pessimistic in calling the journey of Tabío's characters "forbidden and impossible,"[21] especially after recognizing that at the end they "want to leave, but are reminded of the dream and prove reluctant to abandon the exact glimpse of its potential";[22] for it is the potential of the journey that is vital to the film's optimism. Unlike Fernando Pérez's beautifully shot but ideologically cynical *La vida es silbar* (*Life Is To Whistle*, 1998), which ends with a dream of Cuba in 2020 that has designer-clad, Coke-guzzling teenagers rollerblading on the Malecón as if it were Venice Beach, *Lista de espera* holds true to the Socialist dream even as it lets go of its practical existence. The opposite of *La vida es silbar*, in which an omnipotent narrator decides the fate of characters who neglect their beliefs in favor of personal liberties that are tantamount to selfishness, *Lista de espera* posits the rebirth of the coach station as a collective effort that nurtures a late autumn blooming of Socialism and is, as Tabío says, "a hymn to human solidarity from the collective's point of view."[23]

Tabío and his fellow co-screenwriters, Arturo Arango and Senel Paz, won the prize for best screenplay at the 2000 Havana Film Festival and *Lista de espera* enjoyed limited international distribution in Canada and most of Europe (except the United Kingdom) on the back of its screenings at the Toronto, Cannes, and Polish Latin American film festivals, as well as the nomination for best film and the best supporting actor award for Perugorría at the 2000 Cartagena Film Festival. In Spain, where it grossed a reasonable €1,595,375 and where Perugorría was becoming a popular character actor and occasional leading man, *Lista de espera* was nominated for the 2001 Goya for best foreign Spanish-language film (losing to Argentina's *Plata Quemada* [*Burnt Money*, 2000]), while Thaimí Alvariño won the best actress award from the Malaga Film Festival. *Lista de espera* was especially well received in Germany, where one critic declared that the film "in Caribbean spirit, talks of love, hope and freedom and above all delivers the message: Anything is possible!"[24]

Instead of championing progress or getting misty-eyed over revolution, *Lista de espera* is a film about facing stagnancy and imminent change with patience and stoicism. Although it refers to such transnational elements as foreign films and the Spanish boyfriend of Jacqueline, *Lista de espera* is defiantly more inward-looking than *Fresa y chocolate*, which ended with Diego's leaving Cuba, with *Lista de espera* suggesting that Jacqueline stays. Unreleased in the United States except on unrated DVD in 2004, *Lista de espera* failed to obtain for Tabío the status he deserves of being at least equal to his late friend and collaborator Alea. His 2003 film *Aunque estés lejos* (*So Far Away*) cowritten with Arango, starring Alea's widow Mirta Ibarra and coproduced by the Spaniard Gerardo Herrero suffered the demands of Spanish investors for local Cuban flavor and could not manage a convincing criticism of the stereotypes that it presented. Since the release of *Lista de espera*, Fidel Castro has attempted to wean Cuba off tourism by building industrial and commercial links with Venezuela's Hugo Chávez and restricting the free circulation of American dollars on the island. In 2004 the U.S. Coast Guard intercepted 1,498 Cubans attempting to cross the Straits of Florida,[25] while the average Cuban's standard of living remains at a lower level than before the post-Soviet depression of the 1990s, and the country still owes an external debt of over $12 billion to Russia. For all the advances in health and education, Cubans are prohibited from buying computers or accessing the Internet without permission and the infrastructure that supported tourism is being neglected. Cuba is changing so fast that the specific political meaning of *Lista de espera* has been lost to the humor and sentimentality of a film that now represents nostalgia. However, if the Cubans must all awake from the revolutionary dream, this film, like fragrance on a pillow, at least provides a memento of what once had seemed so real.

Notes

1. Michael Chanan, *Cuban Cinema* (Minneapolis: University of Minnesota Press, 2004), 2.

2. Senel Paz, *Fresa y chocolate* (Navarra: Editorial Txalaparta, 1998).

3. Reynaldo González, *Cine Cubano: El ojo que nos ve* (Havana: Plaza Mayor Colección Cultura Cubana, 2002), 197. "*El tejido anecdótico y el enfoque reflejaron una problemática en la que marginados y marginadores quedaban apresados en la lucha entre la tradición y la necesidad de ruptura, la acquiescencia con cañones heredados y la urgencia por superarlos.*"

4. Ann Devroy and Daniel Williams, "Lawmakers' Warnings Influence Change in Clinton's Cuba Policy," *The Washington Post*, vol. 115, no. 23 (May 5 1995): 2, www.tech.mit.edu/V115/N23/lawmaker.23w.html (August 20, 2005).

5. Chanan, *Cuban Cinema*, 9.

6. Chanan, *Cuban Cinema*, 10.

7. Roy Armes, *Third World Film-making and the West* (Berkeley: University of California Press, 1987), 183.

8. Armes, *Third World Film-making*, 183.

9. Georg Sorensen, *The Transformation of the State: Beyond the Myth of Retreat* (Great Britain: Palgrave Macmillan, 2004), 83–102.

10. The World Factbook, www.cia.gov/publications/factbook/geos/cu.html (accessed August 21, 2005).

11. Michael Myerson, *Memories of Underdevelopment: The Revolutionary Films of Cuba* (New York: Grossman, 1973), 18.

12. Chanan, *Cuban Cinema*, xi.

13. Chanan, *Cuban Cinema*, 13.

14. Chanan, *Cuban Cinema*, 10.

15. Mikhail Bakhtin, "From the Prehistory of Novelistic Discourse," in *The Dialogic Imagination* (Austin: University of Texas Press, 1981), 41–83.

16. Juan Carlos Tabío, "Making of *Lista de espera*" on Region 2 DVD.

17. Tabío, "Making of," "*Un pretexto para hacer un homenaje a muchos amigos.*"

18. Tabío, "Making of," "*Belleza desaliñada del lujo.*"

19. Mikhail Bakhtin, *Problems of Dostoevsky's Poetics* (Minneapolis: University of Minnesota Press, 1984), 129–30.

20. González, *Cine Cubano*, 197.

21. Chanan, *Cuban Cinema*, 194.

22. Chanan, *Cuban Cinema*, 194.

23. Tabío, "Making of." "*Un canto a la solidaridad humana desde el punto de vista colectiva.*"

24. Susanne Wolf, "Kubanisch Reisen," www.allesfilm.com/show_article.php?id=20347 (accessed August 18, 2005). Thanks to Claire Gubbins for the translation.

25. *The World Factbook*, www.cia.gov/publications/factbook/geos/cu.html (August 14, 2005).

CHAPTER NINE

The Power of Looking
Politics and the Gaze in
Salvador Carrasco's *La otra conquista*
Miriam Haddu

Many of the filmmaking tendencies of the 1990s in Mexico were concerned with reestabishing a sense of national identity on the screen. Tired of celluloid images that reflected a bygone era of revolutionary nationalism, contemporary Mexican filmmakers during the last decade of the millennium began to look within, to redefine what is meant by *lo mexicano*, or a sense of Mexicanness. Crucial to the transnational commercial success stories of recent cinema from Mexico, such as Alejandro González Iñárritu's *Amores perros* (*Love's a Bitch*, 2000) or Alfonso Cuarón's *Y tu mamá también* (*And Your Mother, Too*, 2001), lies the self reflective and introspective period of filmmaking witnessed during the 1990s.[1] The cinematic work conducted during the 1990s allowed for the progression and growth of an industry that had, toward the late 1980s, looked considerably threatened. To address this problem, during the late 1980s the ex-president, Carlos Salinas de Gortari, consolidated the Mexican Film Institute (IMCINE) as an independent body. At the core of the reconfiguration of IMCINE lay the attempt to instill a sense of autonomy among the Mexican filmmaking community, with the aim of encouraging the growth of an independent national cinema. Strategic to this scheme was the implementation of a cofinancing policy for new and prospective projects, which gave way to the flourishing of ideas, alongside a focusing on the task of fundraising on behalf of the filmmakers. On completion, such efforts translated themselves into cinematic success stories, paving the way for one of the most fruitful periods of domestic filmmaking since the Golden Age. Moreover, during the 1990s, films such as Alfonso Cuarón's *Sólo con tu pareja* (*Love in the Time of Hysteria*, 1991), María Novaro's *Danzón* (1991), Dana Rotberg's *Angel de fuego* (*Angel of Fire*, 1991), Alfonso Arau's *Como agua para chocolate* (*Like Water for Chocolate*, 1992), and Guillermo del Toro's *Cronos* (Chronology, 1993), set in motion a period that would be characterized by international and national critical acclaim, as well as a growing interest in Mexican cinema as a viable industry. Furthermore, the filmic success of the 1990s, headed by a generation of young and dynamic directors, put Mexican cinema on the international map by gaining recognition in the form of positive reception and awards and thus securing distribution for acclaimed films. The films of this period are linked thematically by a search for a contemporary sense of Mexican identity on the screen, with its multiple cinematic visions and a fragmented sense of self. As a result, during the 1990s moviegoers saw a multiangled interpretation of Mexican identity projected onto their screens as revealed by the industry's newest arrivals. Further, what this new generation of filmmakers also sought to reevaluate were the archetypal representations of *mexicanidad* as articulated in the cinema of the Golden Age and to reflect the sociopolitical and economical changes that Mexican society had witnessed in the past forty years. Thus a reassessment not only of past cinematic identities, such as the Mexican macho or the archetypal female role, took place in the cinema of the 1990s, but also a reconsideration of both historical and previously unrepresented histories took narrative form. Moreover, the evaluation of important historical events took shape in several significant filmic narratives from the 1990s and produced the history genre in contemporary Mexican filmmaking.

The shifts in representation that was observed in the filmmaking tendencies of the 1990s allowed for the progression and development of a confident, multigeneric and complex cinema that continues advancing well into the twenty-first century. In addition, a critical evaluation of the cinematic productions of the 1990s is necessary to formulate an accurate picture of the filmmaking arena in contemporary Mexico and also for a specific contextualization of Mexican cinema's recent success at home and abroad seen in the aforementioned *Amores perros* and in *Y tu mamá también*. Despite the obvious positives of the success of both Iñárritu and Cuarón's films (in terms of highlighting Mexican cinema as a world player within the international filmmaking arena) back at home, the increasing awareness of the potential gains stemming from commercially successful films ran the risk of affecting the decision-making tendencies behind the financial support and backing of proposed future projects. An inclination toward this line of thinking can be seen to have developed toward the latter part of the 1990s, when Mexican cinema witnessed an increase in the production of films that projected an internationalized vision of Mexican society, witnessed, for example in *Sexo, pudor y lágrimas* (*Sex, Shame and Tears*, 1999) directed by Antonio Serrano (a film that incidentally was the first contemporary Mexican film to be taken up by Twentieth Century Fox). *Sexo, pudor y lágrimas* proved to be the result of a potentially winning formula for commercial success, originally devised in the mid-1990s by Rafael Montero's *Cilantro y perejil* (*Recipes to Stay Together*, 1994), a production that enjoyed considerable popularity in Mexico. Films imitating both *Cilantro y perejil* and *Sexo, pudor y lágrimas*, pretexts for exploring gender divisions in contemporary Mexican society, saw an increase in production toward the latter part of the 1990s, exemplified in Fernando Sariñana's *Todo el poder* (*Gimme Power*, 1999), and later in Nicolás Echevarría's *Vivir mata* (*Living Kills*, 2002). These films sought to rework the gradually becoming familiar picture of metropolitan life as seen from the point of view of the young, professional members of society. Heavily influenced by the Hollywood studios' offerings of modern life's twists and woes, alongside the indisputable flavoring of satellite television's projections of young *Friends*-type urban living, Mexican cinema dutifully borrowed techniques, frameworks, and stylistics from its northern neighbors to represent its own up-and-coming youth, thus giving form to the romantic comedy genre, a development unique to the contemporary period of filmmaking. However, almost as an antithesis to the above romantic settings lies the work of artists who continued, in a diversity of ways, to penetrate beyond the façade of modern living, to explore the roots of the current Mexican nation, a task that had also begun during the early 1990s. This quest for a contemporary sense of national identity took on several representative avenues and was shaped by various contexts and locations. Women directors, more prominent in the contemporary period than ever before in the history of national cinema, took the search for a sense of feminine realities in Mexican society one step further, by providing visions and cinematic constructions specifically framed from female points of view, seen for example in the work of María Novaro, Maryse Sistach, Dana Rotberg, Busi Cortés, and Guita Schyfter, to name but a few. The emergence of women's narratives in contemporary Mexican cinema relocates the thematic search for *lo mexicano/a*, from a gendered vacuum, to a multiplicity of representative spaces.

Whereas many directors took on board the changing nature of gender discourse in modern society and explored these on the screen, others chose to observe important moments in Mexican history as points for departure for further cinematic explorations of identity. These narratives looked to the past for explanations of the current nation state and attributed the modern condition to specific figures, moments, and events from Mexican history. An analysis of these explorations is thus vital to an understanding of this filmic search for identity undertaken by contemporary Mexican filmmakers. Therefore this chapter will center on an example of the cinematic quest to explore the origins and fragments of Mexican identity, so crucial to the investigations taking place during the filmmaking of the 1990s. Discussions in this chapter will focus on one of the highest grossing Mexican films in the nation's recent cinematic history, and the analysis will seek to explore some of the issues raised by the film and by its reception. Salvador Carrasco's *La otra conquista* (*The Other Conquest*, 1998), a highly acclaimed *opera prima*, highlights both in its narrative content and in its reception, one of the primary concerns for representing a cinematic Mexico and turns its attention to a crucial episode in Mexican history to find answers to national cinema's quest for identity on the screen. Carrasco took six years to complete his project (which began filming in 1992) because of the financial burdens of seeing through an ambitious project with limited funding. Notwithstanding the financial constraints, in 1999 the film was screened in Mexico City and then in 2000 in Los Angeles to packed theatres. Yet despite the success of *La otra conquista*, Carrasco's film has failed to attract adequate distribution and awaits nationwide release in the United States. Furthermore, the case of *La otra conquista* raises interesting questions regarding the role of distribution and its impact on the possible shelf life of a film, regardless of its commercial or artistic value. The polemics of representation witnessed by Carrasco's film both because of its subject matter (the narrative of which is set against the backdrop of the Spanish conquest of Mexico) alongside the (perceived) challenges the film provides for commercial reception, also opens the debate regarding the boundaries and restrictions governing transnational success.

Contextual Frameworks (Re)Vising 1992

During the early 1990s, echoing a growing interest in the subject matter of the Conquest, contemporary Mexican cinema produced films such as Juan Mora Catlett's *Retorno a Aztlán* (*Return to Aztlán*, 1990), Sergio Olhovich's *Bartolomé de Las Casas* (1992), and later, Felipe Cazals's *Kino* (1993). In addition, Nicolás Echevarría's contribution to the trend culminated with his prize-winning *Cabeza de Vaca* (1992), the story of a spiritual and geographical journey undergone by the Spanish conqueror of the same name. A few years later, Salvador Carrasco's *La otra conquista* portrays the Conquest as seen from the perspective of the conquered peoples of the Mexican central valley. Here Carrasco's narrative delves into the mind of the *mexica* nation, personified in the character of Topiltzín, an Indian struggling to make sense of the loss of his ancient world, while attempting to find a space amid the "New World" that has been thrust on him. Independently made, Carrasco's feature film addresses an area of Mexico's past that is significant to modern day notions of national identity.

October 12, 1992 signaled the 500-year anniversary of the controversially termed "Discovery of the Americas," a date that in Spain saw the propelling of a series of commemorative events to mark the occasion. However, such proceedings ignited a wave of protests from Latin American voices from the region, where the validity of Spain and Portugal's past claim of sovereignty over the territory was brought into question. Here criticisms were also made on the use of exploitation and violence as a means of control during the ensuing Colonial period. In addition, the year 1992 marked the 500-year anniversary of indigenous resistance in the Americas, which called for a celebration of Native American cultures across the continent, and highlighted the perceived injustices and marginalization suffered by such communities since the Conquest.

In the international filmmaking arena, and in accordance with the transatlantic commemorations, Hollywood's mainstream cinema reflected the need to capitalize on and represent those symbolic first European steps on American soil. Keeping in line with these events the studios delivered blockbuster features with their visions of Columbus' historic crossing, seen for example in Ridley Scott's *1492* (1992), starring Gérard Depardieu as Christopher Columbus. Further conventional readings of history were adopted with John Glen's *Christopher Columbus: The Discovery* (1992). By contrast, Michael Mann directed the more culturally sensitive *The Last of the Mohicans* (1992) starring Daniel Day-Lewis.

Contemporary Mexican cinema, like much of Latin America's indigenous and mestizo population, took a different view of events. *Retorno a Aztlán*, in which the dialogue is conducted entirely in Nahuatl (with Castilian subtitles) perhaps marks the first significant shift toward an attempt at the rewriting of history on the contemporary screen. In turn, *Bartolomé de las Casas* pays homage to the humanitarian friar of the same name. Moreover, *Kino* explored an alternative view of the Spanish Friars in the Americas, by moving away from traditional notions of such friars as being indifferent to Indian suffering and solely driven by missionary ambitions. Here Padre Kino is portrayed as an adventurous missionary who combines the fearless qualities of the conquistador with the piety characteristic of a man of his vocation. Situated within this series of quincentury films, *La otra conquista* takes its place as a prime example of a much wider cinematic project at the forefront of Mexican filmmaking during the 1990s. Such a project, as highlighted previously, sought to re-present important historical events on celluloid to re-define the present national condition. However, the release of *La otra conquista* caused a stir in the media, which found critics divided in their responses and subsequent analyses of the film. What was predominant and consistent however, was the audiences' positive response to the work, which translated itself into record-breaking box-office success. Whereas some saw the project as being overambitious because of the film's subject matter, others appreciated it as a step toward responding to a cinematic need that had been inherent in Mexican filmmaking for decades. This need saw the desire for representation on the screen in contexts that mattered most to the Mexican public.

The overwhelming public response to Carrasco's film articulated the Mexican nation's thirst for self-representation on the screen in a manner, context, and framework that was relevant and important to its audience. Carrasco's film, therefore, filled the gap in a cinematic area that had been significantly lacking in representation. As film critic Arturo Arredondo notes in his review of *La otra conquista*:

> It is now time to create films set in this period [the Conquest], without fear or doubts, even without money. Only by wasting does one learn and in this portion of historical cinema we have a lot to waste, and a lot more to learn. Welcome therefore *The Other Conquest*, since it opens a space in the horizons of a Mexican cinema in much need of bravery and inventions.[2]

Moreover, the Conquest, which is understood to be the crucial event in Mexican history that gave form to the current infrastructure and character of the nation, has surprisingly received little attention in Mexican cinema. It was this need for a filmic interpretation of the events and effects of the Conquest that both drove Carrasco to finalize his project and saw the flocking of Mexican moviegoers to the theatres, where, during the film's four-month run *La otra conquista* drew in an audience of more than one million.[3] Contrary to other generically defined success stories of contemporary Mexican filmmaking, such as the mid-1990s romantic comedies set in the city mentioned previously or the gangster films depicting the violent nature of the nation's capital made in the late 1990s, *La otra conquista* appealed to a cross-section of Mexican society, who, regardless of creed, race, or gender attended cinemas to witness a section of their past being re-presented on the screen.

The Other Conquest

Carrascos's film provides an insightful reflection on the effects of the Conquest on the conquered mexica people, who were in a short space of time faced with the destruction of their spiritual and material worlds. The narrative tells the story of Topiltzín, the illegitimate (and fictional) son of the Aztec emperor Moctezuma, who lives to witness the eradication of his family, their possessions, and eventually their way of life. Topiltzín is spared his own life through the intervention of his half-sister Tecuichpo, now Hernán Cortés's new mistress.[4] Tecuichpo recognizes Topiltzín during his trial in the presence of Cortés. In this scene Topiltzín stands accused of attempting to take the life of a man of God. His alleged victim is Fray Diego de la Coruña, a gentle monk deeply troubled by the aggressive tactics of his fellow countrymen. The assault in question occurred during an incident involving the capture and subsequent escape of Topiltzín from the Spaniards, after his arrest for heresy. Having been discovered performing the act of human sacrifice in honor of Tonantzín, the mother goddess, Topiltzín and his family are attacked and arrested by Spanish soldiers, who are accompanied by the observant Fray Diego. In an effort to escape from the Spaniards, Topiltzín simulates an enchantment with the icon of a fair Virgin Mary, the latter accompanying the Spaniards and the friar on their journey. However, instead of falling prey to her charms (as the friar hopes) Topiltzín begins to throw stones at his oppressors, injuring the friar and thus causing enough commotion to enable him to flee into the dark night. Following his escape spectators see Topiltzín living in isolation in the jungle, in an attempt to secretly continue his pre-Hispanic way of life. He is, however, betrayed by his half-brother, Alanpoyatzín, and is arrested once more by the Spaniards. And it is because of his past attack on Fray Diego that Topiltzín now finds himself before Cortés, standing trial for assault. Under the influence of Tecuichpo, however, Cortés sentences Topiltzín to the lesser punishment of a public lashing (rather than being burned at the stake), and a forced conversion to Catholicism. Cortés also orders that Topiltzín's spiritual welfare be entrusted to Fray Diego. A firm believer in the willing conversion of the natives as the only true way to convert, Fray Diego takes Topiltzín under his wing and makes the Indian's spiritual conversion his main mission in life. Thus Topiltzín is renamed Tomás and is sent to live in the fictional monastery of Our Lady of Light. Here Topiltzín finds refuge within the monastery walls and returns to his vocation as a scribe, a trade for which he was admired in pre-Hispanic Tenochitlán. In addition, Tecuichpo has been instructed to teach her half-brother the colonizers' tongue, Castilian, and it is during these classes that the siblings bond, rekindling an affection for one another that will drive the two toward incest in a desperate attempt to continue the Moctezuma (and pre-Hispanic) lineage with their planned offspring.

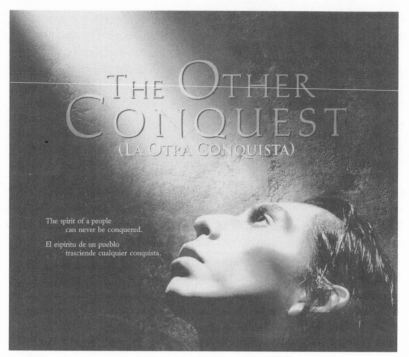

Topiltzín/Tomás (Damián Delgado) is illuminated by the sun. Photo by Andrea Sanderson, courtesy of Carrasco & Domingo Films.

The Spiritual Conquest

The narrative of *La otra conquista* deals with the struggles associated with the process of hybridization, embodied in the image of Topiltzín, and to a certain extent, in Fray Diego. However, *La otra conquista* aims to delve deeper than other Conquest-themed films from Mexico, attempting to penetrate the mind of the conquered peoples and thus decipher the psychological implications of a cultural and so-called "spiritual conquest." Through the character of Topiltzín, Carrasco examines the effects of the process of conquest, assimilation, and finally, hybridity on the mexicas, from a cinematically unexplored angle. Coinciding with the 1992 commemorative projects, Carrasco's film seeks to interpret the roots of the current Mexican nation by examining the spiritual conquest of a people, which in many ways was more devastating to the Aztec empire than the territorial invasion itself. His film marks a turning point in the Conquest debate on celluloid, by representing his mexicas in a nonvictimized form and by casting doubts on an essential spiritual conquest having taken place in Mexico. Instead Carrasco seeks to ask "who conquered whom" within the process of conquering, rebuilding, and consolidating the New Spain.[5] This query is relayed in the film's title and then answered in its tagline: "The spirit of a people can never be conquered."

Carrasco situates his narrative ten years before the recorded apparition(s) of the Virgin of Guadalupe in Mexico. Such apparitions to an Indian boy, Juan Diego, in 1531, significantly advanced the purported spiritual conquest of the nation that was initiated during the early 1520s by the Spanish clergy in the current Mexico. At the core of Carrasco's filmic exploration lies the relationship between his main character, Topiltzín, and the image of the fair Madonna brought over from Spain by the friars. Topiltzín's relationship with the Virgin, which begins with resentment and rejection, progresses onto curiosity, fascination, and then appropriation, disclosing the process of hybridization that occurred on Mexican soil at the time of the Conquest. The Indian appropriation of Christian icons through the process of interpretation and cultural translation paved the way for the creation of a hybrid spiritual belief system in post-Conquest Mexico. The image of the Virgin of Guadalupe thus encapsulates this spiritual hybridity. Her brown skin (mirroring the skin color of the indigenous Mexicans) and her chosen apparition to an Indian confirm the Virgin's symbolic embracing of the indigenous population as her own. Furthermore, the Virgin appeared to Juan Diego at the site where the Aztec mother goddess, Tonantzín, was once worshipped. The symbolic nature of such an event is crucial to an understanding of the process of assimilation inherent in the aforementioned "willing" spiritual conversion of the conquered mexicas. The mothering roles of Tonantzín and the Virgin are thus united as one in the mexica psyche, and Carrasco chooses to focus the intellectual thread of his film on this process of appropriation of the Virgin Mother, the most influential icon in Mexico today.

The Mother
At the beginning of the film the viewer is told that after the Conquest the mexica nation was left in a state of orphanage. Indeed the viewer sees an empire in tatters, with its central city, Tenochitlán, deserted in the aftermath of the Templo Mayor massacre. The city-state is thus embodied in Topiltzín, whose desolate figure is shown rising from a heap of bodies. In a desperate attempt to free himself from the destruction around him, Topiltzín climbs to the top of a nearby pyramid, from where he is able to view the extent of the destruction below, and from there cries out to the sun god Huitzilopochtli, bemoaning the deity's abandonment of his people. The narrative commences with a tragedy and ends with the "miracle" of acceptance seen in the image

of a lifeless Topiltzín embracing the statue of the fair Madonna. The journey from despair, abandonment by the gods, and acceptance of a new way of life and belief system is the central theme of the film, whereby Topiltzín serves as the vehicle both for questioning the new religion being forced on him and as a mouthpiece for a past way of life at risk of becoming destroyed. His talent as a scribe further propels Topiltzín toward using his vocation to represent the lost world of the mexicas and their experiences by creating codices that narrate their histories.

La otra conquista not only attempts to portray an endangered pre-Hispanic way of life on film but also proposes alternative forms of reading history on the screen. Carrasco positions the moral spectrum of both sides of the cultural clash within easy access for the viewer. He displays a critiquing of both Spanish brutality from the viewpoint of the Indian and in turn, shows the sometimes violent nature of human sacrifice as seen from a Spanish perspective. The element of human sacrifice, a much-debated topic within studies of pre-Hispanic civilizations, was a convincing motive behind Spanish condemnation of the "savage" nature of the mexicas. It was also significantly used by Spanish friars in their criticism of the worship of Aztec deities; blood sacrifices were considered especially "barbaric." Carrasco plays with our perceptions of the barbaric and the savage by allowing both Aztecs and Spaniards to call one another by these terms. In one of the early scenes in the film, which depicts Topiltzín at home with his grandmother, Nanahuatzín and half-brother, Alanpoyatzín, the latter refers to the Spaniards as "barbarians" when discussing the family's plans to make an offer to Tonantzín, the mother goddess. Later, when the Spaniards stumble on the human sacrifice being carried out in the secrecy of an internal chamber in an abandoned pyramid, they refer to the ceremony as "an act of barbarity," with Fray Diego's observation "you really do come from another world" underlying the narrative questioning throughout the film. The juxtaposition of ideologies is paralleled in the film with the contrasting of images, in an attempt to paradoxically highlight the similarities of both cultures. An acknowledgement that the current spiritually hybrid state of Mexico would have been impossible without the presence of parallel ideas linked to religious icons constitutes the driving force behind Carrasco's exploration of the meaning of the spiritual conquest. Such a notion is symbolized in the image of the fair Madonna with whom Topitlzín engages in an all-consuming obsession. His first "vision" of her occurs after the Spaniards have destroyed the statue of Tonantzín, following their discovery of the forbidden practice of human sacrifice. After a struggle in which several members of the party are killed (including Topiltzín's grandmother), Topiltzín witnesses the replacement of their deity with the image of the fair Madonna. This image he finds alien, yet alluring, and his curiosity is aroused by Fray Diego's reassurance, "Yes, yes, take a good look at her. That lovely woman is Mary, Mother of God. Yours is nothing more than a handful of stones." Fray Diego misinterprets the Indian's perplexity before the image for what he believes to be Topiltzín's emotional engagement with the icon. The irony contained within Fray Diego's words is that the replaced mothering icon is, of course, a statue also.

The War of Images

In his seminal study of the role of images in the conquest of Mexico, Serge Gruzinski notes that the territory which the Spaniards fought to conquer was not only ripe for the picking because of internal political disputes between the Tlaxcalans (who sided with Hernán Cortés in his battles to defeat the Aztecs) and the powerful Triple Alliance of the Aztec empire but also that the mexica state was a nesting ground for a subsequent clash in images that would mould the current character of the nation. As Gruzinski acknowledges, both Spaniards and Aztecs belonged to a highly visual culture in which icons dominated their spiritual ways of life. Such fervent support of icons would nourish the process of hybridity and would help feed the public imaginary in the formation of a dual deity embodied in the Virgin of Guadalupe, the proclaimed Mother of all Mexicans. Thus the process of appropriation of Spanish icons by the indigenous raises questions as to the accurateness of using the term "spiritual conquest" in relation to the Mexicans, because it is also possible to see the current hybrid belief system as the result of an indigenous "conquest" (and thus adoption) of Christianity. The ending of La otra conquista points toward this conclusion, whereby Fray Diego construes Topiltzín's physical appropriation and replacement of the Virgin in his cell, as a "miracle." In this scene the friar interprets the vision of Topiltzín embracing the Virgin as a further example of the possibility of a new race emerging from the chaos, helped by the application of love and tolerance.

Gruzinki makes a further observation on the role of the visual in the conquest of Mexico when he analyzes the importance of the gaze in this setting. Here he reflects on the positioning of the gaze in the process of rejection or appropriation of religious icons from the perspective of both parties. From the point of view of the Indian, the crucial moments of "seeing" the conqueror's icons constituted the first step toward the fragmentary appropriation of a different belief system and way of life. Furthermore, during the Conquest the "matter of images played such a role in the Spanish strategy that the Indians could not help closely associating, even identifying, the invaders with their practices, which were alternately idoloclastic and iconophilic."[6] For the

Spaniards however, the vision of Indian idolatry constituted the epitome of evil:

> Endowed from the very beginning with a demonic identity, function, and form, the 'evil and lying,' 'dirty and abominable' idol could only exist in the gaze of the one who discovered it, was scandalized by it, and destroyed it.[7]

Gruzinski further notes that the gaze played a significant role in the concretization of a hybrid spiritual belief system whereby the "cross and the images of the Virgin were commonly mixed with the [Indian] 'idols' . . . thus prophesizing a future religious syncretism that continues to exist in present-day Mexico."[8] The juxtaposition of images combined with the subsequent iconoclastic measures adopted by the conquerors during the process of conquest reveals not only a clash of ideals represented in the images harbored by both Spaniards and mexicas but also a war of images that would lead to the fusion deity embodied in the current Virgin of Guadalupe. This ideological cross-fertilization, which led to eventual mass conversion, is the topic for Carrasco's psychological exploration of the "conquered" nation, ventured through Topiltzín's mind. The impetus for the director's intellectual enquiry was heightened by what he saw as a considerable lack of academic investigation into the years between 1521 (dating the fall of the Aztec Empire) and the year 1531, when the apparition of the Virgin of Guadalupe to Juan Diego is reported to have occurred:

> [I]n all of my research I found quite a bit of literature until August 13th 1521, when Cuahutémoc surrendered. Then [suddenly] there's a black hole of ten years. There's very little [written] on what happened in the following ten years . . . I thought . . . what happened the morning after? We all know how it ended when Cuahutémoc surrendered, but imagine the psychological and emotional scars.[9]

Thus Carrasco saw the filling of this historical void as a "creative challenge," and it is for this reason that the director chooses to set his narrative in the years leading up to the apparition of the Virgin of Guadalupe, commencing his tale in 1521, after the Conquest.[10]

The encounter between polar images described above is represented in the film on two levels. Firstly, the icons of Tonantzín and the fair Madonna are constantly juxtaposed, their images eventually fusing into one during a sequence in one of Topiltzín's delusions. Secondly, the hallucinations experienced by both Topiltzín and Fray Diego provide an insight into the characters' tormented minds, as well as serving to articulate the process of hybridization experienced by both the Indian and the friar. Contextualized within the hallucinations, the images of the Aztec and Catholic icons take center stage, revealing a conflict of images, which wrestle for visual supremacy contained in the realms of the imaginary. In the case of Topiltzín, the hallucinations suffered after the arrest and imprisonment of his half sister, Techuichpo, reveal a struggle between his yearning for the mother goddess, who at first appears as the fair Madonna, and his rejection of the new theology being imposed on him. Within this delirious setting the rebellious Topiltzín takes it on himself to sacrifice the Catholic icon to the Aztec gods, helped by the presence of his deceased grandmother and Tecuichpo, alongside two other women. In this setting Topiltztin takes center stage and replaces the Aztec priest as performer of the sacrifice, only to recede once the fair Madonna metamorphoses into the image of Tonantzín. This is not the first time the two mothering deities have met in the film; after the Spaniards have ransacked the scene of the human sacrifice in honor of Tonantzín earlier in the film, the Spanish soldiers place a covered Madonna next to the statue of the Aztec mother goddess. Once the Spaniards have destroyed the icon of Tonantzín, and she is nothing more than "a handful of stones" on the floor, the conquerors replace her image with the icon of the fair Virgin, brought over from Spain for Cortés' palace. A distressed Topiltzín begs forgiveness from his mother goddess, now a shattered mass of rubble, of which nothing survives except for the mask that reveals her dual features of life and death. As soon as the Virgin is unwrapped, Topiltzín is captivated by her image, pertaining more to curiosity than fascination, yet at this point in the narrative the Virgin's gaze does not return Topiltzín's own uninterrupted stare. It is only at the moment of Topiltzín's excruciating pain under torture that their eyes connect, and the Virgin's gaze returns Topiltzín's own desperate look. At this moment in the film, assisted by the camera angles, the Virgin loses her aloofness and responds to Topiltzín's suffering with a wistful expression on her until-then-inexpressive face. And as if answering Topiltzín's call and sharing in his grief, the camera frames a single teardrop released from one of the Virgin's observant eyes. From there forward in the narrative Topiltzín becomes fascinated with this mothering deity, and in his mind he questions the Virgin's capacity to both physically and spiritually replace the image of Tonantzín. The end result of this struggle sees a harmonious framed image of Topiltzín and the Virgin lying side by side, after the former has become reconciled with his hybrid state and has appropriated the icon as his own, shown at the end of the film.

Hallucinatory images also trouble Fray Diego; they appear in the form of nightmares whereby the clash of images is played out in the realm of his subconscious state. Tossing and turning under the crucifix hung on the wall above his bed, Fray Diego is haunted by the image of Tonantzín. As we follow his nightmare, the camera enters the interior of a cave, zooming in to a wall covered in dry grass, the blades of which invite the viewer's gaze by opening up like curtains, to reveal the dual face of life and death of the Aztec mother goddess. The friar awakens from his nightmare with a sense of impending doom and orders the Spanish soldier, Rolando, to guard Topiltzín's cell for the remainder of the night. The hallucinations return toward the end of the friar's life, which in narrative terms is situated at the beginning of the film. These images convey the shadows on the wall of what appears to be Fray Diego converting an Indian, then an Indian mirroring the gestures of the friar's benediction, "converts" Fray Diego. His willingness to die (since his return from New Spain the friar has not uttered a word and has stopped eating) suggests an element of guilt on the part of Fray Diego for his role in the conversion of Indians. It also indicates recognition of the Indian spiritual belief system (through the role reversal of the conversion in his hallucination) and the possible introduction of doubt on the validity of the friar's own religion. On his deathbed, the friar mutters the words "a last journey" leading his companions to believe that he is describing a glimpse of the afterlife. When asked to explain where this last journey will take him, the old friar simply replies, "where all mortals go" thus refusing to elaborate on his thoughts and discrediting his vocational belief in absolutes.

Indications of the process of hybridization between Fray Diego and Topiltzín being reciprocal are reinforced when after the latter's death, Fray Diego speaks to Topiltzín's lifeless body in Nahuatl, acknowledging with his words and their contents, the possibility of a new race emerging from the encounter between the two apparently different worlds. Such actions contradict the friar's earlier position regarding the merging of both cultures, which he saw as impossible because of the perceived fundamental differences between the two. In a scene shared with Topiltzín, the friar lectures his protégé on the impossibility of a fusion of both cultures and urges Topiltzín to adapt to the new world being forced on him, because, unfortunate for his culture, this is the reality facing the mexicas. In this scene the camera visually divides the two parties, representative of both worlds and ideals, by locating each character on either side of the frame. However, bridging the two men stands the statue of a smiling cherub, a direct replica of the cherub at the foot of the Virgin of Guadalupe, prophesizing a future mestizo nation and undermining the friar's words.

Reversing the Negative Paradigm

In addition to his exploration of the effects of the so-called spiritual conquest on the mexicas, Carrasco's innovation in his cinematic portrayal of post-Conquest Mexico lies in his treatment of the women in the film. In line with his deliberate antivictimized stance regarding the representation of the mexicas, Carrasco portrays his filmic women as strong, independent, and intelligent participants in the process of the Conquest and the subsequent formation of a new state under Spanish sovereignty. Just as he reverses the effects of conqueror and conquered in the depiction of Fray Diego and Topiltzín and their struggles to reconcile a newly hybrid state of being, Carrasco reverses the negative paradigm maintained through the image of *La Malinche* or Doña Marina with his portrayal of the Aztec princess-turned-Colonial-governess found in Tecuichpo. In the film, Tecuichpo stands as the antithesis to La Malinche, Cortés's first Indian mistress, who assisted the conqueror during his travels in Mexico, acting as his interpreter and companion and who, toward the end of the relationship, bore him a child. According to sources, Malinche's firstborn, the mythologized first Mexican mestizo, represents the current nation state. The Mexican poet and essayist Octavio Paz notes in his essay, "*Los hijos de la Malinche*" (*Sons of La Malinche*), that the root of Mexican machismo lies at the heart of what he sees as a complex relationship with the two mothers: the Virgin of Guadalupe, the virtuous, all nurturing mother, and La Malinche, the betraying, blemished woman who offered herself voluntarily to the oppressor.[11] La Malinche thus embodies the biological mother of the Mexican state, and her binary opposite is to be envisaged in the Virgin, the nation's spiritual mother. Paz suggests that the Mexicans blame La Malinche for the fall of the Aztec Empire, because her interpreting skills were put to great use during Cortes's ventures into the central valley. Indeed Aztec codices depicting the encounter between Cortés and Moctezuma demonstrate an actively involved Malinche at Cortés's side, providing the latter with verbal assistance. She did not only just act as Cortés's interpreter, however; historians believe that in many ways La Malinche was Cortés' gateway to understanding the Aztec psyche in that she was also able to translate indigenous beliefs, customs, and fears to Cortés for his use during the Conquest. On the other side of the debate, feminist analysis reclaims La Malinche from historical oblivion and proclaims her a victim of the patriarchal order.[12] Such arguments condemn what is seen as a demonization of La Malinche's image and forward this as an example of the elaborate powers of male-dominated discourse at play. Her marginalization from Mexican history and the condemnation of her role in the Conquest have, feminists argue, contributed toward the oppression of women in Mexico and the repression of female sexuality, with the belief held that La Malinche's greatest sin was that she "gave" herself voluntarily to the conqueror. Historical data however, sheds doubts on such claims of sexual abandonment because La Malinche was originally sold to Cortés for his pleasure, and once discovered, her interpreting abilities were later put to great use. In his film, Carrasco chooses to move away from polarized visions of La Malinche, offering instead a nonvictimized, nonglorified, and nondemonized replica of the paradigm in his interpretation of Teciuchpo's persona. Here he projects an image of a complex, intriguing character who is tormented by the memory of her late father, Moctezuma, and murdered husband, the Aztec rebel warrior, Prince Cuahutémoc. Her choice to remain by the side of Cortés, her late husband's enemy, is made out of a combination of necessity (because she is now alone after the fall of the Aztec Empire), political ambition, and a thirst for revenge. She is not however, a victim. Tecuichpo is portrayed as a strong woman who endures both sexual and psychological harassments from Cortés on a regular basis. Emotionally and spiritually, however, she maintains the upper hand over the conqueror, because she does not return Cortés's affections and sustains an enduring affinity with her half brother, Topiltzín. Along with Topiltzín, Tecuichpo embodies the underlying narrative thread of the film, which concludes that the spirit of a people cannot be conquered. Indeed, toward the end of the narrative Cortés begrudges Tecuichpo's indifference toward him and laments his inability to "reach" her.

This is My Body, This is My Blood

Our first encounter with Tecuichpo in the film immediately recalls the Malinche paradigm, as she steps in from the shadows and reveals her face to a surprised Topiltzín, who is kneeling before Cortés while awaiting his sentence. Tecuichpo takes her place by Cortés's side, recalling Aztec depictions of her predecessor, and when she begins to interpret Cortés's words to Topiltzín, initial preconceptions of the negative paradigm seem confirmed. However, Tecuichpo's first words in the film are conducted in Nahuatl, and their contents beg Topiltzín to spare her his judgment. It soon becomes apparent that Techuichpo is Cortés's interpreter in the true sense of the term, paraphrasing his words according to her interpretation of the events. The relationship between Tecuichpo and Cortés appears tense and confrontational. The power struggle occurring between the two continues to dominate their relationship until the end of the film, when a heavily pregnant and imprisoned Tecuichpo turns the tables on Cortés and reveals that the child she is carrying is not his. Cortés appears to be consumed with the desire to possess Tecuichpo both in mind and body. However, although Tecuichpo "surrenders" herself physically to her "lord" she remains spiritually unmoved and psychologically untouched by him. His forceful attempts to possess and break her will ends in his frustration, and this obsession haunts the conqueror until the end of the film. Tecuichpo, on the other hand, although not officially recognized as Cortés's spouse, will manipulate her political position and emotional domination over Cortés to enable a lesser sentence to be passed on to her half brother. Later in the narrative we see her plotting to avenge her father and husband's death by falsifying Cortés's signature in a politically harmful document destined for the King of Spain. Carrasco's Tecuichpo is well aware that her "condition" as a woman has meant that she was bypassed as the rightful successor to her father's empire, and thus adapts to her current situation by capitalizing on her position as the object of Cortés' desire. From there she is able to guarantee the safety of Topiltzín both at the time of his sentencing and by calling a halt to his torture when she implores Fray Diego to intervene. Rather than being a passive victim of the new regime in place, Tecuichpo quickly adapts to the new society and its norms (note her change of attire within the space of a few years), while at the same time secretly plotting the continuation of the pure Aztec race through her sexual relation with Topiltzín. Despite the repeatedly unsolicited possessions of her body by Cortés, Tecuichpo is able to confront her lord one last time from her cell in the dungeons of his palace, and thus reenforces her control over her own body and the conqueror's lack of control over Tecuichpo's mind. Her words in response to Cortés's accusations, firstly spoken in Nahuatl, and then repeated in Castilian, "this is my body, this is my blood," confirms Tecuichpo's sense of autonomy. Tecuichpo, despite the threat of violation and death, chooses to protect her own blood and ensure its continuation. Her words uttered in defense against Cortés's accusations, are directly lifted from a previous scene in the film involving Topiltzín's public torture and forced conversion to Catholicism. Here, while Topiltzín is being lashed in front of a crowd of Indians, the camera frames the intimate moment being shared between a young indigenous mother and her white-skinned baby. A nearby Spanish soldier is moved by this image of maternal tenderness, as the unnamed Indian mother whispers soothing words in Nahuatl to her newborn, "this is my body, this is my blood. Even though your skin is white, I will never abandon you." Indications of a new race being born as a result of violent means are held here, however, the resulting offspring of the aggression rather than being rejected, is being met with love and acceptance.

National and International Reception

Although domestic and U.S. moviegoers alike responded positively to the film, in Mexico, official bodies, including the well-regarded IMCINE, were less supportive of the project. Not content with disclaiming the film's worth during and after production, a number of officials publicly set about discrediting Carrasco's film. Such reactions to the film reveal a politics of production that is at the heart of the current conflict of representation experienced within Mexican filmmaking. How to or how not to represent Mexico and its inhabitants constitutes the fundamental preoccupation behind the fundraising and promotional activities of the filmmaking community. Intent on representing a modernized, internationalized, and therefore, commercially successful film at home (which in turn constitutes an art house movie abroad), national cinema is experiencing limitations on how Mexico should be represented on the screen. Furthermore, as revealed in the introduction to this chapter, such limitations are beginning to creep onto the decision-making agenda, thereby curbing the possible future success and therefore, transnationalization, of films that contain a specific cultural context within their narratives. That said, the recent *Amores perros*, along with *Y tu mamá también*, although specifically Mexican in context, are able to transcend national frontiers because of both the independent nature of their funding, and through the intensive and highly successful marketing strategies employed in the "selling" of the films. Somewhat paradoxically, after completion, *La otra conquista* was adopted by Twentieth Century Fox and duly distributed under their Latin American wing in Mexico and in Los Angeles, however when it came to a national U.S. and subsequent worldwide release, the company dropped the film. Despite it being the highest grossing Latino film in U.S. box-office history (prior to *Amores perros* and also *Y tu mamá también*), *La otra conquista* at the time of writing has yet to receive a worldwide release date, seven years after its opening in Mexico and in Los Angeles. The case of *La otra conquista* raises questions as to how Mexico ought to be and is represented on the screen. In the aggressively competitive world of filmmaking, a concern with the film's protagonist's racial origins and therefore, the potential (or otherwise) commerciality of his image, point toward a distinctive desire to leave behind the country's Indian roots in an increasingly uniform cinematic Mexico. Long gone are the days when Mexican cinema turned to the image of the Indian as exemplary of the roots of the nation, witnessed in the Gabriel Figueroa/Emilio Fernández productions from the Golden Age. What seems to be largely popular, and therefore, commercially successful, are cinematic images of a predominantly cosmopolitan, modern, and internationalized Mexico, recognizable and identifiable to audiences everywhere. A filmic narrative mainly conducted in Nahuatl, such as occurs with *La otra conquista*, and which speaks of a 500-year-old conflict, was not, in many eyes, a commercially viable investment to make. These fears however, proved unfounded, as Carrasco was able to show through the unprecedented success of his first film. The question of a cinematic representation of contemporary Mexico, raised through Carrasco's decision to proceed with an indigenous protagonist contributes toward the debate that sees the multiple-angled interpretation of the nation on the screen. However, independent films, such as the Mexico-Spain coproduction, *Aro Tolbukhin, En la mente del asesino* (*Aro Tolbukhin, in the Mind of a Killer*, directed by Isaac-Pierre Racine, Agustí Villaronga, and Lydia Zimmermann, 2002), or Jesús Magaña's *Sobreviviente* (*Survivor*, 2003), both of which, although critically acclaimed and with successful attendance at home, failed to make it as far as mainstream screening abroad. That Mexican filmmakers who venture to interpret a less glossy version of the country in their films should be penalized with poor distribution and therefore, the noninternational exposure of their work remains a much-needed point for revision within Mexican cinema and provides critics with food for thought regarding the future of the nation's truly independent cinema.

Notes

1. This chapter is also published (in a revised form) in Miriam Haddu, *Contemporary Mexican Cinema: History, Space and Identity (1989–1999)* (Lewiston, N. Y.: Edwin Mellen Press, 2007).

2. As the films are known and were released under their Spanish titles, I have made reference to the Spanish titles in the case of both these films

3. See Arturo Arredondo, "*La Otra Conquista*, de Salvador Carrasco," *Novedades* 16 April 1999, 4 (N). "*Es tiempo ya de crear las películas de esta época [la conquista], sin miedo sin temores, aun sin dinero, sólo echando a perder se aprende y en este renglón del cine histórico tenemos mucho que 'echar a perder' y mucho que aprender. Bienvenido 'La Otra Conquista' porque abre una brecha en los horizontes del cine mexicano, tan necesitado de inventos y valentías.*"

4. Judith Michaelson, "Conquista Conquering" *Los Angeles Times* March 25, 2000, 2–4.

5. Tecuichpo or Doña Isabel, is in fact a real historical character. She was Hernán Cortés's lesser-known mistress, whom, it is believed, replaced Malinche or Doña Marina as the conqueror's aide and translator. In the film, Hernán Cortés proclaims Tecuichpo governess of the kingdom of Tacuba.

6. Salvador Carrasco in an unpublished interview with the author conducted on August 13, 2004, Hollywood, Los Angeles, California.

7. See Serge Gruzinski, *Images at War: Mexico from Columbus to* Blade Runner *(1492–2019)* (Durham, N.C.: Duke University Press, 2001).

8. Gruzinski, *Images at War,* 39

9. Gruzinski, *Images at War,* 42

10. Gruzinski, *Images at War,* 39

11. Carrasco, unpublished interview with the author.

12. See Octavio Paz, *El laberinto de la soledad.* (Madrid: Cátedra Letras Hispánicas 1995), 202–227.

13. See for example Ann Marie Remley Rambo, "The Presence of Woman in the Poetry of Octavio Paz," in *Woman as Myth and Metaphor in Latin American Literature,* eds. Carmelo Virgillo and Naomi Lindstrom (Columbia: University of Missouri Press, 1985), 94–107. See also Sandra Cypress Messinger, *La Malinche in Mexican Literature: from History to Myth* (Austin: University of Texas Press, 1991), 2. See also Jean Franco, *Plotting Women: Gender and Representation in Mexico* (London: Verso, 1989), 129–147.

CHAPTER TEN

Peruvian Cinema and the Struggle for International Recognition
Case Study on *El destino no tiene favoritos*
Sarah Barrow

Throughout its history, Peruvian cinema has been badly affected by a lack of infrastructure and proper support from business and political sectors. Yet, since the first moving images were screened to admiring audiences in Lima, constant efforts have been made to emulate the critical and commercial successes of filmmakers elsewhere in the world. While the number of significant achievements in this regard is limited compared to those of countries such as Brazil and Mexico there have been some memorable Peruvian films and filmmakers during the medium's first century of development, and the desire to create films remains, it seems, as strong as ever despite the challenges. This chapter will provide an overview of some of the important breakthrough moments in recent Peruvian cinematic history and explore attempts by emerging national filmmakers to break into the international market. Through a detailed analysis of one such director's first feature, Alvaro Velarde's *El destino no tiene favoritos* (2003), this chapter highlights and explores some of the reasons for Peru's continuing position on the margins of international cinematic recognition.

In doing so, special regard needs to be paid to the sociopolitical, economic, and cultural contexts of the 1990s when President Alberto Fujimori (1990–2000) instituted a number of changes that dealt a severe blow to the slow but steady progress of national cinematic practices. For example, by deciding to abolish rather than to revise a cinema law that had benefited national filmmakers via tax incentives and guaranteed screenings, Fujimori's regime in effect wiped out the flawed yet supportive infrastructure that had given rise to a degree of continuity since 1972.[1] The mid-1990s hence experienced a period without a single national film release, during which time Hollywood studio–sponsored multiplexes began to appear in the more affluent areas of Lima and filled their screens with seductive and lavishly made Hollywood blockbusters. Most of the smaller cinemas were meanwhile forced out of business, partly because of competition but also because of a decrease in audience figures resulting from the fear and disruption caused by two decades of terrorist activity and military response.

Since Fujimori's departure, the political turmoil and years of recession have inevitably meant that plans for a new film law have been put on hold. Nevertheless, as at earlier times of crisis, Peruvian filmmakers have continued to make their case and to fight for funds and support to develop what they believe to be an important means of expression of national identity. However, from year to year the situation fluctuates. Hence national film critic and historian Isaac León Frías reported optimistically in 2003 that:

> the 2002 Peruvian Film Congress stressed the need for a new legal framework to support production within the liberal economic model . . . and film-makers have begun to put pressure on the new government of President Alejandro Toledo to do more for their industry.[2]

Yet just one year later, this optimism had been dampened, and his tone was more cautious, with his review of the year this time forced to acknowledge that:

> the long-awaited new film legislation has remained in a kind of limbo, while Peruvian legislators are preoccupied with more pressing social concerns . . . that make the plight of the film industry seem trivial, and make it virtually impossible for CONACINE (*Consejo Nacional de Cinematografía*) to improve the situation.[3]

Bearing such political and economic circumstances in mind, this chapter will take a brief look at the political developments of the 1990s that affected Peruvian film activity and provide a detailed reading of Velarde's *El Destino no tiene favoritos*. This, his first feature, is constructed as a parody of the racial and ethnic prejudices and divisions entrenched in the class system of Peruvian society and a pastiche of the highly popular Latin American television format of the *telenovela*. As an exercise in comedy, the film makes some pertinent and timely comments about Peruvian national culture in an entertaining and indirect fashion that represents a departure from the more traditional Peruvian approach of social/dramatic realism. It also provides an opportunity to consider the immense challenges faced by Peruvian directors in their efforts to bring their work to the attention of international audiences.

Peruvian Cinema in the 1990s

Throughout its first century, Peruvian cinema enjoyed just a few brief moments of international attention. Furthermore, the worsening economic climate and remnants of harsh political violence of the 1990s gave rise to even more challenging circumstances for national cinema in Peru, and John King's comment that "local film production remained intermittent"[4] was perhaps something of an understatement. The protectionist "Cinema Law" established in 1972 was repealed in 1992, and a new one introduced in 1995 that focused instead on funding competitions and a new requirement to find external investment. The kind of benefits that had been on offer for twenty years, such as tax incentives and guaranteed screenings for national films, were entirely absent from the new proposal. Filmmakers were furious, having themselves put forward a new law that built on the advantages of the previous one. Indeed, Nilo Pereira del Mar, filmmaker and President of the Filmmakers Association of Peru, gives some indication of the anger that was still felt by many in a speech given at the first national prize-giving ceremony for shorts and feature film projects in December 1996:

> As everyone knows, these last four years have been devastating for national cinema . . . prior to this, national cinema had reached a maturity of content and professional quality which opened up an international space thanks to prizes and screenings all over the world. Twenty years of unbelievable effort by more than 200 filmmakers over two generations were about to be sent into oblivion. Nevertheless, we persevered with our dreams. And for four years we battled tirelessly to achieve a new legal framework that would allow us to really get on with our work.[5]

These problems were exacerbated by cinema closures, declining audiences, rampant video and DVD piracy, and stiff competition from terrestrial and cable television networks. For a few years, it seemed as if only established director Francisco Lombardi, with his ability to attract international investment and "intelligent use of mainstream conventions,"[6] could keep going under such circumstances. As King states: "only one Peruvian film [was] released in 1994 and 1995 and none at all in 1997."[7]

By the end of the decade, however, the government's modified system of support for its filmmakers, while limited in scope, had begun to reap some rewards; several of the productions that had been underway when the state withdrew from film funding in 1992 were able, at last, to be completed, and there was renewed interest in short filmmaking, as will be seen in the section on the work of Velarde. Since 2000, in fact, a small but important number of new filmmakers has begun to emerge, some (such as Velarde) returning from education and training in the United States, while others (such as Josué Méndez) had gained experience in Peru through television work and participation in workshops run by veteran director Armando Robles Godoy.[8] These young directors, unaccustomed to total reliance on the mechanisms of state support, have quickly turned their attention to sources of funding beyond the national institutional framework, including festivals, such as Sundance, Rotterdam, and Cannes, which have a policy of supporting new filmmakers from around the world, and to transnational coproduction projects, such as Ibermedia, which draw together resources from Spain and Latin American countries to support the development of a Hispanic cinema. The ways in which such sources have been helpful to Velarde, and the extent to which they have been useful, will be explored in the analysis that follows.

Alvaro Velarde

Alvaro Velarde's film career began just as Peruvian national cinema was experiencing yet another barren period in its development, the early to mid1990s. In 1993, he put a potential career in economics to one side and went to study for a master's degree at the New School for Social Research in New York, supported by a grant from the Ford Foundation.[9] He spent three years at the school, working at the same time in the cinema section of the city's famous Museum of Modern Art, and returned with two 16 mm short films in 1996, during the same year when not a single national film was released in his home country.

The first short, 98 *Thompson* (1994), recounts the tale of a man just arrived in New York who is trying to find his way round. It was applauded for its tight structure, use of silent slapstick comedy, and careful cinematography. The second, C. *Lloyd: A Tale of Crime and Punishment* (1996), developed the use of comedy (slapstick, verbal pun, and satire) alongside a tale of terror for a film student. Both shorts won cash prizes from the new national film awards in Peru (coordinated by government sponsored body CONACINE), which in turn set the scene for Velarde's insertion into the national cinema framework. His first "Peruvian" short film, *Roces* (*Frictions*, 1999), presents a group of archetypal urban characters (a priest, a gay man, a secretary, a street-seller, etc.) who are brought together at a bus stop when their bus is delayed. The way they are shown (without the use of dialogue) to interact (or fail to) was described by de Cárdenas as a "mosaic of prejudices and exclusions, conveyed visually by the way various characters deliberately avoid sitting next to or even near to each other."[10] This portrait of social intolerance is overturned by the director with a single powerful image in the final scene that shows everyone squashed together in the packed bus. The film won two prizes—from the critics and from the audience—at the Festival of Peruvian Short Films, as well as another cash award from the government-sponsored competition and was selected for screening at the prestigious Berlin International Film Festival. These achievements all but assured Velarde of a place among the more established filmmaking community in Peru, and the films themselves, as confirmed by Ricardo Bedoya himself, "forecast the atmosphere, tone, style and interests that would emerge" in his first feature.[11] They also created a great air of expectation and placed a considerable burden of responsibility on one of the few emerging national filmmakers with recognized talent.

El destino no tiene favoritos was finally released in Peru in late 2003, almost six years after being awarded a government script prize, which provided 30 percent of the predicted budget, having suffered "an interminable post-production process" all too familiar to Peruvian filmmakers who do not have access in their own country to high-quality editing and sound-mix facilities.[12] Nevertheless, a world premiere screening was secured in January at the Rotterdam Film Festival as a result of a grant from the prestigious Hubert Bals Fund for World Cinema, a fund established in 1987 and supported in part by the Dutch Ministry for Foreign Affairs.

Despite having only one 35 mm print and a limited distribution and marketing budget, Velarde's film was selected for and screened at a number of other festivals, including Los Angeles, New York, Korea, Raindance (London), and Viña del Mar (Chile). In light of this international attention, support was finally secured from a Peruvian newspaper, *El Comercio*, to support its domestic release, at which point the film was warmly received by most national critics and audiences, with an award for Best Actress going to Tatiana Astengo (who plays the maid Oliva) at the Seventh Latin American Film Festival in Lima in 2003.

Nevertheless, the film's commercial release in Peru had only limited box-office success and subsequent plans for international distribution have been thwarted at every turn. This misfortune comes despite the selection of the film to represent Peru at the Goya Awards in Spain in 2004 and despite the film winning yet another audience award at the Comedy Film Festival of Móstoles (Madrid) in June 2004, at which the actress Astengo (herself the recipient of an honorary award at the same festival) collected a check for €6,000 from the hands of Cuban cinema veteran Juan Carlos Tabío specifically to assist with the film's distribution costs. Before taking a closer look at some of the possible reasons why *El destino no tiene favoritos* has been unable to build on its initial success, the chapter now turns to an analysis of the film's content and form in an effort to understand its potential appeal to audiences from a range of different cultural backgrounds.

El Destino No Tiene Favoritos: Analysis

El destino no tiene favoritos has been described by renowned Peruvian critic and academic León Frías as "excellent genre film-making, examining class and the relationship between reality and fiction with an ironic eye."[13] Velarde has admitted in interviews that he prefers to express his ideas through comedy, as is clearly shown through his short films, and firmly believes that life can be hard to take without a big dose of humor and fantasy.[14] For him, the film is above all an exercise in comedy. He was keen to say something interesting about his own national culture but eschewed the more didactic approach of social realism. In terms of characterization, he constructs emblematic characters that represent easily recognizable "types" of people, specific to a Peruvian context but which also work on a broader level. The mistress, for example, represents the fast-disappearing (white) upper class, the maids the oppressed and rebellious lower classes of indigenous heritage. Visually, the garden and house he uses as the setting represent a closed world, cut off from most outside influences, within which class battles are enacted. Comedy is a rare genre for Peruvian cinema, and Velarde's example encompasses the more familiar comic ingredients of mistaken identity and misunderstanding, coincidence, slapstick, pastiche, and farce that makes its audience laugh (at the film but also at itself), and also makes provocative social comment and at the same time delivers a parody of a popular televisual form.

El destino no tiene favoritos, then, is a parody of the telenovela, a popular TV genre referred to by Sinclair as a "fusion of commercial exploitation and popular culture"[15] that has become, according to López, "the basic staple of all Latin American TV programming."[16] The protagonist of Velarde's film is Ana (Monica Steuer), a rich, repressed, and bored housewife, who has been left alone in the house with two maids while her husband Ernesto (Javier Valdez) is away on business. Much to her annoyance, Ernesto has rented their garden for the production of a telenovela, called *Destiny Has No Favorites*. However, in her boredom, Ana quickly finds herself totally absorbed by watching the shooting of the program from her window, while the maids Oliva (Tatiana Astengo) and Martina (Rebecca Raez), much more excited about these visitors from the world of television, become eager observers of the action from the kitchen. Ana makes the acquaintance of Nicolás (Paul Vega), the director of the telenovela, who casts her for a role, much to the dismay of the other actors, not to mention the two maids. They start blackmailing their employer, threatening to disclose her true identity to the television crew and her developing relationship with the television director to her husband if they do not also get roles in the show. While real events and the intrigue of the telenovela begin to intertwine and reality merges with fiction, Ana finds herself entangled in a soap opera all of her own. On the surface, order appears to have been reinstated by the end of the film when the husband returns, but the audience shares Monica's secret and knows otherwise.

As Ana M. López explains, while Latin American telenovelas share plenty of historical and formal features with their U.S. and U.K. "soap-opera" counterparts, telenovelas have been "imagined differently" and tend to have, for example, "clear-cut stories with definite endings that permit narrative closure."[17] Jesús Martín-Barbero observes that the telenovela offers "a complicity with certain markers of cultural identity,"[18] such as class and race. López indeed suggests that "the devaluation of melodrama [in Latin America] is explicitly class-based [rather than gender-based as in the US/UK versions]" and that "the telenovela's melodramatic antecedents were all . . . scorned . . . as entertainment with no cultural or redeeming value."[19] Nowadays, however, they are seen to be of tremendous economic and cultural importance. López herself points out that telenovelas are "widely exported and definitive of the Latin American star system" and that to "work in a telenovela today is often to have reached the apex of one's professional career,"[20] whereas cinema is more often the goal for most soap stars in the English-speaking screen context. Martín-Barbero has offered a slightly elitist rationale for this, suggesting that it is "the crisis in cinema and politics [in all Latin American countries that] has driven many artists, writers and actors into television and the telenovela."[21] Both he and López acknowledge that telenovela writers are highly respected, extremely well-paid and "often better known than their literary counterparts,"[22] and that the appeal of this genre to its audience is rooted in its provision of dramas that locate "social and political issues in personal and familial terms," thereby helping to make sense of "an increasingly complex world."[23]

Velarde appears to have had much of this televisual context in mind when devising his film script around the telenovela format, and turning most of the generic and spectatorial conventions on their head. In accordance with the main function of parody, that is "to exploit and contest that which came before,"[24] Velarde indeed plays with audience expectation of and familiarity with the telenovela format to redefine the relationship between himself and those viewers he knows are fully aware of the conventions of that popular form. In doing so, he also involves them in the work of distinguishing between the "reality" of the film's narrative, and the fiction of the "*novela*" within the film. For example, he intertwines the different levels of fiction by using the generic convention of the freeze-frame when he is supposed to be dealing with the reality, and some of the "real" protagonists repeat some of the dialogue already spoken by their telenovela characters. Hutcheon has posited that parody "both incorporates and challenges that which it parodies"[25] and indeed with *El destino no tiene favoritos*, Velarde offers both a celebration and critique of the form, content, and mass appeal of telenovela culture. In so doing, the audience of a work of parody such as this has to "play continual catch-up,"[26] trying to make sense of the multiple levels of intertextuality, juxtaposition, and jibe.

Stephen Mamber has suggested that "the activities of parody have been directed towards an exploration of the processes of creation" and the notion of the "failed artist" is an important aspect of cinematic parody that Mamber has outlined in this regard.[27] Velarde's film offers several examples to support this idea: Nicolás is the frustrated television director who seems to believe he was destined for greater things than churning out telenovelas. His actors are less than mediocre, and attention is drawn to their lack of talent via the late-night discussions between Nicolás and Ana. Furthermore, while scriptwriter Magda (Celine Aguirre) firmly believes herself to be an underappreciated artist, she is portrayed as being deluded to the point of insanity about her own capabilities.[28] Her writing skills have been seriously undermined by Ana's interventions, and her dream of seducing Nicolás with her words has been thwarted by the same woman's easy imitation of her trade. Ultimately Nicolás falls pretentiously in love with nothing more than a bizarre figment of his own imagination, an idea that is visually underscored by his wearing of a head bandage that mirrors the towel turban that Ana wears around her head every time he visits the house.

Of course it is assumed that the film's viewer (domestic and international), steeped in telenovela/soap-opera culture, will pick up on such devices and delight in a sense of knowingness of being able to share the joke with the director, while at the same time becoming the unwitting butt of such jokes. For if an intense knowledge of generic conventions is required to fully appreciate the parody, part of the critique must surely be focused on the viewer's own obsession with such cultural forms, with the sentimental appeal of melodrama, the universally understood themes of class and ethnic prejudice (here loosely inflected by the Peruvian context), and the familiar and predictable narrative structures. As Mamber himself concludes, "critiques of fandom are built into [such] films."[29]

Within this framework of parody, it is Velarde's attention to detail and the way he turns to the abstract and the surreal that has been most highly praised by national critics, such as Bedoya, who has suggested that this approach is modeled to a certain degree on the comedies of such globally renowned 1930s directors as Ernst Lubitsch and Mitchell Leisen. Bedoya even suggests that "making a film in this way is much more ambitious than creating a social drama or period film [since it's more important in comedy to] get the tone just right and lead the actors to express emotion via gesture, facial expression and attitudes that owe nothing to psychology nor to naturalism."[30] One such example of this can be seen at the moment when telenovela director/writer Nicolás finally recognizes the actress Ana as being the owner of the house with whom he has fallen in love. One side of her hair has been cut short by Martina, the vengeful maid, and a series of surreal dissolves reminiscent of Buñuel's *Un chien andalou* reveal that Nicolás has suddenly realized who he has been working with all along. He sadistically demands that her face be covered in cream and slaps a slice of cucumber onto her cheek, replicating the ridiculous "disguise" of the face mask worn by Ana in the house to hide her identity from Nicolás. In the end he forgives her, and their "love" is consummated back at the house. Further revenge on Ana is enacted via the agonizing death scene of her telenovela character, which has been written into the script by the lovelorn Magda, encouraged by Martina, and the denial for her of a traditional happy ending. While Mamber has written that in most successful telenovelas, "heavy doses of humor and violence intermingle in uneasy, shifting disharmonies,"[31] the resolution to Velarde's film takes this to a humorous extreme.

Thematically, as well as stylistically, the film functions as a parody. It relocates and violates the conventions of the Latin American telenovela by taking a wry approach to the popular theme of social and ethnic difference based primarily on European versus indigenous heritage, and by lampooning the common device of romantic love used to break through such socially constructed barriers. Velarde's film also undermines a range of political and cultural responses to such barriers, highlighting the inadequacy and irrelevance of each. The film thus exposes, through comedy, the fragility of the values on which such popular programs are based. Even traditionally Marxist modes of resistance are sent up through the older maid, Martina's, apparent obsession with a Guevara-like rebellion against her employer and then her abandonment of that course of action in favor of signing up for a starring role as a telenovela actress. Such gags function by provocatively revealing

María (Angie Cepeda) strikes a pose.

the limited nature of traditional ways of dealing with class and ethnic barriers, by poking fun at the superficial and nostalgic appropriation by the star industry of cult political figures (Guevara posters in Martina's room), and by pointing mockingly to the unwavering dominance of the global cult of celebrity. In short, Velarde's film serves both to "mirror and ridicule the supposedly more serious and central dramatic activities" of the telenovela.[32] The final "epilogue" scene shows Ana and Oliva, both pregnant, together preparing a meal for the new television crew to whom Ana's husband has rented out his property.

The fact that Velarde's first feature follows certain generic elements of the popular telenovela form ensures that, despite its parodic intentions, this film is highly watchable and had the potential to achieve success at the box office. In general, *El destino no tiene favoritos* was warmly received by public and critics alike. In a round-up of the best and worst of the cinema of 2003, most contributors to the Peruvian journal *Butaca sanmarquina* ranked it as the top national film of that year, praising, for example, its "artistic direction and elliptical rhythm."[33] However, in the same article, another critic drew attention to the fact that one of the worst aspects of Peruvian cinema in 2003 was the "relatively low number of spectators who went to see *El destino*."[34] It turned out that, despite its success at a string of international festivals and acclaim from almost of all of the domestic critics, Velarde's film did not achieve the financial return that would enable its director to guarantee investment in his next project. Nor has it yet attracted a distributor outside of Peru, despite tremendous efforts made by Velarde himself. There are a number of possible reasons for this, unrelated to the quality and appeal of the film itself, that need to be explored if one is to begin to understand the current challenges faced by Peru's national filmmakers.

First, it should be noted that the director believes he experienced a difficult relationship with his initial producer, Gustavo Sánchez (long-time collaborator of Francisco Lombardi) who was keen for commercial reasons to include a stronger element of nudity and sexual innuendo within the film. This was part of the motive for casting the voluptuous and eye-catching Venezuelan star Angie Cepeda to play the role of "María," the star of the telenovela we see being filmed.[35] Velarde objected, keen to maintain the integrity of his piece and unwilling to compromise his vision of a more subtle brand of humor for the sake of perceived audience demand for crude titillation. Director and producer ended up parting company, the result being that Velarde was forced to take over Sánchez's business responsibilities, leading in turn to a series of situations that might have been foreseen by a more experienced producer.[36]

Once the shoot was over, the postproduction phase of the film took much longer than planned because of a lack of funds, delaying the release date and making promotional plans difficult to put in place. The final investment eventually came from national Peruvian daily *El Comercio*, and in return for ownership of the domestic rights to the film, the paper agreed to place a series of advertisements at the time of its commercial release at the end of September 2003. This promotional agreement extended to spots on the cable television channel owned by the paper and thus reasonable coverage was guaranteed by such a deal. And yet this strategy was useful in the short term only. The newspaper, inexperienced in film distribution and exhibition, failed to organize such basic but effective promotional activities as poster distribution, for example. Furthermore, they contracted out the film promotion side to the same company that was dealing with the only other Peruvian film on release at that time, a disastrous move that set up an unnecessary and avoidable rivalry.[37] Furthermore, Velarde's film opened at only eleven screens in Lima, compared with fifty for the Hollywood blockbuster released at the same time, *The Matrix*, which attracted 240,000 spectators. After eight weeks of domestic release, *El Destino no tiene favoritos* had attracted a creditable but frustrating 50,000 viewers.[38] This unfortunate experience reflects a broader need for the development of skills in and support for marketing and distribution activities related to national films. It was hoped that this would form part of the remit for CONACINE when it was first established, and that the development of promotional activities, such as FINPROCI, would generate a certain infrastructure in this regard, but promised government support for such initiatives is yet to be made properly available and without proper funding there is little of substance that these organizations can achieve.[39]

Velarde is adamant that his film would have benefited from a longer run at certain cinemas, and box-office figures bear this claim out to a certain degree, because income was higher for the third week of release than for the first. But cinema exhibitors cannot afford to wait for "word-of-mouth" to take its effect, and without tough negotiations from an experienced distributor, *El destino no tiene favoritos* was forced to make way for the next guaranteed money-spinner from Hollywood. In the end, Velarde's first feature made $100,000 at the box office, 60 percent of which remained with the exhibitors while only 40 percent (one tenth of the total cost of the movie) was returned to the film's main investors.

During an interview with the author in July 2004, Velarde admitted to further complications when attempting to gain distribution for his film in the United States. *El Destino no tiene favoritos* had been well received at screenings at, for example, the Los Angeles Latino Film Festival 2003, resulting in approaches from a number of agents with promises of distribution support. A deal was struck with one of these but after just six months of bad decisions and botched administration, Velarde severed the tie and reluctantly took back the roles of producer/distributor/promotional agent. By April 2005, he decided that the festival circuit had been exhausted and that he should take satisfaction from the many awards that he, the film, and his actors had re-ceived for their efforts. Still hopeful of an overseas commercial cinema dis-tribution deal to come out of the Cannes 2005 event, he nevertheless de-cided to close a deal with a North American distributor for DVD release in the United States and Canada. As for a similar DVD release in Peru, who knows. For the time being, Peruvian cinephiles will be forced to buy from the United States, as is the case with so much of Latin American cinema. The irony seems to be that overseas viewers with access to the Internet and DVDs now have greater opportunities to explore the cinema of this region than those viewers located within the national boundaries of a country that sorely needs the support of its domestic audience.

Conclusion

Facing such challenges with regard to funding, audience support, and the lo-gistics of production and distribution, how then should Peruvian filmmakers proceed? As this chapter was nearing completion in May 2005, Norma Rivera (director of the National Film Archive in Lima) reported that "no Pe-ruvian films [had yet been] released" that year.[40] And while the prestigious Cannes 2005 "spotlight on Peruvian film" was undoubtedly of major signifi-cance and cause for celebration for the younger directors in particular, there were no guarantees that new distributors would become interested as a result, such was the strength and quantity of films seeking promotion at that event.[41] The situation remains tough for Peruvian cinema in terms of break-ing out of national boundaries, despite persistent efforts. None of those films shown at Cannes was taken on by an international distributor and only Mendez's feature was screened beyond the festival circuit. Moreover, in 2005, only four new Peruvian features were released in national theaters, and none of them gained an international distribution deal.[42] In terms of the produc-tion context, most feature projects continue to depend upon the support of European funds such as the Netherlands' Hubert Bals Foundation, Switzer-land's Monte Cinema Verita, the UK's Film Four or TV5 in France, in addi-tion to the Ibermedia programme, which receives contributions from many Ibero-American countries, and in which Spain has a prominent role. Indeed it is sadly unlikely that many, if any, of the four Peruvian titles selected for screening at Cannes would have attracted the attention of commercial buy-ers, however attractive their content and form, due in large part to the ac-knowledged dominance of North American products at the festival and the increasingly market-driven environment of the festival circuit more gener-ally.[43] Peruvian cinema needs strong, experienced producers to work alongside its writers and directors if it is to stand a chance in a world in which the remorseless drive for "audience-friendly globalized cinema" has become just one more cinematic strategy for the likes of Hollywood moguls, such as Harvey Weinstein.

Renowned commentator on Latin American cinema Michael Chanan has written that the region, cinematically speaking, can be divided into three groups, the first comprising of the "three largest countries, Mexico, Argentina and Brazil, where the size of the home market [has] allowed indigenous industries to function."[44] He then suggests that the smaller countries be divided into two groups, in accordance with the degree of state support provided to them, insisting on the need for "decisive state action" for a national film industry to become part of the second group. While proactive state action was indeed taken in Peru with the establishment of the 1972 Cinema Law, the abolition of this twenty years later, the delay in developing new legislation, and the current government's lack of enthusiasm for supporting any kind of national cultural policy has resulted in Peruvian cinema's position falling back to being amongst "the smallest countries, where everything would seem to be against the idea."[45] While the Toledo-led government remains focused on more pressing social concerns and the frustration of decreasing political power, national filmmakers, like Velarde, are instead having to rely on complex coproduction arrangements with overseas partners and to contend with the harsh economic realities of international distribution. In the inaugural edition of *Tren de Sombras*, the editorial team of the newest Peruvian film journal acknowledged that while the release of half a dozen new national films in 2003 is cause for some optimism, it should not be forgotten that the state has yet to honor its commitments to the new cinema law in any substantial way, pointing out that "a competition for short films called by *Conacine* in early 2004 does not change the reality of the lack of real support."[46] Indeed, if Peruvian cinema is to make its mark on the international scene outside of the increasingly competitive festival circuit, then substantial incentives for investment by the private sector into the areas of production, distribution, exhibition, and training need to be put in place as a matter or urgency.

Notes

I would like to thank the following for supporting the preparation of this chapter: the School of Arts & Letters at APU, Cambridge for a grant to conduct research in Peru in summer 2004; Norma Rivera, director of the *Filmoteca de Lima*, for endless archive resources, contacts, and general advice; and Alvaro Velarde, for giving generously of his time to answer questions and supply regular e-mail updates on the progress of his first feature.

1. For further detail on the development and abolition of the 1972 Cinema Law in Peru, see Sarah Barrow, "Images of Peru: A National Cinema in Crisis," in *Latin American Cinema: Essays on Modernity, Gender and National Identity*, ed. Lisa Shaw and Stephanie Dennison (Jefferson, N.C.: McFarland, 2005), 39–58.

2. Isaac León Frías, "Peru," in *Variety International Film Guide 2003: The Ultimate Annual Review of World Cinema*, ed. Daniel Rosenthal (London: Button Publishing, 2003), 266–67.

3. Isaac León Frías, "Peru," in *Variety International Film Guide 2004: The Ultimate Annual Review of World Cinema*, ed. Daniel Rosenthal (London: Button Publishing, 2004), 234–35. *Consejo Nacional de Cinematografía* refers to the National Advisory Board for Cinema.

4. John King, *A History of Cinema in Latin America* (New York: Verso, 2000), 281.

5. José Perla Anaya, *Los Tres Primeros Años: Memoria 1996–1998* (Lima CONACINE 1998), 19.

6. John King, *Magical Reels*, 2nd ed., (London: Verso, 2000), 282.

7. King, *Magical Reels*, 284.

8. Méndez's first feature, *Días de Santiago*, was released in Peru in late 2004 after having gained enormous critical acclaim at festivals throughout the world. It focuses on a young soldier returning from conflict and follows him as he tries, and fails, to reintegrate himself into civilian society. It has been applauded not only for its tight narrative structure and compelling performances but also for its complex stylistic choices in terms of sound and color, which have led it to be compared favorably with the work of, for example, Scorsese and Kieslowski. It was hailed by León Frías in his 2005 round-up of national cinema as "the best Peruvian film of recent years." See "Peru," in *The Guardian International Film Guide 2005*, ed. Daniel Rosenthal (London: Button Group, 2005), 235.

9. Federico de Cárdenas, *"El Destino no tiene favoritos*: Review," *Domingo, La Revista*, October 26, 2003, 30.

10. De Cárdenas, "Review," 30.

11. Ricardo Bedoya, *"Inexperiencia con talento,"* *El Dominical*, November 2, 2003, 4.

12. Claudio Cordero, *"La Hora del Culebrón,"* *El Comercio*, October 19, 2003, c7. In fact, this was the only negative review of the film, with the main criticism being focused on its perceived "emotional distance."

13. Isaac León Frías, "Peru," in *The Guardian International Film Guide 2005*, ed. Daniel Rosenthal (London: Button Group, 2005), 234.

14. The director's views in this paragraph are drawn from interviews by the author of this chapter with Velarde via e-mail and in person between 2001 and 2005.

15. John Sinclair, "The Telenovela," in *Latin American Television: A Global View* (Oxford: Oxford University Press, 1999), 158–62.

16. Ana M. López, "Our welcomed guests: Telenovelas in Latin America," in *To be continued . . . Soap Operas Around the World*, ed. Robert C. Allen (London: Routledge, 1995), 256–75.

17. López, "Our welcomed guests," 258.

18. Jesús Martín-Barbero, "Memory and form in the Latin American soap opera," in *To be continued*, 276–84.

19. López, "Our welcomed guests," 260.

20. Ibid.

21. Martín-Barbero, "Memory and form," 282.

22. López, "Our welcomed guests," 261.

23. López, "Our welcomed guests," 261.

24. Barry Laga, "Decapitated Spectators: *Barton Fink*, (Post)History, and Cinematic Pleasure," in *Postmodernism and the Cinema*, ed. Cristina Degli-Esposti (New York: Berghahn, 1998), 187–207.

25. Linda Hutcheon, "Beginning to Theorize Postmodernism," *Textual Practice* 1, no. 1 (1987): 17.

26. Stephen Mamber, "In Search of Radical Meta-Cinema," in *Comedy/Cinema/Theory* ed. Andrew S. Horton (Berkeley: University of California Press, 1991), 80.

27. Mamber, "In Search of Radical Meta-Cinema," 88.

28. Mamber, "In Search of Radical Meta-Cinema," 83.

29. Mamber, "In Search of Radical Meta-Cinema," 86.

30. Ricardo Bedoya, "*Inexperiencia con talento*," *El Dominical*, November 2, 2003, 4.

31. Mamber, "In Search of Radical Meta-Cinema," 87.

32. Mamber, "In Search of Radical Meta-Cinema," 80.

33. Melvin Ledgard in "*Lo Mejor y lo Peor del 2003*," *Butaca Sanmarquina* 19 (December 2003): 29–31. My translation.

34. Emilio Moscoso in "*Lo Mejor y lo Peor del 2003*," *Butaca Sanmarquina* 19 (December 2003): 29–31.

35. Until her appearance in this film, Angie Cepeda was best known in Peru for her starring roles in *Luz de Maria* (1998, a tremendously popular telenovela) and Lombardi's tenth feature *Pantaleon y las Visitadoras* (1999), both of which take full advantage of Cepeda's physical form.

36. From personal interview with Velarde, July 2004.

37. This film was *Paloma de Papel* (*Paper Dove*), directed by locally well-known television and film actor Fabrizio Aguilar. It attracted an unprecedented (for the 1990s) domestic audience of 230,000 spectators with its simple yet effective tale based on political violence recounted from a child's point of view. The release coincided with the publication of the long-anticipated report from the Truth and Reconciliation Commission on human rights abuses committed during the Dirty War between *Sendero Luminoso* and military forces. Furthermore, the investor in *Paloma* owned a chain of movie houses throughout Lima, thereby guaranteeing it the most appealing time slots.

38. From personal (e-mail) interview with Velarde, April 2005.

39. *FINPROCI* was set up in 1997 by the Peruvian Filmmakers' Association, with support from *CONACINE*, using resources provided by conversion of external debt into aid. It was supposed to support the promotion of national cinema activity, but without the promised funds it has been unable to achieve anything in this area.

40. Via e-mail, May 12, 2005.

41. The Peruvian films screened at Cannes were: Francisco Lombardi's *Bajo la Piel* (*Under the Skin*), first released in 1996; Velarde's *El Destino*; Josué Méndez's *Días de Santiago* (*Days of Santiago*); and a new documentary from Aldo Salvini, *El Pardo Caudillo* (*The Brown Shirt Commander*).

42. The four Peruvian films released in 2005 were: *Cuando el cielo es azul* (Sandra Wiese); *Manana te cuento* (Eduardo Mendoza); *Un dia sin sexo* (Frank Perez-Garland); and *Piaratas en el Callao* (Eduardo Schmidt).

43. Nick James, "The Right Stuff," *Sight and Sound*, July 2005, 16. In his review article of the Cannes 2005 Festival, Nick James begins by pointing out that this "strong . . . festival showed North American filmmaking in resurgence with thinner pickings from the rest of the globe," and focuses on the idea that 2005 could augur the "end of a golden age of world cinema" that arguably began in the late 1980s.

44. Michael Chanan, "The Economic Condition of Cinema in Latin America," in *New Latin American Cinema Volume One: Theory, Practices and Transcontinental Articulations* ed. Michael T. Martin (Detroit: Wayne State University Press 1997), 185–200.

45. Chanan, "The Economic Condition of Cinema in Latin America," 196.

46. "Cine Peruano," *Tren de Sombras* 1 (March 2004): 36.

Selected Bibliography

Allen, Robert C., ed. *To be continued . . . Soap Operas Around the World*. London: Routledge, 1995.

Armes, Roy. *Third World Film-making and the West*. Berkeley: University of California Press, 1987.

Chanan, Michael. *Cuban Cinema*. Minneapolis: University of Minnesota Press, 2004.

Cohan, Steve, and Ina Rae Hark. *The Road Movie Book*. London: Routledge, 1997.

Elena, Alberto, and Díaz López Marina, eds. *The Cinema of Latin America*. London: Wallflower, 2003.

Falicov, Tamara L. "Argentina's blockbuster movies and the politics of culture under neoliberalism, 1989–98." *Media, Culture and Society* 22–23 (2000): 327–42.

Foster, David William. *Contemporary Argentine Cinema*. Columbia: University of Missouri Press, 1992.

García Canclini, *Culturas híbridas: estrategias para entrar y salir de la modernidad*. Mexico: Grijalbo, 1989.

———. Néstor. *La globalización imaginada*. Mexico: Paídos, 1999.

Granado, Alberto. *Travelling with Che Guevara: The Making of a Revolutionary* (trans. Lucía Álvarez de Toledo). London: Pimlico, 2003.

Gruzinski, Serge. *Images at War: Mexico from Columbus to Blade Runner (1492–2019)*. Durham, N. C.: Duke University Press, 2001.

Hershfield, Joanne, and Maciel, David R., eds. *Mexico's Cinema: A Century of Film and Filmmakers*. Wilmington, Del.: Scholarly Resources, 1999.

Martin, Michael T. ed. *New Latin American Cinema Volume One: Theory, Practices and Transcontinental Articulations*. Detroit: Wayne State University Press, 1997.

Martin-Barbero, Jesús. *Communication, Culture and Hegemony*. Newbury Park, Calif.: Sage, 1993.

Myerson, Michael. *Memories of Underdevelopment: The Revolutionary Films of Cuba.* New York: Grossman, 1973.

Noble, Andrea. *Mexican National Cinema.* London: Routledge, 2005.

Noriega, Chon, ed. *Visible Nations: Latin American Cinema and Video.* Minneapolis: University of Minnesota Press, 2000.

Shaw, Deborah. *Contemporary Latin American Cinema: Ten Key Films.* London: Continuum, 2000.

Shaw, Lisa and Stephanie Dennison, eds. *Latin American Cinema: Essays on Modernity, Gender and National Identity.* Jefferson, N.C.: McFarland, 2005.

Shohat, Ella and Robert Stam. *Unthinking Eurocentrism: Multiculturalism and the Media.* London: Routledge, 1994.

Smith, Paul Julian. "Transatlantic Traffic in Recent Mexican Films." *Journal of Latin American Cultural Studies,* vol. 12, no. 3 (2003): 389–400.

Stock, Ann Marie. *Framing Latin American Cinema: Contemporary Critical Perspectives.* Minneapolis: University of Minnesota Press, 1997.

Vieira, Else R. P., ed. *City of God in Several Voices: Brazilian Social Cinema as Action.* Nottingham, U. K.: Critical, Cultural and Communication Press, 2005.

Index

About the Contributors

Sarah Barrow is senior lecturer of film and communication studies at Anglia Polytechnic University, Cambridge. She is working on a monograph of contemporary Peruvian cinema. Recent publications include: "Strategies of Hybridity in Contemporary British-Asian Cinema" in Morgan-Tamosunas, Rikki & Rings, Guido (eds.) (2003) *European Cinema Inside Out: Images of the Self and Other in Postcolonial European Film* (2003) and "Images of Peru: A National Cinema in Crisis" in Stephanie Dennison and Lisa Shaw (eds.) *Modernity, Gender and Nationhood* (2004).

Nuala Finnegan is the director of postgraduate research and director of the Centre for Mexican Studies at the University College Cork. She is the author of *Monstrous Projections of Femininity in the Fiction of Mexican Writer Rosario Castellanos* (2000) and has published a number of articles in the field of Mexican women's writing and Mexican film in prestigious Hispanic academic journals. She is currently in the final stages of completing her book *Ambivalent Modernities: Women, Writing and Power in Mexico since 1980*.

David William Foster is chair of the department of languages and literatures and Regents' Professor of Spanish, Humanities, and Women's Studies at Arizona State University. His research interests focus on urban culture in Latin America, with emphasis on issues of gender construction and sexual identity, as well as Jewish culture. He has written extensively on Argentine narrative and theater, and he has held Fulbright teaching appointments in Argentina, Brazil, and Uruguay. He has published numerous works in these areas and his publications include *Violence in Argentine Literature: Cultural Responses to Tyranny* (1995); *Cultural Diversity in Latin American Literature* (1994), *Contemporary Argentine Cinema* (1992), *Mexico City in Mexican Filmmaking* (2002), and *Queer Issues in Latin American Filmmaking* (2003).

Miriam Haddu is a lecturer in Hispanic studies at Royal Holloway University London. She has been awarded an AHRB grant to complete her monograph, *Contemporary Mexican Cinema: History, Space and Identity*, and she has published a number of articles in the field of contemporary Mexican cinema.

Geoffrey Kantaris is senior lecturer in Latin American culture in the department of Spanish and Portuguese and the Centre of Latin American Studies, University of Cambridge, and Director of the MPhil in European Literature and Culture. His current research is on contemporary urban cinema from Colombia, Argentina, and Mexico, and he has published several articles in this area. He is also the author of *The Subversive Psyche* (1996), on postdictatorship women's writing from Argentina and Uruguay.

Deborah Shaw is senior lecturer in film studies at Portsmouth University. She is the author of *Contemporary Latin American Cinema: Ten Key Films* (2003) and has published widely in the field of women's writing in Mexico and Latin American and Spanish Cinema.

Lisa Shaw is reader in Portuguese and Brazilian Studies at the University of Liverpool. She has published widely in this field, and her publications include *The Social History of the Brazilian Samba* (1999), and she coauthored, with Stephanie Dennison, *Popular Cinema in Brazil, 1930–2001* (2004). She has also coedited *Latin American Cinema: Essays on Modernity, Gender and National Identity* (2005).

Rob Stone is the author of *Spanish Cinema* (2002), *Flamenco in the Works of Federico García Lorca and Carlos Saura* (2004), *Julio Medem* (2005), and coeditor of *The Unsilvered Screen: Surrealism on Film* (2005). He is the course leader of film studies at the University of Wales, Swansea.

Else R. P. Vieira is Professor of Brazilian film and cultural studies at Queen Mary University of London. She has a particular interest in the rights of minorities and the politicization of the expression of the dispossessed and has published widely in this field. She has recently edited City of God *in Several Voices: Brazilian Social Cinema as Action* (2005). She is currently working on an AHRC-funded research project, *Screening Exclusion: Brazilian and Argentine Documentary Film-Making.*

Dr. Claire Williams is Lecturer in Portuguese and Brazilian Studies at the University of Liverpool, where she has been teaching since 2001. Her doctoral research analyzed the figure of the encounter in the works of Brazilian writer Clarice Lispector, who has been the focus of subsequent projects, including the edited volume of essays *Closer to the Wild Heart* (2002). She has published articles on contemporary lusophone women's writing, especially the work of Maria Gabriela Llansol, Lília Momplé, virtual orality, maternal genealogies, and literatura "light." Her current research project addresses the changing representations of the Brazilian favela (shanty town) in literature, film, art, essay, and the media.